THE SURVIVAL OF THE NOVEL

D0539875

00002 0087

The Survival of the Novel

British Fiction in the Later Twentieth Century

Neil McEwan

MACMILLAN

First edition 1981
Reprinted 1983, 1985

Published by
THE MACMILLAN PRESS LTD
Houndmills, Basingstoke, Hampshire RG21 2XS
and London
Companies and representatives
throughout the world

Printed in Hong Kong

ISBN 0-333-30092-0 (hardcover)
ISBN 0-333-34885-0 (paperback)

823

For My Parents

Contents

Preface

I have aimed to put a case about the nature of the novel's survival in England and to provide an introduction to a limited number of novelists and novels. The book takes an optimistic view. It is not an apology for English novelists on the grounds that they are catching up late in the day with American or French innovations. Nor is it a defence of a conventional — static — type of fiction, as opposed to 'intellectual puzzles'. My argument is that, well within the literary world of fabulation and *nouveau roman*, writers in Britain have achieved a creative relationship with the traditional novel. As a result, they have managed to keep their work close enough to common experience to make their experiments meaningful and to ensure the novel's continuing life.

So much good fiction has been produced in the last thirty years that any selection must be a personal choice. Some major authors — including Greene and Waugh — have been left out because they flourished in an earlier period.

Part 1 deals with five novelists whose experimental attitude to tradition seems to me characteristic of modern English fiction. In Part 2, I consider the problem of assessing and accounting for fiction in the present state of criticism and look at two very successful novels in the context of interpretation they have received.

Because I am also concerned with criticism, I have throughout referred to, quoted from and sometimes disagreed with the relatively few critics who clearly are the best in the field. Malcolm Bradbury and David Lodge are critics who are also novelists. Bernard Bergonzi's *The Situation of the Novel*, which takes in a wider view than I do, cannot be ignored.

I am grateful to Professor A. N. Jeffares and to Mr Stephen Wall for encouraging me to write, and to my colleagues M. Michel Dupont, Dr Roger Boase and Mr Nick Bell for help and advice. My sister-in-law Mrs Pauline McEwan was a patient typist.

J. N. McE.
July 1980

Part 1

1 Introduction

In Lawrence Durrell's *Clea* (Faber, 1960), Pursewarden reminds 'Brother Ass' of how London used to appear to young writers arriving from the provinces, full of promise and laden with manuscripts:

> The metropolis seemed to quiver with the portent of our talent, our skill, our discernment. Walking along the Mall, we wondered who all those men were — tall hawk-featured men perched on balconies and high places, scanning the city with heavy binoculars. What were they seeking so earnestly? Who were they — so composed and steely-eyed? Timidly we stopped a policeman to ask him. 'They are publishers,' he said mildly. Publishers! Our hearts stopped beating. 'They are on the look-out for new talent.' Great God! It was for *us* they were waiting and watching! Then the kindly policeman lowered his voice confidentially and said in hollow and reverent tones: '*They are waiting for the new Trollope to be born!*' Do you remember, at these words, how heavy our suitcases suddenly felt . . . A million muffin-eating moralists were waiting, not for us, Brother Ass, but for the plucky and tedious Trollope! [Chapter 3]

This sense of exasperation with the state of the modern English novel has often been expressed by observers overseas. But attitudes are beginning to change and a new interest in our fiction can be detected abroad — even in France. The *nouveau roman* is no longer new; Roland Barthes, who did so much to publicise the anti-novel, came to modify his views, admitting that story-telling may be worthwhile.[1] English writers are no longer automatically assumed to be clinging to exhausted traditions, cut off from the important work going on in France and America. It is coming to seem likely that the English novel, technically adaptable even though stubbornly realist, will be an influential form of writing, in an increasingly anglophone world, at the end of the century.

Trollope's own reputation has increased since Durrell wrote. Pursewarden's 'plucky and tedious' looks a very crude judgement after the recent critical studies by Juliet McMaster, R. C. Terry and Robert Tracy.[2] The degree of artistry and imaginative control that can go with popular story-telling has been shown in other Victorian novelists, especially Dickens, as critical and scholarly work on nineteenth-century fiction has advanced over the last thirty years. We can see now that polemicists in the 1940s and 1950s were declaring 'conventional narrative' to be exhausted before they could properly appreciate what it had achieved. Trollope is still read, moreover; and although television has made much of him, serialisations appear to create a readership rather than supplant one. Prophecies about how the novel would be 'replaced' as a form of entertainment have not come true. In critical prestige and potential readership, his sort of novel is flourishing.

But we understand the conditions in which Trollope and the other great Victorians wrote too well to suppose that a modern writer can carry on as if, as Bernard Bergonzi puts it, 'the nineteenth century were still a going concern'.[3] British novelists have not attempted any such thing, and several of them, and most notably Iris Murdoch, have explained why it is pointless to try. Many recent critics have been concerned to refute (a task not complete) the view put forward by Rubin Rabinovitz in *The Reaction against Experiment in the English Novel, 1950–1960* (1967), and by B. S. Johnson in his introduction to *Aren't You Rather Young to Be Writing Your Memoirs?* (1973),[4] that British novelists are 'neo-Dickensian' and unaware of Joyce's *Ulysses*. My intention is to dispel any remaining doubt, and to show how unVictorian even the most Victorian-seeming modern English novelists are.

My object is to examine the originality of a number of writers in relation to the Victorian novel. Bernard Bergonzi has emphasised in *The Situation of the Novel* the unavoidable knowledge which author and reader share of what has been done before. This consciousness has indeed influenced novelists; but it seems nonetheless that they have been able to take advantage of their readers' awareness of the gap between Trollope and a modern mind and have used the resources of nineteenth-century fiction with a creative — not ar-chaeological — sense of the past.

Bernard Bergonzi draws attention also to the survival in English life of much that has vanished elsewhere. England can seem, he says, 'a living fragment of the nineteenth century' and it often appears to

Americans and Europeans that 'as a cultural phenomenon the country has all the pathos and unreality of an Indian reservation . . . ' (p. 62). Totalitarian pressures, he fears, are likely to overwhelm our 'quaintly preserved' values. Most Englishmen who have worked abroad must have returned with similar thoughts. Yet if this comparison, made with America and Europe in mind, is just, a different impression can be formed by looking at other parts of the world. The transition brought about in most developed countries (apart from Britain) by economic forces and by war is far from complete elsewhere and ways of life belonging to separate epochs commonly coexist. Modern Britain offers contrasts of the same kind, if less extreme; this helps to explain the (usually disregarded) interest in English fiction in Third World countries. English novelists cannot simply copy Victorian novels but nor can they ignore them. The same is true of Victorian ways of life which continue in close proximity to the very different conditions of post-industrial Britain.

Daniel Martin in John Fowles's most recent novel *Daniel Martin* (1977) remarks on this situation. He has, he tells us, had to escape (to California) from his 'Victorian' childhood in the 1930s: 'My contemporaries were all brought up in some degree of the nineteenth century, since the twentieth did not begin until 1945. That is why we are on the rack, forced into one of the longest and most abrupt cultural stretches in the history of mankind' (Chapter 8). Daniel's 1930s, in a West Country vicarage with an eccentric (Trollopian) father presiding calmly over a rural parish, were not like the official decade in the history books. His twentieth century began in 1945; the nineteenth century still persists, elsewhere, as he finds when he comes back from California. Furthermore, according to Daniel at least, the English differ from the Americans in 'allowing hypotheses about ourselves, and our pasts and futures, almost as much reality as the true events and destinies . . . We paint an ideal, or a dream-self on the glass and then wallow in the discrepancy'. In making a novel out of his own life he has to confront real experiences and fantasies which he feels belong to the nineteenth century, and their 'discrepancy', given all he knows about the twentieth.

Daniel Martin is conceived as an important novel, a seven-hundred-page opus, which re-creates traditional procedures: international situation; detailed background; prolonged discussion of themes among the characters. It brings Victorian methods to bear on ways of life — at Oxford, on a farm, on a great estate — which are still partly Victorian. Fowles's earlier novel *The French Lieutenant's Woman* (1969) tells a Victorian story from a contemporary point of view; and the disparity between content and method which is so startling there is present to some degree in most British novels.

In the case of *The French Lieutenant's Woman*, the result is a modern classic, discussed at length in the next chapter. The interest it has aroused is connected with what Malcolm Bradbury calls, in a recent essay, 'an essential evolution of consciousness and society, from the nineteenth to the twentieth century, which has taken us across some essential divide in the matter of reality'.[5] Such a divide explains the strong views of critics like B. S. Johnson, who complained about 'nineteenth-century readers' who ignore the chaotic nature of modern reality, or like Susan Sontag and John Hawkes in America. In Britain, most of us seem to be nineteenth-century readers in part when we come to contemporary fiction, because we still read the Victorians, and because our society is in many respects anachronistic. (We may also feel that what Johnson calls 'nineteenth-century reading' corresponds to a basic human need for stories and characters.)

While an intellectual *avant-garde*, including readers of John Hawkes, has developed in the way Bradbury suggests, many readers remain confused about 'the essential divide in the matter of reality' between the nineteenth and twentieth centuries, where the novel is concerned, and hence the hostility to 'postmodernist' fiction here. Perhaps the best-known statement of the divide is Graham Greene's:

. . . with the death of James the religious sense was lost to the English novel, and with the religious sense went the sense of the importance of the human act. It was as if the world of fiction had lost a dimension: the characters of such distinguished writers as Mrs Virginia Woolf and Mr E. M. Forster wandered like cardboard symbols through a world that was paper thin . . .[6]

Trollope's clergymen, he goes on to say, stumbling through muddy lanes and fumbling with umbrellas, possess an importance in another world which makes them exist as characters 'in a way that Mrs. Woolf's Mrs. Ramsay never does'.

Virginia Woolf and E. M. Forster, like Joyce and Proust, the first 'modernist' generation after the Victorians, can be called 'classical modernists' to distinguish them from Greene's generation. Modernist writing is about seventy years old, and the analysis of its stages is a delicate task. David Lodge's chapter called 'Postmodernist Fiction' in *The Modes of Modern Writing* (1977) provides a clear brief account. He calls Beckett and writers who broke away from Joyce and Proust in the 1940s and 1950s 'postmodernist', and a subsequent phase of innovators in the 1960s and 1970s he calls 'new postmodernists': they include John Barth, Thomas Pynchon and John Hawkes in America, and John Fowles and Muriel Spark in Britain. These are commonly used distinctions. Some would say that fictional worlds have become increasingly paper-thin with each generation of new methodologists.

It has until recently been usual to say that British fiction has reacted against these experimenters, first against stream-of-consciousness techniques and complex time-schemes, both opposed by Waugh, then against Beckett's uncertain worlds, and the *nouveau roman*, opposed by social satirists like Kingsley Amis and Angus Wilson. Obviously the history of fiction since James and Hardy is not one of steady departure from their sort of novel, or from what Lawrence called, when writing *The Rainbow*, 'the old stable ego of character'. But Greene's distinction between the characters of Trollope and those of Virginia Woolf holds for the broad difference between Victorian and modern novels. Iris Murdoch has discussed this long-distance contrast in a famous essay, 'Against Dryness' (1961): 'We no longer see man against a background of values, of realities which transcend him. We picture man as a brave naked will surrounded by an easily comprehended empirical world. For the hard idea of truth we have substituted a facile idea of sincerity.'[7] The nineteenth-century novelist, Iris Murdoch explains, lived in a world transcended by God or, for George Eliot, by an absolute Duty. The human condition was taken for granted by novelists (on the whole, though not by poets) and they dealt with individuals 'struggling in society'. The modern novelist sees man making his own world, and, in Britain, hoping for a working compromise to deal with society. There are two types of modern novel, she says, the journalistic and the crystalline. The journalistic is a looser, weaker version of the social novel of the Victorians; the crystalline is symbolist, not to do with social life or 'characters' but with the human condition. Iris Murdoch does not give examples. Presumably C. P. Snow would be journalistic, Virginia Woolf crystalline. Neither sort is really satisfactory, she contends, and the nineteenth-century sense of real people is what the modern writer should aim to recover. Elsewhere, Iris Murdoch has written of 'the vanishing of the philosophical self together with the filling in of the scientific self' in the present century, which has weakened moral thinking (and the novel), and in her philosophical writings she argues the need to discover a new moral philosophy.[8] While she sees how we have lost touch with the traditional purposes of the novel, she wants to recover and renew them. This is the position of many English writers. Malcolm Bradbury's satirical novel, *The History Man* (1975), shows how conscious he is of the case against Iris Murdoch's, and that he remains on her side. In America, in France, and in parts of the world subject to American or French influence, confidence in moral philosophy and in the novel is much feebler.

Lecturing at Harvard in 1970, Lionel Trilling remarked on the sad state of narrative. In the book, *Sincerity and Authenticity* (1972), based on the Charles Eliot Norton lectures for 1969–70, he writes about the 'reduced status of narration, of telling stories':

> It is the exceptional novelist today who would say of himself, as Henry James did, that he 'loved the story as story', by which James meant the story apart from any overt ideational intention it might have, simply as, like any primitive tale, it brings into play what he called 'the blessed faculty of wonder'. [p. 134]

He cites the modern view (expressed by Walter Benjamin) that story-telling and teaching through stories have become 'inauthentic for our time'. The significance of Aristotle's beginning, middle and end is considered spurious; it is unacceptable, Trilling notes, to modern historians like G. R. Elton and J. H. Plumb who have tried to free their work from such narrative oversimplifications. As for the novel, although T. S. Eliot's view that Flaubert and James had put an end to it has not quite come true, the best that can be said is that 'the novel does seem to persist in some sort of life' (p. 134).

Lionel Trilling is perhaps the greatest of American liberal critics; *Sincerity and Authenticity* is both a study of 'the attenuation of self' in the last two centuries and a defence of humanism against most currents in American postmodernist culture. At one point he refers to Susan Sontag's objections to 'interpretation' and to 'pleasure' in relation to art, seeing her as the outcome of an ultimate romanticism, removing 'the artist' altogether from the audience, whose wishes no longer have to be taken into account at all. If one believes that, one must consider the novel to be out of date. Some critics in America think it ought to be. Leslie Fiedler connects the rationalism of Western art with the imperialism of the West and sees both as corrupt. Others share something like this attitude, and attack modernism for its élitist preoccupation with artistic truths, meanings, and tastes of a minority. Ideas in origin Marxist (though detached from Marx) are combined with popular versions of 'phenomenology' which declare that reality does not exist or that meaning is dead. The significance of all this for the novel is summed up in a well-known statement by John Hawkes: 'I began to write fiction on the assumption that the true enemies of the novel were plot, character, setting and theme.'[9]

Another much-quoted slogan is Richard Poirier's 'Literature is now in the process of telling us how little it means'. Reviewing the 'New American Writing' Spring issue of *Granta* for 1979, in the *Guardian* on 16 August, David Lodge writes that 'even when they seem to be speaking directly of their own experience, these writers complicate the simple pleasures of recognition by stylistic device, foregrounding the textuality of their texts. This, however, is not always an unqualified blessing.' David Lodge, an expert on postmodernism who still believes in and writes entertaining fiction, is introducing John Hawkes, Joyce Carol Oakes, Susan Sontag and James Purdy to *Guardian* readers whom he presumes to be used to more conventional reading. 'Foregrounding the textuality of their texts' is a technical summary of a method which some British novelists as well as these Americans have adopted as a means of emphasising the limitations of literature.

For those unfamiliar with modern American writing, Laurence Sterne's *Tristram Shandy*, published between 1759 and 1767, provides a good example of this process: at one point the narrator rebukes a lady-reader for inattention and sends her back to reread more carefully. Most of the characteristic postmodernist 'disruptions' of the traditional novel — discontinuity, randomness, excess, permutation — can be found in *Tristram Shandy* which has become an honorary modern classic. Dr Johnson called it odd, disapprovingly ('Nothing odd will do long'), and although it has always been enjoyed, it has been seen as outside the main tradition of psychological and social realism in the English novel. If its modern successors are to be found in America, this may be because the American novel was always more inclined to the fantastic and absurd possibilities of fiction. Lionel Trilling, in *Sincerity and*

Authenticity, quotes Henry James's view that nineteenth-century American society was 'thinly composed', lacking 'the stuff out of which novels were made' — novels in the British sense at least.[10] Fowles's *Daniel Martin* can be seen as an assertion that there is still, today, more novelistic 'stuff' in Britain than in America. Certainly the most brilliant (and entertaining) of emphatically fictive works from the United States, John Barth's *Chimera* or Nabokov's *Pale Fire*, tend to be remote from ordinary American life.

'Ordinary life' is a conventional concept and belongs to what the French critic, Roland Barthes, called 'the essential enemy, the bourgeois norm'.[11] Barthes was the champion, over the last twenty-five years, of the cause of freeing literature from common sense and of separating modern fiction from all past traditions. The nineteenth century, in Barthes's belief, is shrouded in bourgeois myths which frequently persist into modern life and need to be dispelled: the worst of these for the novelist is the myth of realism. Barthes campaigned against it steadfastly, despite the contradictions and inconsistencies of his intellectual career. The idea that fiction has a real content is the main object of attack in his best-known work, *S/Z* (1970), his critical commentary on *Sarrasine* (1830), a story by the master-realist Balzac. An infinitely explorable universe, he declares, is revealed in the combinations of meaning Balzac's words evoke — though he explores it by means of a modest five 'codes' or semantic classes. *S/Z* does reveal the extent to which literary language is richly suggestive and exposes the fallacy that fictional creations have a life of their own. The more a writer encourages his readers to create meanings for themselves, as Barthes defines it, the more 'modern' he is, rather than 'classical', the more 'open' his text, rather than 'closed'. Joyce is modern and open, and more so in *Finnegans Wake* than in *Dubliners*. Balzac comes between the classical and the modern. Ideally, according to Barthes, readers are free to 'rewrite' for themselves. Modern novelists should abandon altogether the conventions of nineteenth-century fiction: Alain Robbe-Grillet and Michel Butor, authors of the French New Novel, have produced the 'correct' fiction for today, where the reader must reconstruct everything in his own imagination. It was under the influence of such ideas that B. S. Johnson attacked 'nineteenth-century readers', and issued his novel *The Unfortunates* (Panther, 1969) with the gatherings unbound, in a box, to force his readers to participate. 'I live in the age of . . . Roland Barthes,' the narrator tells us in *The French Lieutenant's Woman* (Chapter 13); he cannot, therefore, condone any surrender on our part to the story's illusion.

The great effectiveness of Barthes's work was in forcing issues into the open, and although he ignored prewar English critics who had already expressed many of his ideas, English readers — if not English novelists — had often disregarded them too. Barthes's impact in England in the 1960s and 1970s, directly and indirectly, added to the challenge of American experiments in making us aware of the two issues of central relevance to English fiction: its relations with tradition and its relations with 'mimesis' (or realism). Should a modern novel aim to be judged as if it were by George Eliot or Trollope? Should it pretend to mirror the world in the same sort of way?

Literary-minded Frenchmen, told that Roland Barthes is not well known in England, tend to reply that F. R. Leavis is not well known in France. Leavis was responsible, through the influence of *Scrutiny*, the journal which ran from 1932 to 1953, his book on the novel *The Great Tradition*, and the writings of 'Leavisite' followers, for a theory of the novel quite unlike Barthes's: moral, liberal and English. This insisted on the contemporary significance of a particular 'line' of novelists: Jane Austen, Dickens, George Eliot, James, Conrad and Lawrence. Little subsequent fiction, it was implied, lived up to their standard or merited serious 'adult' reading. Leavis's dictatorship of opinion was mocked and resisted, of course, although his outlook and the quality of his criticism of approved texts have always been respected; with Q. D. Leavis he produced, in *Dickens the Novelist*, by far the best book on the subject for the centennial year, 1970. The critical passion of Leavis's work, which would condemn Balzac and Flaubert (let alone Alain Robbe-Grillet) as superficial, is accompanied by a more flexible and tolerant commitment among writers in England who support 'decency' and a common-sense view of reality. In the 1950s Leavis provoked English critics into an attempt to re-establish reputations (Hardy's, Thackeray's, Trollope's) he had swept aside; by the 1960s, French influence made it seem necessary to defend the basic Leavis principle of literature as a force for good.

Bernard Bergonzi published *The Situation of the Novel* in 1970. He notes in the Preface to the revised second edition (1979) that 'a baffled liberal haunts this book' and suggests that the shaken liberal nerve of the late sixties has steadied during the last decade. The view he develops in a chapter called 'The Ideology of Being English' — that English literary culture is untheoretical, that where American critics cry 'exciting' English critics cry 'rubbish', that fear of experiment and political innocence limit what can be achieved here — seems unduly defensive. Such a book as Philip Thody's 1977 study of Roland Barthes illustrates the ability of an English academic writer to assess theory, and sometimes put it through the wringer;[12] our sense of the difference between rubbish and originality is preserved by the variety of approach, and by the most astringent, satirical wing of literary journalism. The capacity of English novelists to experiment and the extent to which they have been doing so throughout the last thirty years have become increasingly clear in the 1970s. Nineteenth-century novelists are mentioned and quoted with reference to the current state of fiction throughout Bernard Bergonzi's book. Yet when he quotes Margaret Drabble, as a novelist influenced by Victorian models, saying, 'I'd rather be at the end of a dying tradition which I admire than at the beginning of a tradition which I deplore,'[13] the alternatives imply an unnecessarily negative attitude to the uses a novelist today might make of George Eliot or Anthony Trollope.

A critic who has done much over the last ten years to revive confidence in British fiction is Malcolm Bradbury, himself an English novelist as well as a professor of American Studies. His *Eating People is Wrong* (1959), the first of three university novels, is an entertaining, somewhat whimsical account of a liberal-minded and bemused provincial university professor. The third, *The History Man* (1975), is a portrait of a sociologist at a new university (who would have the professor for breakfast): this is a new type of don, an anti-liberal, anti-bourgeois cliché-spinner, versed in structuralism, who tells his pupils that reality does not exist yet, and drives the one student who disagrees with him out of the university. Bradbury knows the History Man from inside, but retains his own sense of proportion; and the same ability to absorb theory without losing sight of what Christopher Ricks calls 'the Unignorable Real' pervades his criticism of fiction in the 1970s: *Possibilities: Essays on the State of the Novel* (1973) and the Introductions to two recent collections he has edited. *Possibilities* is, true to its title, a stimulating book, positive in its liberal, Jamesian belief in the novel and influential in its sense of imaginative options. Introducing *The Novel Today* in 1977, he writes 'it now seems . . . important to stress that many of the best English writers of the 1950s were not intrinsically anti-experimental; more often they were simply defined as such by the critics who read them' (p. 17). In the Preface to *The Contemporary*

English Novel in 1979 he confirms that view. Professor Bradbury points out that most books on modern British fiction are by Americans (Rabinovitz, Frederick R. Karl and James Gindin) who have created a myth of the conservative, insular, nostalgic British novelist who wants to write 'premodernist' novels. Such a regression is in any case impossible, and certainly not to be looked for from novelists like Iris Murdoch, Amis, Wilson or Golding, as far removed as Bradbury himself from naïvety about the formal and theoretical problems of fiction after the modernists.

Criticism in the 1970s has not succumbed to the algebraic technicalities of French structuralist studies by disciples of Barthes like Julia Kristeva. But certain new technical words have come to be used, by Bradbury himself and by other critics writing in, for example, *The Contemporary English Novel*. 'Fictiveness', 'textuality', 'fabulator' and 'fabulatory' are among these. Other old terms have developed new emphases and new connotations: 'narrative' itself has acquired fresh resonance. The abstractions of French poetics are behind some of these changes: *le récit*, as a phenomenon liable to formalist analysis, is behind the new use of 'narrative'. But the work of an American professor, Robert Scholes, has introduced the concept of 'fabulator' and, in *The Nature of Narrative* (1966), written with Robert Kellogg, altered the scope of the word 'narrative' and our attitude to what it means.

Scholes's *The Fabulators* (1967) is inspired by a pleasure in the artificial nature of fiction. He admires the ability of John Barth and Iris Murdoch to create illusory paper-worlds which make us pay attention to their fictiveness. An older type of novelist like Trollope engages in incidental fabulatory jokes with his reader — in such blatantly invented names as Duke of Omnium or Sir Omicron Pie. But the fabulator proper gives such games a central role and reverses the traditional novelist's stress on the real historical world in the book to stress its unfactual, invented nature instead.

In *The Nature of Narrative*, Scholes and Kellogg argue that we should stop regarding Victorian fiction as the ultimate achievement of narrative, as we have been led to do by the 'realist' orientation of works like Auerbach's *Mimesis*. Petronius's *Satyricon* or *Sir Gawain and the Green Knight* should not be thought of, Scholes and Kellogg say, by novelists as primitive versions of their own art but as examples of different options in narrative fiction. If our literary outlook should become less 'novel-centred' we might be less inclined to see Joyce undermining the genre established by James, and more able to recognise *Ulysses* as another new departure in the long tradition of European story-telling. *The Nature of Narrative* studies common problems of 'character', 'plot' and 'point of view' in novels and in Renaissance, medieval and ancient types of narrative.

The thrust of these two books is clearly directed against any such supreme tradition of Victorian fiction as F. R. Leavis proposed and against the whole tendency of university English departments to elevate the 'classics' of the nineteenth-century novel, in so far as that tends to deter or demoralise the contemporary writer who feels unable to rival Dickens or James. For a novelist who takes Scholes and Kellogg seriously this need not mean losing touch with the older novel, but it might have an emancipating effect by removing the impossible duty of competing with James and Dickens. Instead a close relation might be expected to exist between modern narratives and the Victorian novel without the latter giving the former a false sense of inferiority. And this does indeed seem a more accurate version of what English novelists have been doing than the account which presents them as crudely and feebly neo-Victorian.

Among French analysts of narrative, the Soviet critic Mikhail Bakhtin has been increasingly influential. He is coming to be better known in England, especially among academics interested in structuralism; Roger Fowler refers to his concept of 'dialogic structure' in his *Linguistics and the Novel* (1977). Bakhtin is attractive to structuralists because of the broad range of literature he deals with and because of his willingness to compare works from totally different backgrounds. In *Problems of Dostoevsky's Poetics* (1929, 1963; translation 1973), he discusses the novelist in the light of what he calls a 'carnival' attitude to the world and provides an account of menippean literature from ancient times up to Dostoevsky. As a category of narrative, Bakhtin's menippea suggests possible antecedents, if we attempt to take the long view proposed by Scholes and Kellogg, for recent developments in the novel.

Petronius, Apuleius and, most fully, Lucian illustrate menippean writing in antiquity. Rabelais, Swift and Voltaire are literary summits of 'this carnivalized genre, extraordinarily flexible and as versatile as Proteus', which, Bakhtin writes, 'has had enormous, but as yet underestimated significance for the development of European literatures'.[14] Chapter 4 of *Dostoevsky's Poetics* sets out 'fourteen basic characteristics'; a brief summary of them suggests many features of contemporary fiction at its most distinctive.

Bakhtin's menippea is a comic, satirical, fantastic mode of

literature, close in spirit to carnival but basically committed to pursuing the truth. The hero goes to hell or to heaven, he sells himself as a slave in the market, or immolates himself at the Olympics, or gets changed into an ass: but his real purpose is always 'to test the truth'. Fantasy and symbolism are combined with 'crude underworld naturalism' (low life). The adventures take us, in pursuit of the truth, into taverns, prisons, brothels, markets, graveyards, highways: in ancient menippea, philosophy was said to be 'decked out as a hetaera'; but 'bare ultimate questions' (rather than detailed philosophical problems) are still the real interest.

The menippean world is complex and unstable. Heaven and hell are close at hand; peculiar vantage-points — as, later, in *Gulliver's Travels* — provide weird changes of scale; abnormal states of mind are explored; so are madness, dreams and day dreams, suicidal and erratic inclinations of all kinds. 'Man's unfinalizability and disunity' are better realised here than in the official genres of classical literature. Similarly, scandalous and eccentric behaviour disrupts the 'seemly course of human affairs' and provides another departure from epic and tragic assumptions about the 'integrity of the world'. Society is seen as unpredictable: the emperor can become a slave; a prostitute is nobly virtuous; *mésalliances* are normal. Dreams and journeys lead to social utopias. Current affairs and schools of thought are alluded to or discussed: 'this is in its way the "journalistic" genre of antiquity'. Different genres are mixed. Stories, letters, speeches, debates, verse and parody are absorbed into the menippea. 'There is formed here,' says Bakhtin, 'a new attitude to the word as the material of literature.'[15]

This interpretation is far broader than the orthodox account of a 'Lucianic' or menippean satirical line to be traced to Ben Jonson, Fielding or Peacock. Northrop Frye's *Anatomy of Criticism* defines 'menippean' as a comedy of ideas rather than of people. 'Squire Western belongs to the novel' but Thwackum and Square 'have menippean blood in them'.[16] Douglas Duncan's recent study, *Ben Jonson and the Lucianic Tradition* (Cambridge University Press, 1979), agrees with this, but suggests that 'Lucianic' should replace Frye's 'menippean' (p. 11). Lucian is still very readable; he seems, to borrow Roland Barthes's distinction, more 'modern' than 'classical' and there is more to him than just a brand of satire: an attractive 'I' persona, a creative use of narrative (including space-travel), blends of sexual and intellectual comedy, the power to elaborate a fantasy. His sceptical, amused view of conflicting philosophies and superstitions in the second century AD, when read in an idiomatic translation like that of Paul Turner's selection in Penguin Classics, is likely to appeal to readers familiar with Flann O'Brien, Anthony Burgess and Michael Frayn.

Lucian, like Petronius (of whom much less has survived), shows ancient menippean writing at its best, but a literary tradition which eventually includes modern novelists can be better accounted for by such a loose, flexible mode as Bakhtin's 'menippea'. For, although the social mobility, intellectual agnosticism and sexual freedom of contemporary Europe make us feel at ease with Lucian, his literary world was ruled by epic and drama, while, on the other hand, we have the great traditions of the novel—and hence our intense interest in people, of an inwardness and subtlety inconceivable in ancient literature. In Bakhtin's author, of course, the psychological vision is of a different order from anything in the past: Dostoevsky may have known Lucian's work but he transcended it.

The relevance of Bakhtin's menippea to contemporary fiction is in the assertion it makes of a revitalising power, and here Dostoevsky is a reminder of how much was excluded from the nineteenth-century novel in English: his influence in English has been closely involved with modernism. Connected, as Bakhtin sees it, in Rabelais or in Dostoevsky, with principles of 'carnival' throughout European cultural history, the menippea is a medium of renewal, quick to absorb and rework other genres but always true to its basic, unsettling, unseemly drive. Just such a renewal can be seen in the present-day novel and its relations with Victorian fiction.

Contemporary fiction seems to us livelier and healthier than their conventions allowed Victorian novels to be—despite their solid achievements—in certain areas and these correspond to the menippean mode. Our fiction is strong in fantasy, in scandal and sexual humour, in eccentric forms of life, in philosophical and intellectual comedy, in its radical social irreverences; and in its attitude to genre, its parodies, and its attitude to the verbal nature of the novel. Throughout the criticism of the last decade, the terms 'ludic' and 'playful' have been made to express a positive quality among new novelists. The play has sometimes been laboured and the playfulness claimed by critics for some 'ludic' efforts is heavy-going. But just as Lucian, Petronius, Rabelais and Swift are more widely appreciated today than they were a hundred years ago, so their subversive play with 'the seemly course of human affairs' (as Bakhtin says) is welcome to us, though banned by Victorian public taste.

Trollope's Archdeacon Grantly reads Rabelais in private. Swinburne's brilliant burlesque-novel, *La Fille du Policeman*, featuring Queen Victoria in the midst of an English revolution of 1848, was written in French and not published until 1964.[17] Unacceptable to the nineteenth century, it is a work which takes liberties with society and with fiction itself. John Fowles's Victorian novel exploits both fictional scenes and attitudes to fiction that were outside the permitted limits of the nineteenth-century novel. Ancient menippea combined formal aesthetic licence with social and religious scepticism and so do our own novels. Very conservative societies (like Professor Bakhtin's) tend to inhibit both. Dickens and Thackeray (up to *Vanity Fair*) were relatively unpredictable in the ways they used fiction and the uses they put it to, but the Victorians made a great artistic institution of the novel before the end of the century.

The initial impetus of modernism away from Victorian restrictiveness has been continued in postmodernist writers, set on breaking all rules of discretion, politeness, clarity and order, until what might be seen in Joyce as a menippean revival in the novel has shifted in such writers as Robbe-Grillet and William Burroughs from the principle of 'testing the truth'. In many American writers there has been a tendency to leave the common experience of social life altogether and to concentrate on marginal elements even of 'underworld' society. In the *nouveau roman* an extreme devotion to reason (which a Lucian would enjoy ridiculing) has moved fiction away from common interest in ultimate questions of life and the common sense of what is reasonable which is so strong in Lucian or Rabelais or Swift. David Lodge points out in 'Postmodernist Fiction' (in *The Modes of Modern Writing*) that since the progressive stages of modernism are essentially rule-breaking, each stage becomes more rarefied as the rules seem more remote.

That process is one of trying to keep the genre new, and the feeling of exasperation at a 'novel no longer novel', in Bernard Bergonzi's phrase, has been a reaction against the authority of the later, high-serious Victorian fiction. Early modernists took the novel's high status for granted, although they often disagreed with the Victorians about how to achieve it. For people like Michel Butor, Ortega y Gasset and Alberto Moravia, the novel was a great genre in its death throes.[18] They might have looked a little further back to a different idea of fiction. In 1851, David Masson, comparing Dickens and Thackeray, called them 'friendly competitors for the prize of light literature'.[19] This less academic attitude seems closer to the point of view of writers like Amis, Murdoch, Wilson, Powell and Burgess, in the period after 1950. The recognition that James and Flaubert were no longer suitable models in the 1950s created, by a confused association of narrative with 'late-nineteenth-century novel', a dissatisfaction with John Hawkes's declared enemies: 'plot, character, setting and theme'. Narrative, satire, comedy, fantasy, debate, moral fable do not depend on 'the status of the novel', however defined. The advantage of Bakhtin's broad extensive concept is in reminding us of the depth of the novel's roots in the history of literature and in our curiosity about life. Attenuation is the danger to contemporary fiction, especially when it experiments within too narrow a vision of its own genre.

It is not surprising that British novelists in the 1950s opened up relations with premodernist fiction. The Victorian novel appeared, a generation after Joyce, as a vast and orderly genre reflecting a coherent society, which had since broken up, leaving its surviving relics in an uncertain world. This historically misleading view was creatively useful. A postmodernist position, it preserved relations with narrative and with the social framework from which modern life was emerging. Postmodernist disruptiveness is meaningless when it loses contact with literary convention. However conscious of their unviability, modern fiction has depended on Victorian rules for its own sense of freedom.

The relationship takes many forms. Parody, pastiche, allusion and direct imitation were modes in which individual novelists could be used: Dickens, for example, in the work of Angus Wilson. Various myths or collective notions of Victorian fiction could be even more effective. L. P. Hartley took advantage of such schemes. Reviewers of *The French Lieutenant's Woman* could not agree about which novelist — Thackeray? Collins? Hardy? — Fowles was imitating. William Golding's *Lord of the Flies*, an internationally admired modern 'classic', is interpreted as a refutation of Victorian myths of imperialism. Kingsley Amis, in a remarkable variety of novels, has explored Victorian standards in a contemporary state of decay. Anthony Powell, whose twelve-volume *A Dance to the Music of Time* spans the complicated cultural changes between late Victorian and contemporary life, creates an enormous fictional masquerade whose affinities extend beyond the traditional novel into seventeenth-century and Renaissance prose.

It is not my intention to pursue the question of the bearing of Bakhtin's 'menippea' in discussing modern English novelists in the following chapters. But in looking at relations between modern and Victorian styles of fiction in a group of contemporary novelists I want to keep in mind the larger context of narrative possibilities which this concept provides. It may be objected that a Lucianic, Rabelaisian mode is amoral and therefore incompatible with the novelist's scrutiny of individual motive and responsibility. But, on the contrary, the truth-seeking instinct of the menippea corresponds to the concern in the present-day novel to find a way to preserve a moral sense with honesty. Iris Murdoch's *Under the Net* is a good example. With its surrealist sequences, its bohemian worlds poised between fantasy and realism, its socially mobile intellectual adventurer hero Jake, its constant debating of basic financial, political and social problems, its carnivalised atmosphere — it is thoroughly menippean. It is even more so in its questioning of how to behave. Malcolm Bradbury points out that Jake's self-discovery is 'as much philosophical as moral', though reminding us of George Eliot and Henry James; it is less to do with 'moral competence' than with 'knowing the truth' (*Possibilities*, p. 246). If contemporary novelists regard 'moral competence' with more scepticism than their predecessors, they are concerned with testing the truth of the great tradition itself; and this remorseless questioning of life through narrative, far older than the novel, is happily still a going concern.

2 John Fowles: *The French Lieutenant's Woman*

'They are waiting for the new Trollope . . .' Durrell's 'London publishers' peer from their windows in vain. Meanwhile, Bernard Bergonzi speculates, in *The Situation of the Novel* (1970), that the weekly reviewer, confronted with a mixed batch of 'bedsitter epyllion', 'Welsh mining village' and latest 'gritty version' of the New Novel, 'may still be looking out for a new *Dombey and Son* or a new *Wuthering Heights*' . . . though the expectation is unrealistic.[1] John Fowles's third novel, *The French Lieutenant's Woman* which appeared in 1969, delighted reviewers and its own publishers by contriving to offer both a fresh version of a nineteenth-century novel and a definitive exorcism of the elusive 'new Trollope' in the interest of modern consciousness.

Although the novel came out too late for Bernard Bergonzi to discuss it in *The Situation of the Novel* in 1970, he used the Preface of the Pelican edition to express his 'intense admiration' for this book, despite his poor view of Fowles's work up to then. He discusses it at length in the 1979 edition; the 1972 Preface had summed up its achievement: 'John Fowles has made a remarkable re-creation of the sense of life of the Victorian novel whilst preserving a full consciousness of the essentially problematic nature of fictional form in our time.' The result has proved a best-seller and a critical success. It is not surprising that Bergonzi should have singled it out for special praise. *The Situation of the Novel* could be seen as an open invitation to write such a work; novel and critical survey in fact were composed almost simultaneously. The novel was given the welcome accorded to books (like *Vanity Fair* and *Jane Eyre* in 1847) which seem to say very clearly what everyone has vaguely had in mind, and reveal a new talent, fully developed.

The French Lieutenant's Woman was received as the book of the moment certainly, and perhaps of the decade. The (then anonymous) *Times Literary Supplement* reviewer, in a congratulatory notice (quite unlike Michael Mason's savage *TLS* review of *Daniel Martin* in 1977) suggested why:

> This imagined novelist is himself one of the subjects under discussion: he is at once a mask for John Fowles, and his butt, while representing an admission that Fowles and his readers are still much governed by Victorian concepts — and uncertain whether a more acceptable convention for novel-writing has yet been discovered (12 June 1969).

Fowles had been one of the English novelists most conspicuously at work to discover it. He was best known in 1969 for *The Magus* (1966), although better known and liked in America than in England. Bergonzi attacks *The Magus* in *The Situation of the Novel* as the work of an Englishman, who ought to know better, aping American pretentiousness. Malcolm Bradbury, on the other hand, complains in *Possibilities* that the intellectual sluggishness of the cultural scene in Britain in the 1960s makes it 'uncurious' that *The Magus* was ignored and surprising that so wide-awake a novelist should have emerged from such a background. He sees it (the 1966 version; a revised text came out in 1977) as a creatively experimental work relevant to our philosophical and aesthetic problems. Malcolm Bradbury is an obvious example of a novelist with a keen sense of these problems but his novels are more entertaining than Fowles (in 1966 or 1977) in *The Magus*. The old-fashioned rules of the Victorian story-teller provide a discipline in *The French Lieutenant's Woman* for Fowles's prolix, intellectualising inclinations. *The Magus* is too theoretical for the ordinary British reader.

Pretentiousness is a hard charge to rule on. Any writer seriously influenced by French thinkers of the last thirty years is in danger of seeming pretentious in England, and as structuralism comes to be discussed (twenty years late) in English universities this problem grows more acute. Bernard Bergonzi's account of *The Magus*, whose schoolmaster protagonist Nicholas Urfe, teaching on a Greek island, suffers as Bergonzi says 'a succession of appalling things', lists the atrocities that go on, and creates the impression that Fowles must lack a proper sense of proportion (p. 75). Proportion, decency, humour are criteria that English reviewers have used to resist the excesses of ultra-modernist fiction, and the only good objection to them is that they keep out what is intellectually adventurous. One attraction of *The French Lieutenant's Woman*, for all but the most austere, was in being intellectually exciting within the bounds of common readability. Another was in testing the conditions of fiction, which were felt to need testing, but doing so in the world of the Victorian novel and restoring, for once at least, its solid narrative comforts, for which there was and still is an obvious hankering.

Yet another appeal can be seen in its coinciding with the beginning of the present craze for the 'vanished civilisation' of the Victorians. John Fowles's account of the book's genesis is revealing about this aspect of its success:

> It started four or five months ago as a visual image. A woman stands at the end of a deserted quay and stares out to sea. That was all. This image rose in my mind one morning when I was still in bed half asleep . . .
>
> It was obviously mysterious. It was vaguely romantic. It also seemed, perhaps because of the latter quality, not to belong to today. The woman obstinately refused to stare out of the window of an airport lounge; it had to be this ancient quay . . . The woman had no face, no particular degree of sexuality. But she was Victorian; and since I always saw her in the same static long shot, with her back turned, she represented a reproach on the Victorian Age. An outcast. I didn't know her crime . . .[2]

Mysterious, romantic, reproachful, the image from Fowles's idea of the past attached itself to a particular quay near his home and reminded him of 'obscure books and forgotten prints' from his collections. Such images can affect us as photographs do from the especially remote-seeming period just beyond what anyone alive can remember: it is a feeling reflected in the many anthologies of photographs of Victorian towns and counties. There is a narrative interest in many of the photographs and Fowles's novel caters for a similar curiosity in its scenes of Lyme and London. Fowles calls his image of the girl 'mythopoeic'. We are drawn by such images because they help us with the myth-making which George Steiner discusses, by which we try to define ourselves (see Chapter 7 below). The reproachful figure is particularly evocative and useful in this way, and suggests yet another kind of interest in the novel.

The counterpart of current nostalgia for the nineteenth century has been a fascination with Victorian scandal. Revelations in studies like Steven Marcus's *The Other Victorians* (1966)[3] are rivalled by many passages in *The French Lieutenant's Woman*. Chapter 35 is an essay answering a question raised in the story: 'What can an innocent country virgin know of sin?' The narrator turns his best didactic, rhetorical Victorian manner on Victorian hypocrisy about sex:

> What are we faced with in the nineteenth century? An age where woman was sacred; and where you could buy a thirteen-year-old girl for a few pounds — a few shillings if you wanted her for only an hour or two. Where more churches were built than in the whole previous history of the country; and where one in sixty houses in London was a brothel (the modern ratio would be nearer one in six thousand). Where . . .

At the head of the chapter is an extract from a Children's Employment Commission Report (1867). Yet it is typical of the novel's method that the narrative voice catches both an indignant Victorian tone (though with greater frankness) and a contemporary smugness. The *TLS* reviewer pointed out that we are still more Victorian — prurient and puritan — than we like to acknowledge in our attitudes to the nineteenth century. This narrator spans the century and his 'revelations' of our predecessors' social problems are more subtly and maturely conceived than in many literary–historical 'exposures'. He uses the 'myth' of the guilty Victorian, which draws us, but disturbs our complacency too.

'What can it have been like, in bed with Mr Knightley?' broods Jane Gray in Margaret Drabble's *The Waterfall* (1969); 'Sorrow awaited that woman' (Penguin, p. 58). 'Emancipated' as we consider ourselves, we are impatient with the reticences of nineteenth-century fiction, what were Casaubon's sexual relations with Dorothea? Lord Steyne's with Becky Sharpe? Fowles's novel seemed to be letting us into secrets about what Victorians got up to. When Charles Smithson goes up to London he spends a riotous evening at his club with a pair of cronies 'discussing' milk punch and champagne as if in a Trollope novel. But Fowles takes him on, after dinner, to a zone of London near the Haymarket said to be 'very nearly unrelieved brothel', to a place 'where damn lucky fellows always go of a jolly night', as one of the cronies explains. 'A Victorian novel no Victorian would have written', *Cosmopolitan*'s reviewer gloated.

There is a sensationalism, typical of the 1960s, about this part of the book, but it can also be seen as a development of the old social commitment of the realist novel. At its most historically responsible our interest in the seamier side of the Haymarket is connected with our interest in cultural continuity, in how our social conditions came about. But although it re-creates an older sort of realism, to serve the old purpose of studying society, *The French Lieutenant's Woman* is quite unlike a realistic Victorian novel. In its capacity to re-create and redefine an older fictional life it is a key to understanding the best of contemporary British novelists whose relations with Victorian fiction and culture, although less conspicuous than here, are often equally intimate and complex.

The novelist points to his mask, to borrow Roland Barthes's favourite image for the self-conscious artist,[4] on the first page. A young couple walk on the quay at Lyme Regis on a March morning in 1867. The story sets off with a perfectly appropriate self-assurance: 'The Cobb has invited what familiarity breeds for at least seven hundred years . . .' The opening paragraph goes on to compare the Cobb to Piraeus, allude to local taxes for its upkeep, mimic the guide books which call it 'redolent' of English history — the Armada, Monmouth — praise it as a piece of folk-art, and finally refer its 'subtle curves and volumes' to Henry Moore and so abruptly let us know that this is a 1960s narrative. The prose is meant to seem more like that of the 1860s: Thackeray's perhaps, if he had lived on after 1863, his writing become crisper after *Denis Duval*. It has a fluent control of its circumlocutions, a wordiness and formality not quite pompous and a socially superior way with the reader: we are well-travelled, or at least we know about Athens; we can look down financially on the small provincial taxes of Lyme; we have better taste than some guide-book readers; we understand art. Thackeray creates this kind of relationship with his reader. Mentioning Henry Moore makes us aware of mimicry, and of parody even in the format: the verse of Hardy as epigraph to the chapter is in the manner of George Eliot and Hardy (imitating Scott and preVictorian novelists). 'I don't think of it as an historical novel, a genre in which I have very little interest,' Fowles has said.[5] Yet with sixty-one chapters, many of them with two epigraphs, this device provides a chorus of historical images and ideas: Hardy, Clough, Tennyson (especially *Maud*), Arnold, Carroll, Newman, Leslie Stephen are mingled with Darwin and Marx, and only interrupted occasionally by G. M. Young.

In fact, the opening chapters establish a principle of contrast: Thackeray, Arnold and Clough on one side; Fowlesian style and content on the other. The perspective, though, is constantly shifting; we wonder which side Marx belongs to; the 'omniscience' of the narrator makes him ambiguous, belonging to both ages, an effect explained by the *TLS* reviewer by supposing him a hundred and fifty years old. Sometimes he is demurely Victorian (perhaps Trollope): 'Of the three young women who pass through these pages Mary was, in my opinion, by far the prettiest' (Chapter 11). At other times the century of hindsight gives him an elevation beyond that of any godlike pre-Jamesian narrator: 'Charles did not know it, but in those brief poised seconds above the waiting sea, in that luminous evening silence broken only by the waves' quiet wash the whole Victorian age was lost' (Chapter 10).

The first dozen chapters, as in a well-constructed, old-fashioned novel, introduce us to the characters, the situation, the background, and to the range of tones — pleasantly informal about Mary, tantalisingly portentous about the whole Victorian age. We get accustomed to the reassuringly predictable 1860s circumstances: the clever cockney servant Sam chasing the pretty country girl Mary, the well-born Charles engaged to the wealthy Ernestina. We enjoy the hints of destiny riding above the characters' heads: 'needless to say Charles knew nothing of the beavered German Jew quietly working, as it so happened, that very afternoon in the British Museum library' (Chapter 3). We may perhaps recognise that in talking to us about Marx or Darwin, or about the social revolution in the manservant's struggle to improve himself, the narrator, true to Victorian practice, is flattering us (saying in effect 'learned reader') while still assuming us to have only a modest, middle-brow knowledgeability. However well-up we may or may not be in Victorian studies, we enjoy the sense that a literary game is in process, under control and meant to be accessible to the reader (in Vladimir Nabokov, and other 'fabulating' writers, it often seems that the reader is meant to be excluded). We also share the kind of interest Victorian readers would have brought to a good dramatic situation: will Charles be faithful to his fiancée Ernestina, or will he yield to the strange charm of Sarah Woodruff, the proud, abandoned 'French Lieutenant's Woman'? Will Mrs Poulteney, Sarah's fiercely righteous protectress, find out about her secret meetings with Charles? Recognising a fashionable sort of game with novel conventions, we are free to enjoy a good story at the same time until the end of Chapter 12, which teases with an old-fashioned note: 'Who is Sarah? Out of what shadows does she come?' Chapter 13 answers, 'I do not know' and cuts into the illusion with B. S. Johnsonian impatience:

> I do not know. This story I am telling is all imagination. These characters I create never existed outside my own mind. If I have pretended until now to know my characters' minds and in-nermost thoughts, it is because I am writing in (just as I have assumed some of the vocabulary and 'voice' of) a convention universally accepted at the time of my story; that the novelist stands next to God. He may not know all, yet he tries to pretend that he does. But I live in the age of Alain Robbe-Grillet and Roland Barthes; if this is a novel, it cannot be a novel in the modern sense of the word.

Most of Chapter 13 is a discussion of the terms on which the novel is written, given the competing claims of omniscient narrator and independent action in the characters. 'When Charles left Sarah . . . I ordered him to walk straight back to Lyme Regis. But he did not . . . Oh, but you say, come on — ' Freedom for the characters, not authority in the narrator, is our first principle today, Fowles tells us. As for illusion-breaking he sounds very like Butor: 'fiction is woven into all, as a Greek observed'; our lives, Butor says in 'Le roman comme recherche' are steeped in narrative. '*Hypocrite lecteur*' Fowles says, for pretending to think that a character is real or imaginary; we can't help fictionalising our lives. 'We are all in flight from the real reality.' If we think the digression has nothing to do with the 'capitalised ghosts in the night', Time, Progress, society, evolution, the narrator says, 'I will not argue. But I shall suspect you.'

This is, despite *Tristram Shandy*, a very modern rhetoric of fiction. Joining in, as we are invited, we might say that the authority is harder to abdicate than Fowles thinks; that his whole digression is authoritarian, that writing itself is so, in the sense he means. Also that our lives necessitate a constant effort to separate the fictional from the real, and that novelists are meant to help, not to confuse the issue. And finally 'Oh, but come on — ' and break off, since he has thought of what we are saying himself.

There is another serious jolt to the course of the narrative at the end of Chapter 44 and the start of 45. Repeated meetings with the unhappy though formidable Sarah have made a conquest of Charles. Meanwhile his prospects of inheriting from his rich old bachelor baronet uncle are dashed when Sir Robert gets engaged. Ernestina's Papa, the great store-owner, now begins to patronise him with hints that Charles might take an interest in trade. Summarising brings out the hackneyed nature of the plot which, to read, is compelling. A crisis approaches as Charles returns to Lyme from London, feeling tainted by the menace of 'trade'. He must pass through Exeter where Sarah, an almost fallen woman, having fled from Lyme, is poised over the social abyss. Will he go to her or cling to his engagement and safety? Chapter 44 takes him home to Ernestina and a clean breast. 'And so ends the story', says the narrator (though we can see it doesn't), and fills in the aftermath with the routine bounty of a Victorian last chapter: seven children for Tina, twin heirs for Sir Robert, a successful future in trade, after all, for Charles. The villainously upright Mrs Poulteney, after a pleasing Byronic *himmelspforten* scene, goes to hell, 'a thoroughly traditional ending' as the text observes.

An equally Byronic panache now attributes this ending to Charles's daydream in the train: we are reminded of how we all fictionalise our lives. We are meant to have a sharper sense of a character's 'freedom' when Charles puts up at the Ship in Exeter and goes to call at Sarah's lodging. The next sequence takes him from Sarah's bed to the altar of an Exeter church and ends with him scrubbing Sarah's bloodstains off his shirt in a tub at the Ship. He has chosen Sarah but — a Hardyesque touch — his message goes astray and next morning she has vanished. The rest of the novel deals with his Rochester-like wanderings about Europe and America while his lawyer tries to trace her. The novelist as narrator makes several further interventions. In Chapter 55 he appears in Charles's railway carriage, in the guise of a Victorian novelist, and we see him brooding over Charles — his own fictional creation — and tossing a coin to show his power. He continues to discuss Victorian fiction in the text; the narrator comments on the intrusive figure (bearded and suggestive of Trollope) of the novelist we are meant to see in the carriage (the 'I'): his 'look' as he contemplates Charles is an omniscient creator's. 'Not at all what we think of as a divine look; but one of a distinctly mean and dubious . . . moral quality.' Should Charles be simply abandoned for ever in the train? No; 'the conventions of Victorian fiction allow, allowed no place for the open, the inconclusive ending'. How is an author to dictate the outcome and still respect his characters' freedom? He concludes that two endings are needed to establish 'objectivity', and the figure in the railway carriage spins a coin to decide which comes first.

Charles is brought back to London from America by a telegram — 'She is found' — and so to undesirable riverside Chelsea where Sarah is living with the Rossettis. The historical interest is done just in the manner of a Victorian novel about an earlier period with much coyness about the famous names: ' "That gentleman in there — is he not . . .?" She nodded . . .' A liberated Sarah, dressed as a New Woman, receives him with a dignity he hadn't expected: 'How came you here, Mr Smithson?' But the scene works out happily with Charles holding their baby daughter in his arms. Outside in Cheyne Walk, by the sewage-laden Thames, is the vulgar figure of a 'successful impresario'. This new version of the novelist takes out his watch and turns it back a quarter of an hour.

The final scene is 're-run'. As Sarah clasps Charles's arm, he revolts at the thought of her independence, integrity and new role among the Rossettis, and he leaves. This is offered as an equally plausible ending. The narrator's discussion of the implications seems more than ever like the critical in Fowles thwarting the creative since the world of the novel remains so real, and the effort to deny its cogency so persuasive. The overall result, Malcolm Bradbury writes, is 'a very elegant endeavour at assessing the mental distance that must lie between a modern reader' and a Victorian novel (*Possibilities*, p. 260). Existentialist philosophy is the formula which is used in discussing that distance. Since we no longer take our world for granted, we should not do so with the world of fiction; its characters must somehow match the existential freedom of a modern reader, fully 'aware' of his own predicament.

Yet few readers live up to the rigour of Sartrean existentialist philosophy, and we let ourselves be absorbed in a story as we do in our lives. We listen to 'John Fowles' the theorist with exceptional attentiveness because his old-fashioned story-telling power works so well. Christopher Ricks, who reviewed *The French Lieutenant's Woman* in the *New York Review of Books* (XIV, 3, p. 22) in 1970, under the title 'The Unignorable Real', must be as fully aware as any reader of the distance between modern and Victorian minds, but he found the manipulation of our sense of an ending 'a tease'. He stressed the comparison with Dickens's problem of how to finish *Great Expectations*; Dickens rewrote his original version of the ending more optimistically, giving Pip a hope of Estella (on the advice of

Bulwer Lytton), but he didn't try to have it both ways. Fiction, Christopher Ricks insisted, has to be coercive:

> For there would not be, in life, two possibilities but virtually an infinity of them. To reduce this infinity to two alternatives is no less manipulatory and coercive — though because of its quasi-abnegation it is far more congenial to modern taste — than was the Victorian novelistic reduction of this infinity to one eventuality.

'But then,' he finishes, 'perhaps such is enigmatic Mr Fowles's point. After all, he is not credulous about modern taste.' Two American authors, William Palmer, in *The Fiction of John Fowles* (University of Missouri Press, Columbia, 1974), and Peter Wolfe, in *John Fowles, Magus and Moralist* (Bucknell University Press, Lewisburg, 1976), interpret him as an existentialist. The reader's existential freedom is to be respected, they say. He is, according to William Palmer, to choose the ending that suits him. Many novel readers want to be dictated to, however, and enjoy the old sort of pretending, and Ricks is right to assume that Fowles knows it.

Malcolm Bradbury's statement of the novel's enigmatic poise sums up its subtlety, and can hardly be improved on: it could be, he writes, in *Possibilities* (p. 258), 'a very Whig novel about emancipation through history, with Victorian hypocrisy and ignorance yielding up to modern truth and authenticity'; but it can also be read as 'a novel of ironic counterpointings in which the present may make no such triumph over the past, in which emancipation is . . . a loss as well as a gain'. Or, again, it is possible that 'the modernist fiction is . . . being questioned' by the Victorian 'substance and realism'. *Daniel Martin* confirms that Fowles wants somehow to re-create the positive aesthetic quality of Victorian fiction for modern experience. One reason for the phenomenal success of Fowles's books is that he communicates very strongly his own interest and enjoyment in them. His pleasure in the older novelist's role makes his Lyme in 1867 attractive to a readership far beyond the critical-minded community Christopher Ricks and Malcolm Bradbury have in mind, which is, perhaps, after all, what makes it a real novel.

Great Expectations, Fowles tells us in the introduction to the revised second edition of *The Magus*, has a special place among his favourite novels, and influenced the original *Magus* without his knowing it. We are likely to think of it here: just as Biddy and Estella stand for two alternative types of girlhood and Pip needs to meet no others, so Charles and Ernestina, Sarah and Mrs Poulteney represent the social forces of the time. Charles is a gentleman born, Ernestina, the daughter of a gentleman from 'trade'; Sam is a clever London servant moving up in society, Mary a pleasant country girl ready to adapt. The Lyme lady, Mrs Poulteney, incarnates the narrow, bigoted, inhumane religiosity we feel we know all about (not unlike Dickens's Mrs Clennam). Sarah, deserted by the ungentlemanly French Merchant Navy officer she nursed after his shipwreck, has a conscious sexuality unacceptable in middle-class life in that time.

Defining their roles like this shows how closely they correspond to archetypal figures in our knowledge of the Victorians. Charles is the heir to a baronetcy; Tina's Papa is a draper: Fowles has made the details conform to a classic scheme of the arranged marriage in England. 'I brought the breeding and you brought the dough,' sing the children sending up the pre-1914 world of their parents in Angus Wilson's *No Laughing Matter*. Christopher Ricks quoted a line from Tennyson (unused in the text of *Maud*) to illustrate the reality of what Fowles imagines: 'Buy me, o buy me and have me, for I am here to be sold.' Equally central and exemplary — almost as if devised for a history lesson — is Charles's quarrel with Ernestina's Papa, over Darwin: 'He did say that he would not let his daughter marry a man who considered his grandfather to be an ape. But I think on reflection he will recall that in my case it was a titled ape' (Chapter 2). The account of Charles's relations with the rustic, claret-drinking baronet uncle is equally typical, as are the details of his education. He crams classics, drifts into a bad set, thinks of Holy Orders and is cured of such thoughts in Paris, takes to agnosticism and amateur science, and is trapped at thirty-two by a clever, suitable girl into the society marriage which is soon to complete the almost textbook correctness of his life so far. We are not allowed to miss the point that he belongs to a species competing to survive. Of course the Victorian convention justifies this: George Eliot's Lydgate in *Middlemarch* and Trollope's Louis Trevelyan in *He Knew He Was Right* are possible models for Charles; they have similarly full sets of generic traits. As with Victorian characters, we see Charles in clear relation to his roles, as heir, fiancé and scientist, and these seem to authenticate the incidental touches of detail: his paddling in a rockpool, dawdling for a glass of milk or peeping at girls. The imputation, that he's as fine a sample as the fossils he studies, does not take away from his vivid individuality.

The same is true of Ernestina, Mrs Poulteney, Sam and Mary, Uncle Robert, Papa, and the two single Lyme worthies, Tina's Aunt Tranter and Charles's friend Dr Grogan. Only Sarah is imagined apart from the roles in which the other characters see her. Our sense of how fully they belong to their own time is stronger than could have been achieved in a Victorian novel, even one set back thirty years or so; we might compare *Henry Esmond*, but the nineteenth century is more important to us and more dramatically different than the Augustan period was to Thackeray's readers, and also more intimately known to us because of its novels. Certain occasions are particularly familiar from fiction, and in them our impression of the Victorian is strongest: of the details of personal conduct seen in relation to social rules, for example, in the morning call at Mrs Poulteney's, in Chapter 14.

Mrs Poulteney considers Ernestina 'a frivolous young woman', and expects to disapprove of Charles. She feels it is 'almost her duty to embarrass them' therefore, and she always thinks it her duty to inflict a penance on her 'companion', Sarah, in the form of social discomfort. Such an outlook makes the merest formalities dramatic: ' "How are you, Mrs Poulteney? You look exceedingly well." "At my age, Miss Freeman, spiritual health is all that counts," "Then I have no fears for you." '

Mrs Poulteney is prevented from discussing her physical and spiritual state further, but she manages to get the conversation on to the subject of her late husband, whose portrait is 'the house's chief icon', and his 'wishes', which still rule her life. Although gruesome, this scene is not far from comic and prepares for a moment which comes later in the novel when Charles revolts against the idea in Tennyson's 'There must be wisdom with great Death/The dead shall look me through and through', and we are told that 'what he was throwing off haunted, and profoundly damaged his age' (Chapter 48). The 'Whig' spirit of emancipation through history is active in both passages. In the first, the stiff courtesies that modern life goes without are made to appear repressive and morbid. Property and death, politeness and spite are connected; aggression lurks in the dialogue's ambiguities. Sarcasm in the narrative, in terms like 'icon', is a reaction on our behalf not merely to Mrs Poulteney, whose co-Victorians dislike her, but to the whole civilisation she represents so adversely. Sarah is present, silent and resentful, a reproach to her age, as Fowles first imagined her.

When the quarrel surfaces — over a servant-girl's behaviour — and Mrs Poulteney contrives to rebuke Charles for misjudgement, a look is exchanged between Charles and Sarah which is meant to express a spirit of revolt that our own emancipated society would endorse. But the strength and sensitivity of the social order even when seen in this sordid moment produce a different effect and we see what Malcolm Bradbury means by saying that emancipation can appear a loss. Charles is supporting — against Ernestina's opinion — Aunt Tranter's indulgence to the maid Mary: a happy maidservant is a sure sign of a happy house, he says; Ernestina lowers her eyes and tightens her lips; her aunt blushes and looks down, conscious of the compliment. Mrs Poulteney tells Charles he will learn to judge better when he is older; and then all three ladies 'sit with averted eyes' (Chapter 14).

The epigraph for the chapter is from *Persuasion* (the great Lyme novel); Mr Elliot tells Anne that 'good company', as opposed to the best, 'requires only birth, education, and manners, and with regard to education is not very nice'. Jane Austen was writing half a century earlier; her exact social and moral distinctions presented as abnormal the vulgarity which Dickens and Thackeray made pervasive in the relatively amorphous and coarse worlds of their mid-century novels. Yet if Jane Austen had lived (like Aunt Tranter) into her nineties, she could still have recognised in Lyme in 1867 Mr Elliot's principles of good company. They can be seen in the deliberation with which Charles is gallant to Aunt Tranter and Mrs Poulteney is rude to him; in the competing authorities of Charles as a gentleman and Mrs Poulteney as an elderly widow, and in the relative status of the three independent women, in contrast to the companion's complete lack of it. In minutiae like the tightened lips, the blush, the averted eyes, pressure is exerted by the still coherent civilisation which twentieth-century novelists can see disintegrating. To create a comparable effect, a modern expert in awkward moments such as Kingsley Amis would be forced into a comedy of sexual manners; only there would he find equally strong conventions of behaviour obtaining with us. We can see in this passage the 'interest' Iris Murdoch speaks of in Victorian society's possibilities for the novelist, [6] and although it lets us feel superior to its humbug, we can see too the loss of a stable social world, a loss inseparable from the gains.

Chapter 7, which is a brief (1500-word) incident between Charles and his servant, Sam, is a different type of scene because it is one that a Victorian novelist could not have treated so freely. Some were franker than others about servants; Thackeray's reflections on 'our servants' and how little we know about them were stuffy and complacent by Dickens's standards. But no one could free himself — at least in England — from hesitation and embarrassment. Fowles sets a quotation from Marx's *Capital* (1867) at the head of the chapter ('reproduction of the ancient domestic slaves under the name of a servant class') and introduces a social-historical hindsight that would have disconcerted Marx. Our superiority by a hundred years is at its most significant in this scene.

The circumstances for the meeting of master and man are idyllic to a Wodehousean degree. Warm spring air blows through the bedroom window of the inn-room at Lyme: Sam brings razor and steaming jug, while a rider rattles quietly by on the cobbled street outside. The wind stirring the faded curtains, the baa-ing of sheep below and the sight of a shepherd with smock and crook make Charles feel, 'Really the country is charming.' The security and peace of nineteenth-century England are so strongly evoked that the last sentence dispels a suggestion of advertising copy for some product with 'traditional' connotations, with a necessary ironic reminder of the vantage point: that of a rich townsman on a pleasant country morning. Sam, meanwhile, is sulking in the background over a snub received from a country girl across the way, which all the ostlers ('hall the hostlers') heard, and Charles teases him about it with tedious word-play and patronising affability which seem very plausible. Sam's exact place in the history of Victorian servants is explained in Fowles's didactic narrative voice. Thirty years on from Sam Weller, this type of cockney attendant has risen to be a 'gent' or 'snob', clothes-conscious and worried about getting his aspirates right. His master's condescension is seen in perspective too; it is better than the chilly 'distance' of the new rich who try to treat servants like machines. Charles as a gentleman accepts Sam as a sort of companion. Sam puts up with things cheerfully enough for now, and looks down on the rustics. The older rural society which has always made master–servant relations feel natural is distinguished from the industrial, commercial world which Marx was thinking of. The realism which sets a casual conversation so firmly in its social frame is just what many Victorian novelists were aiming at, without Fowles's unfair advantage. The 'individual' and the 'type' merge, as

Iris Murdoch notes of the nineteenth century;[7] and individuals struggling in society are what the novelist sees, with a dispassionate interest not possible for English novelists at the time.

A Murdochian relish for the bizarre which seems humanly significant — not just eccentric — appears in scenes of both types, those familiar from older novels like the Thackerayan visit to Mrs Poulteney, and those beyond the Victorian reach. Among the first are some where Fowles is slightly more free with religion than Trollope would dare to be: Mrs Poulteney consults a clergyman about her immortal soul and its prospects *vis-à-vis* that of Lady Cotton who does good deeds. The vicar is reassuring — 'dear Madam, your feet are on the Rock' — but advises taking on Sarah as a charitable case. There are objections to be overcome: ' "She speaks French?" ' Mrs Poulteney's alarm at this appalling disclosure was nearly enough to sink the vicar' (Chapter 6).

Particularly moving among the second order of scenes is the incident with the prostitute who entertains the drunken Charles after his evening out with Sir Tom and the bishop's son in Chapters 39 to 41. When Charles vomits from his earlier excesses she becomes 'as calm as a nurse as she had promised to be a prostitute'. Charles keeps groaning apologies between retches: 'most sorry . . . something disagreed . . .' He sits 'ludicrously like an old granny' while she looks after him, then fetches him a cab while he looks after her baby. She is mystified when he leaves five times the normal price: ' "O sir . . . thank you. Thank you." He realised she had tears in her eyes; no shock to the poor like unearned money. "You are a brave, kind girl" ' (Chapter 41). A Victorian emphasis on the parallels, giving this girl too the name of Sarah, reminds us that Sarah Woodruff has only sevenpence in the world when she goes to Mrs Poulteney. There are many sympathetic prostitutes in modern English fiction, but often, as with Simon Raven's friendly, tolerant whores, they are presented with sentimentality and cynicism, which Fowles keeps out. Charles's words on parting are appropriate. Setting them beside Mrs Poulteney's horror at knowing French shows the range of social life in the novel and the strength of its old-fashioned realism and humanism. These are effective despite the 'perplexing barrier' Malcolm Bradbury writes of, between Victorian and modern poetics. Our interest in 'individuals struggling in society', in Iris Murdoch's phrase, survives the sense of parody.

The reviewer in the *Times Literary Supplement* in 1969 concluded with an observation that suggests the way Fowles combines the older realism with a modern view of 'the human condition'. Commenting on the book's vision of life as it used to be lived, the *TLS* reviewer wrote: 'There is something very Marxian about his respect for other generations, trapped in their own times' (12 June 1969). The fact that we see these 'self-contained' past lives so vividly is something original. Fowles denied all interest in historical novels, but he has produced a unique version of the genre even so, since his combination of literary visions is new. The result is a new kind of perspective.

It is accompanied by an almost overwhelming — and for some readers excessive — intellectual debate about the history of our culture in the last hundred years. The views of Marx, Darwin, Matthew Arnold and Sartre are marshalled in the last chapter, in Fowles's own synthesis. Throughout the book the array of serious opinion, set out as parody of Eliot or Hardy, threatens to tire the average reader out of patience with the competing claims of so many great thinkers; as popular summaries of the history of ideas tend to do. The modern idea of 'authenticity', however, joined on the last page with Arnold's 'piety', serves as a guide to Fowles's interpretation of man. Sarah Woodruff's gaze, with its unseemly power (in a woman) to silence Charles's prosings, conveys a modern message. The narrator explains:

> When one was skating over so much thin ice — ubiquitous economic oppression, terror of sexuality, the flood of mechanistic science — the ability to close one's eyes to one's own absurd stiffness was essential. Very few Victorians chose to question the virtues of such cryptic coloration; but there was that in Sarah's look which did. Though direct, it was a timid look. Yet behind it lay a very modern phrase: come clean, Charles, come clean.
> [Chapter 18]

By 'cryptic coloration' (Darwin's term), a species strives to escape extinction. Charles and Mrs Poultency are social equivalents whose camouflage the novelist's scrutiny clears away. Mrs Poulteney's kitchen walls, despite her obsession with fighting dirt, are ingrained with arsenic; being charitable matters to her, but her garden is snared with man-traps, and her servants work a hundred-hour week. She has a bowdlerised Bible, yet she dreads hell. Her supposed charity, in taking Sarah in, leads to the real cruelty of

driving her out again. The domestic 'slavery' (Marx is confirmed by
her household) is supported by the poverty of the countryside her
girls come from and the mass prostitution they might otherwise be
driven to. She is sufficiently 'coloured', all the same, for Aunt
Tranter and Charles and Dr Grogan to call on her and pay their
respects. 'Come clean' is the modern challenge to them, the 'Whig',
progressive determination of the novel.

The debate between the two Darwinians, Charles and
Dr Grogan, shows the effort of responsible minds to see through
their illusions, and how trapped they are in their generations.
Charles, more emotionally vulnerable than the doctor, feels the
shock of Darwin as he looks at his fossils' record of the tragedies of
ammonites ninety million years before: 'existence was without
history, was always now'; 'history, religion, duty, social position, all
were illusions' (Chapter 25). Challenged by Grogan over his moral
conduct, he protests at the 'mealy-mouthed hypocrisy' of their time
and pleads for scientific honesty. Grogan replies with plain, liberal
advice: Charles belongs to a scientific elect and must strive for moral
superiority too; elects who fail in this respect are no more than
'despots, sultans'. We see Grogan and Charles as Victorians here,
but we are conscious also of their human situation, trapped by
history and helpless in time. We sympathise with them as men of
their age, and simply as men.

The success of Dr Grogan as a character, his blend of intellectual
freedom and social conventionality, true to the solidity of life the
book creates, vouches for the truth of his humanist belief; his
credibility resists the tricks the technique plays with it. The
narrator's new-novelistic interventions come to seem a form of
unreliability, which does not, finally, interfere with the character's
integrity. 'Real people are destructive of myth' Iris Murdoch
proclaims, and what she means can be seen in Fowles's people.[8] The
Murdochian way of reading is the one we must end up with.
Grogan's moral imperative is circumscribed by layers of scepticism
about his real and fictional rights to exist, but he is still there, and it
still counts. Man is ephemeral in the scale of geology, and character
is absurdly manipulable in fiction, but we are left with our need for
the novel and its moral, humanist dimension, even so.

The French Lieutenant's Woman serves as a revealing introduction to
the work of other modern novelists, who are as conscious as Fowles is
(although less explicitly) of the need to be wary about the nature of
fiction. It might, not unkindly, be suggested that John Fowles

possesses a Victorian quality of earnestness, which in this novel helped him to bring out clearly certain basic artistic preoccupations of the time.

It is a brilliant, but also a conscientious work. In some of his contemporaries there is a more menippean attitude to fiction, a more boisterous, equally entertaining, but sometimes less intellectually scrupulous acceptance of the possibilities of the novel. Iris Murdoch, Angus Wilson and Kingsley Amis have exploited in comedy, as Fowles has explored in this study, the incongruities of fiction today.

3 Iris Murdoch's Contemporary World

Iris Murdoch's novels have always divided critical opinion sharply, for and against. '*Under the Net* is a winner,' wrote Kingsley Amis, reviewing her first novel in the *Spectator* in 1954, and called her 'a distinguished novelist of a rare kind'.[1] The *New Statesman* dismissed the same novel as 'bluestocking fantasy' and 'café writing', not worth serious attention.[2] She has been vilified and eulogised ever since; her novels are attacked as the pretentious equivalent of women's magazine writing, as disguised moral philosophy and as 'non-novels'. Alternatively, she is praised by academic critics like Frank Kermode and by emphatically non-academic reviewers like Auberon Waugh. Amis's original assessment is supported twenty years later by a large body of critical work (quite apart from reviews). But the problem of defining her achievement remains, and is crucial to any interpretation of the state of the novel.

Iris Murdoch has contributed, as a 'polemicist', to use her own term, to the debate about the English novel's relations to its own past and to the New Novel abroad. Even adverse critics show a certain awe of her standing as a philosopher. She published a study of Sartre before *Under the Net*, and a number of works since dealing with moral philosophy and the purpose of art, most recently a study of Plato.[3] Her essay on the novel, 'Against Dryness' (see Chapter 1 above) has become authoritative as a source of ideas and terminology. Anyone who writes about her novels knows that she has already thought of anything he is likely to say.

She is exceptional as an Oxford philosopher in her respect for Sartre and existentialism. She is like Fowles and unlike many English and American novelists in her awareness of modern French fiction. Sartre is certainly more of an influence on her than Butor or the *nouveaux romanciers* (except perhaps Beckett, if he is one of them); and Raymond Queneau, to whom *Under the Net* is dedicated, a whimsical, witty surrealist, is normally considered a guide to its 'new brand of humour' which Amis remarked on in 1954. But Iris

Murdoch herself may have distracted attention from such influences and affinities, especially after *The Bell*, her fourth novel, in
1958, by her praise for the qualities of Victorian fiction and their
relevance to the novelist's present situation. She discusses that
predicament in terms that jar on much that has been said in recent
years by authors and critics in France.

Discussing John Holloway's theory about the English Ideology,
Bernard Bergonzi writes in *The Situation of the Novel*:

> It will be obvious that the stance of such critics as John Bayley,
> Iris Murdoch and W. J. Harvey, and their belief in the novel of
> character, stems directly from the English Ideology, which insists
> on seeing the nineteenth century as still a going concern. So at
> least it would seem to a French or American observer and it is
> hard not to use such phrases without an implied sneer . . . [p. 60]

That is not, he says, his intention; he wants, rather, to maintain a
balance between stubborn Englishness and the dismissal of contemporary British fiction as 'hopelessly rooted in the past'. But he
finds that in her novels since *The Bell* she has failed to achieve the
imaginative openness of the great nineteenth-century novelists and
instead indulges in 'fantasy, myth and manipulation' (pp. 47–8).
The charge of manipulation has been common among reviewers
who value her commitment to the English Ideology and to
generosity of moral concern. The allegation of an 'old-fashioned'
approach, on the other hand, arises in commentators like Robert
Scholes who look at her writing in relation to the 'postmodernist'
works, coming especially from American writers, which Scholes
calls 'fabulations'. The result is that her novels are sometimes
declared untrue, in their exotic patterns and plots, to the best
English tradition, and at other times declared unemancipated from
a traditional novel 'hopelessly rooted in the past'.

'Nothing is more paralysing,' says the existentialist-minded Jake
in *Under the Net*, 'than a sense of historical perspective, especially in
literary matters.'[4] But historical perspective is invited not only by
Iris Murdoch's critical and philosophical thought, and by her praise
of an earlier fictional density and mystery in rendering life, but in
the novels too. There is a deliberate fostering of elements in 'the
Murdoch world' which are intended to strike the reader as
incongruous in their connotations of period. We read her with an
unusually pronounced sense of contrast between what seems, even

affectedly, contemporary, and what seems old-fashioned in the lives of the communities she invents. This disparity can be very creative. Looked at more closely in some of the novels, it can help with interpretation of the stories themselves, as well as with the problem of Iris Murdoch's relations with other types of fiction, past and present.

In the case of *The Bell* (1958), for example, one of the most admired and discussed of the early novels, criticism has tended both to praise it in traditional terms and to find a traditional kind of problem in the central figure of the bell. In A. S. Byatt's study *Degrees of Freedom* (1965), *The Bell* is admired for the 'solid life' of 'the great nineteenth-century novelists' but the bell itself is said to be 'less interesting than the rest of the story' (p. 73). It is called 'a planted symbol' and Dora's dramatic ringing of the old bell is said to be 'a symbolic action . . . substituted for a real one' (p. 75). A. S. Byatt repeats this view in her British Council pamphlet on Iris Murdoch (1976) in the 'Writers and their Work' series which is widely read and has considerable authority. Yet, although the comparison with Victorian fiction seems appropriate, it is far from obvious that the bell acts as a conventional symbol. An article by Stephen Wall in *Essays in Criticism* in 1963, called 'The Bell in *The Bell*',[5] argues that its meaning is 'shifting and not residual', relative to the viewpoints of characters who see it as a symbol; and shows that it works as a narrative device to reveal — 'on George Eliot's principle' — how character unfolds, and not as a symbol in itself. These references to a nineteenth-century 'solid life' and to George Eliot testify to certain definite aspects of the novel's achievement. If we examine the 'solid life' of *The Bell* and the minds of the characters who find symbols in the bell, what emerges is the extent to which traditional and relatively unconventional kinds of meaning coexist throughout the novel. This can clarify both the central figure of the bell and the nature of Iris Murdoch's originality.

The presentation of both setting and characters in. *The Bell* connects a 1950s present with a nineteenth-century past. The life which the leading characters have chosen is one deliberately set apart from the contemporary world in an Anglican religious community. The nineteenth century has set its stamp on Imber Court, the house (adjoining an Anglican nunnery) where the members are lodged. There is a sense of compromise with the earlier, Victorian style of the place which seems to suit them. The old drawing-room has become a chapel, the old stables and lawns a market garden. The characters themselves contend with slightly anachronistic elements in their own make-up. In both Michael Meade and James Tayper Pace, the foremost brothers, Christianity is linked with a rural gentlemanly past. The bishop is spoken of — 'he won't want too Lenten a scene' — as if living up to a Trollopian level of gusto; the gardener is stirred by neo-feudal promptings; other members are devoted to 'crafts' in the spirit of William Morris. Paul Greenfield, the visiting art historian, comes of old German bankers, and patronises the prevailing Anglicanism in a desire to seem English. By way of contrast, Paul's wife Dora's fondness for jazz, men friends and pubs reinforces the impression of pre-1914 staidness in the Imber community. Dora comes from the lower-middle class, which Iris Murdoch sometimes writes of as if it were a remoter part of the Third World. She is said to have made 'a good marriage', and when the bishop turns up she feels that he takes her for one of the maids. She has recently left Paul for a while to live with Noel Spens, a journalist whose progressive views seem as muddled as those of the community. But Dora herself, who arrives at Imber, her luggage forgotten in the train, clutching a rescued butterfly in her hands, is delightfully uncluttered in a way that seems, in this very old-fashioned setting, a positive kind of emancipation.

The treatment of the subject of religious commitment raises a problem in itself, as Graham Greene observes: '. . . with the death of James, the religious sense was lost to the English novel, and with it the sense of the importance of the human act'.[6] In 'Against Dryness' and elsewhere, Iris Murdoch has contemplated the isolated, untranscended man conceived by twentieth-century philosophy, living in a society 'less interesting and less alive' than in the nineteenth century.[7] That there is no sustaining religious or social background for the characters in *The Bell* we can see in the precarious nature of so many features of the Imber world: the chapel in the former Victorian drawing-room; the gardener who respects Michael's social position as hereditary owner of Imber more than Michael does himself. We see both the characters' connection with a bygone cultural and social order, and how vulnerably separated from it they are.

This unease hovers in the background of their thinking about the bell. A new bell to be installed in the convent provides a convenient image for Michael and James who find quite different spiritual meanings in it: James struck by its candour, Michael by its rhythmic aspect, when they preach their sermons to the community. Even the characters find the task of delivering a sermon slightly embarrassing; obviously it is a genre earlier periods were more at ease with. Michael, as an ex-public schoolmaster, may be disturbed by thoughts of Arnold; he was obliged to leave his job after forming a romantic attachment with a pupil, Nick Fawley, who is now living, grown-up and a chronic depressive, on the Imber estate; Michael, meanwhile, has recently fallen for Toby, an engineering student staying with the community. The incongruity in this meeting of the conventional connotations of the Sermon and the more contemporary-seeming licence in Michael's behaviour, made even more pronounced by the unsuspecting James's denunciation of 'sodomy' in his own address, draws our attention to the precarious balance in which Michael and Imber are poised between a Victorian earnestness and a dangerously eccentric stance in the contemporary world. It detracts from Michael's status as a preacher and so from his interpretation of the bell as a guide to the meaning of the novel. The effect of this is to make the relative, subjective nature of the characters' viewpoint so obvious, indeed blatant, that the reader is most unlikely to attach any absolute significance to the various symbols they create. The symbolising habit of mind is in itself likely to come to seem intellectually questionable amid so much subjectivity and unreliability.

The Bell is full of such incongruities; one repeatedly finds a series of decorous, sacramental thoughts and images appearing Victorian in style in contrast to modern unseemliness and profanity. In the night before the arrival of the bishop to baptise the new bell, Toby and Dora raise from the lake the old medieval bell lost according to legend when a nun took a lover centuries before, and in their excitement make love together inside it. Its muted boom which wakes the jealous Paul, Dora's husband, and the sexually-stifled Michael, Toby's admirer, is something of a joke given the inscription '*vox ego sum amoris*'. Any sense of the bell's being symbolic and representing — as critics have suggested — 'ultimate values' or Art seems remote from what is intended here. The realisation that a symbolic bell belongs to a particular style of thought among certain of the characters is increased by the rite whereby the new bell, dressed as a postulant, is to enter the Abbey next day; it has every appearance of the Victorian medievalism to which Imber Abbey owes its existence. The scene begins with bishop, choristers and villagers attending the lake-crossing of the bridal bell, as if in a

Victorian academy painting. But Nick Fawley has sawn through the planks of the causeway, and his sister Catherine, soon to enter the Abbey herself, responds hysterically to the sign, when the bell falls into the lake, in the language of Victorian melodrama: 'God has reached out His hand. A white garment cannot conceal a wicked heart. There is no passing through that gate. Goodbye' (Chapter 23). She dives into the lake and, in what develops like a sequence from surrealist cinema, is rescued by an aquatic nun. There is a carnival spirit of comedy here, as often in the novel, which overwhelms the 'solid life' created by traditional novelistic procedures, including symbolism, encompassing it within a broader, more fantastic vision.

There are hints, in style, of George Eliot and Henry James, in turns of phrase and in a certain formality in the way a sentence is cast: 'Although to the pain of Paul and his friends the expression "let's face it", acquired in her [Dora's] student days, was still frequently on her lips, she was not in fact capable, at the moment, of confronting her situation at all' (Chapter 1). These need not, of course, have been deliberately produced, but even as unconscious echoes (here of James) there is an effect of contrast, which confirms the impression of two opposed modes of fiction, with the brisk and competent modern prose: 'The train was thundering through Maidenhead. Dora wished she had got her book out of her suitcase before the train started. She felt too shy to disturb her neighbour by doing so now. Anyway, the book was at the bottom of the case and the whisky bottles on the top, so the situation was best left alone' (Chapter 1). Delicate and close to ordinary speech, this could be Kingsley Amis. Amis is suggested too in certain incidents. Sent to the station to collect her suitcase, Dora is diverted, as she explains later to Michael: '"I went to fetch the suitcase, you know, the one I left on the train, and I got it, and now I've left it behind again in the White Lion." Her voice ended in a wail' (Chapter 5). This casual pub-going contrasts sharply with Michael's own Hardyesque reflections on his single, fateful trip to a pub with Toby: 'that something so momentary and so trivial could have so much meaning, could achieve so much destruction . . . Our actions are like ships which we may watch set out to sea . . .' (Chapter 12). Having had one cider too many, Michael has kissed Toby: Toby's thoughts next morning are both inappropriate and convincing in a blend that suggests Anthony Powell; he feels 'as if he had taken part, on the previous night, in some exhausting orgy' (Chapter 12). The interplay of two distinct tones derives from two eras of literature and corresponds to two quite separate cultural styles, to be seen, for example, in Nick's or Dora's attitude to sexual freedom and in the opposed Imber view of Dora as an 'erring wife'.

Looked at in this double perspective, the centre of the novel becomes more intelligible. Dora's act of ringing the old bell and rousing the house need not be read as symbolic because symbolic meanings clearly belong to particular characters whose outlook is circumscribed and unstable, and to an associated narrative view which we can see to be partial and relative. Iris Murdoch has often written about the unsatisfactory nature of all philosophies. In the book *Sartre: Romantic Rationalist*, she says in a passage often quoted: 'What *does* exist is brute and nameless, it escapes from the scheme of relations in which we imagine it to be rigidly enclosed, it escapes from language and science, it is more than and other than our descriptions of it' (Chapter 1). Her work is concerned with human freedom in relation to this reality; and with the constant tendency of the mind to deform it by 'fantasy'; also with the moral truth that, in her own words, 'real people are destructive of myth, contingency is destructive of fantasy'. A. S. Byatt discusses the connection between the 'absurd, irreducible uniqueness of people' and what she expresses in a borrowed phrase as 'the solidity of the normal'. That quality, she says, 'connects' with the bell, and in this she is right, though she is wrong to say that a symbolic act is 'planted' here. Dora is seeking to assert her uniqueness in defiance of Paul and the community. In the strange, remote reality of the bell's bulk, its beauty, the marvel of its survival in the lake, its being what Toby calls 'rebarbative', she finds a means to assert herself which seems Sartrean rather than symbolic. The significance of this moment which critics have found so difficult to account for is that symbolic meanings are like explanations of people: inadequate. The relationship between a narrative tone which evokes George Eliot and an almost existentialist consciousness of the individual's isolation is, like the incongruities between Victorian solemnity and permissive irresponsibility, a playful but crucial and central principle of *The Bell*. Several of the characters and especially Michael and Dora are convincing and moving characters of the kind that B. S. Johnson attacked in writers allegedly imitating the act of being nineteenth-century novelists. But *The Bell*'s independence of the Victorian novel, partial but quite consciously so, is worked into the method with a scepticism about 'present-day reality' which B. S. Johnson might have admired. Malcolm Bradbury comments on *A Severed Head* (the novel which followed *The Bell*) that 'the contrast between the weighty, scrupulous Jamesian style and the very unJamesian invention and subject-matter becomes a comic strategy'.[8] In subsequent novels such contrasts were used to develop a variety of strategies; recognising and enjoying the contrast of traditional and unconventional modes of fiction often resolves what has been felt to be critically difficult.

If *The Bell* was admired in 1958 as a re-creation of the qualities of the great Victorians, this was a misunderstanding, attributable to the English Ideology, to Iris Murdoch's praise of the Victorians and to the tendency in her work in the 1950s away from the Queneau-like, fantastic, philosophical, menippean qualities of *Under the Net* as the ruling principles of the novel. The comic strategy in *A Severed Head* to which Malcolm Bradbury refers had been prepared for by the elaborated Victorian manner of *The Bell*. The 'unJamesian' content of the next novel became increasingly conspicuous in her work during the sixties and by the end of the decade there was a strong feeling of bafflement among reviewers. Readers who had found her upper-middle-class world reassuring in the 1950s were disturbed by the recurrence of sexual irresponsibility and irregularity, of sinister myth and ritual in her novels from 1960 onwards. The term 'Gothic' was used in the attempt to find a genre for what she was doing and there are obvious Gothic reminiscences within some of the books. In devising his concept of 'fabulation' in 1967, Robert Scholes made *The Unicorn* (1963) a prime example of 'emphatic fictiveness' but his perceptiveness was ahead of most reviewers. When *The Nice and the Good* was published in 1968, ten years and six novels after *The Bell*, they were mostly bemused.

While a reviewer on the weeklies has to judge too quickly and riskily for his work to be made to undergo general critical scrutiny years afterwards, reviews record opinion, and the contrast provided by the *New Statesman* and *Spectator* accounts of *The Nice and the Good* suggests the degree of disagreement existing among highly competent readers. A. S. Byatt in the *NS* found much to admire: she thought it 'formally more successful and much more rich and alive' than recent, 'more remote and Gothic' books, and a good mixture of light artifice and moral seriousness. She found the 'repetitive patterning' satisfying and some of the human dilemmas 'very

moving indeed' (*NS*, 26 January 1968). In the *Spectator* Martin
Seymour Smith saw the same novel as a total failure. His reasons
and the nature of the disagreement are worth looking at.

The *Spectator* article, on the same day, dealt with Iris Murdoch's
The Sovereignty of Good (1967) as well as with the novel and found her
impressive as a thinker; though the novel, Seymour Smith wrote,
was 'not merely a failure as fiction, but so trivial, vulgar,
sentimental and (apparently) concocted to appeal to the inferior
reader that it is no more than silly'. Such a book coming from such a
writer, and treated elsewhere as a serious work, meant that
something must be badly wrong. Seymour Smith blamed 'critics'
for encouraging her in using the techniques of women's magazine
stories, combined with fashionable clichés, to try to illustrate ideas
from moral philosophy — her proper occupation. He finished by
comparing her with George Eliot. *Adam Bede* was also didactic and
George Eliot also made mistakes but she always saw her characters
in their setting: 'the Poysers at their farm take possession of her and
of us'. Critics today must demand, he said, the same 'robustness',
and resist the composition of 'non-novels' (as Francis Hope had
called *Under the Net*) like *The Nice and the Good*. This was a clear
statement of a case more vaguely and nervously made from time to
time elsewhere.

The Nice and the Good will not stand comparison with *Adam Bede* if
one looks for order, intensity, probability, density of character, the
expectations appropriate to Victorian fiction. Yet it is not surprising
that they should be looked for because, even more than was the case
in *The Bell*, settings and characters are drawn from circles
prosperous enough to preserve country house, private incomes,
servants, and the general conditions of upper-middle-class life in the
Victorian novel. The bachelor lawyer Ducane, for example, is
presented in relation to his manservant; the benevolence of
Ducane's Civil Service colleague Octavian is seen in his having
found the refugee scholar, Willie, a cottage on his estate; Octavian's
brother Theo has done nothing at all for years after leaving India
'under a cloud'. Octavian's wife Katie, who discovers Ducane's
'man' when inspecting his flat in his absence, reflects, as if she were a
character in Saki, that 'she wouldn't mind *having* Fivey' (Chapter
17). Ducane's gentlemanly vulnerability in dealing with women is
not unlike that of Charles Smithson in *The French Lieutenant's
Woman*. Throughout the book, details of situation and style which
recall features of Victorian fiction, in general or particular, are

imposed on plot and themes which are self-consciously unVictorian. An impression of London as a stage where crucial accidental meetings among the characters take place in streets or parks is at times reminiscent of James. Jessica, Ducane's ex-mistress, spies on Kate, whom he now loves, as she calls at his house. The rendezvous of another couple in the National Gallery (London galleries being a standard Murdoch venue), combined with discussion of a Bronzino painting, is likely to remind us of *The Wings of the Dove*. The style too, can be Jamesian: 'He had no doubt that the married pair discussed him. He would not have been mocked but he might have been laughed at. He could hear Kate saying, "John's a bit sweet on me, you know!" Whatever had so beautifully happened was something to which Octavian was privy. There was, in the situation, no danger' (Chapter 3). Elsewhere there are touches that suggest George Eliot: in the relaxed combination of intellectual and domestic preoccupations at Octavian's house in Dorset, or in the notion of 'righteousness' in the description of Kate and Octavian together: 'There was a careless magnanimity about them both, something too of the bounty of those who might have been magnificent sinners magnificently deciding for righteousness' (Chapter 2). The servant Fivey is almost predictably Dickensian: his mother was a mermaid in a circus.

It may be objected that Iris Murdoch naturally writes about the social circles she lives in and echoes the novelists she likes. Even so, she seems to stress the aspects of life in these circles which most recall the world of James and Meredith, and the overall effect has been to confirm reviewers in a wish to read her as a traditional novelist. But the reminiscences of older fiction are only one aspect of a general literary allusiveness and mimicry in *The Nice and the Good*. It irritated Martin Seymour Smith, who accused her of using 'every cliché from spying and whips to Virgilian allusions'. It also establishes that she is writing a type of novel quite unlike *Adam Bede*.

'Spying and whips and Virgilian allusions' is a neat summing-up of various fashionable tendencies in the novel of the 1960s which Iris Murdoch is mimicking in *The Nice and the Good*. John Le Carré's success with *The Spy who came in from the Cold* (Gollancz, 1963) and Kingsley Amis's with *The Anti-Death League* (1966) and his version of a James Bond novel, *Colonel Sun* (1968), gave a prestige to espionage and attempts to extend its artistic possibilities; Anthony Burgess's *Tremor of Intent* (Heinemann, 1966) is a brilliant satire on this genre. A number of writers, including Colin Wilson, treated sadism with a freedom that would not have been allowed before the 1960s. Iris Murdoch begins with violent death, a suicide in a government office. John Ducane, the 'good' man set on an unselfish life, among 'nice', hedonistic Civil Service colleagues, is required to investigate the background circumstances, a task that involves him in spying out the details of magical and curiously erotic goings on in the dead man's past. His visit to the Department basement, where the magic took place, rather frivolously suggests a descent (like Aeneas's) to the Underworld because there are so many other Latin quotations and Roman allusions. We hear about, and from, Propertius, Catullus, Virgil, Roman magical charms, Roman law, the word and concept of '*amor*'. Other references, to 'Helen of Troy' (a London prostitute), to Greek archaeology, to '*kouroi*', begin to set up a rival pattern of Greek allusions, which is certainly no more helpful in 'explaining' the novel (Iris Murdoch is alluding to myth here, not creating it), but might be seen as parody of the intricate patterns of the novels of Robbe-Grillet and Michel Butor. The manner in which all these 'clichés' are handled is light, irresponsible, and likely to annoy, as they did Martin Seymour Smith and others, even if intended only to amuse.

Similarly whimsical, and remote from George Eliot, are the improbabilities of the story — one of the most provocative features of her work in the 1960s. A. S. Byatt has praised this as what she calls 'Shakespearean plotting', quoting Nathalie Sarraute about the crushing effect on modern writers of a sense of their predecessors' achievements, and suggesting that Shakespeare offers 'a way out' of 'the English debate about the preservation of the values of nineteenth-century realism against the need to be modern, flexible, innovating, not to say experimental'.[9] As 'an eternal part of our culture', she argues, Shakespeare provides the example of a comic vision of the preposterous behaviour of people in love.

Certain features of the novels of the late 1960s and early 1970s (disguise, twins, sexual ambivalence, households resembling Shakespearean courts) might make us think of Shakespeare, though it is hard to say whether we need to. Several of the novels introduce cuckoo calls, to embarrass characters with unfaithful partners. The cuckoo haunts *The Nice and the Good*, prompting conversations about cuckolding, and a reader paying attention to other Shakespearean hints might be made to think of this as a Shakespearean touch. There are numerous possible analogues: one is the song at the close of *Love's Labour's Lost*:

The cuckoo then, on every tree,
Mocks married men; for thus sings he,
Cuckoo;
Cuckoo, cuckoo; O, word of fear,
Unpleasing to a married ear!

That play also includes much mention of the allegorical person of Cupid, who figures in the Bronzino painting, 'An Allegory' (Venus, Cupid, Folly and Time) in the National Gallery, which is admired by characters in the novel (and appears on the original jacket). Then the patterns of paired-off lovers, rivalry between the claims of love and study, and vain denials of the power of sex might appear to be common motifs. Letters turn up in the wrong hands in both, and so does a character called Biranne (Berowne); each has an atmosphere of erudite cleverness made slightly absurd because cut off from ordinary folk. But there is no clue here to the meaning. The novels all include elements of fun, a teasing allusiveness, intended to amuse, and sometimes deceptive for their interpreters. Malcolm Bradbury has found a pattern derived from the myth of Vulcan in *Under the Net* and A. S. Byatt agrees with him about it.[10] Iris Murdoch has denied having meant any such thing, which would not of course impress a Roland Barthes but which has forced both English critics to (almost) abandon their reading. Without wanting to yield to Barthes's dictatorship of the reader, one can see their instinct to keep the Vulcan myth (as well as Wittgenstein) in mind when thinking of what the title means, in spite of the author. Her novels ask to be over-interpreted.

Whether or not Shakespeare has any real bearing on it, *The Nice and the Good* lavishly illustrates the wild absurdities possible among lovers in Iris Murdoch. John Ducane admires Kate but cannot get away from the jealous Jessica; he receives love letters from both, with which he is blackmailed by the office messenger. The messenger's wife, 'Helen of Troy', pursues Ducane too, as she does his colleague Biranne, whose wife is separated from him and living with Kate and Octavian. Also living with them is Mary who hopes to marry the Latinist, Willy. Willy loves Octavian's teenage daughter Barbara, as does Mary's teenage son Pierce, whom Octavian's brother Theo loves. Later Mary falls in love with John and he, happily, falls in love with her. There are other complications. Who loves whom as a novelist's device comes close to being made itself an object of ridicule in the course of this deliberately over-elaborate patterning of infatuations and estrangements. The result is to undermine somewhat the traditional reader's interest in and respect for the romantic attachments of characters in a novel.

This unsettling of the established procedures of fiction is the point of comparison with Scholes's other 'fabulators', including Americans like Barth and Pynchon. Looking at *The Nice and the Good* this way, one might argue, as an alternative to A. S. Byatt's 'Shakespearean plotting', a 'classical' or 'pagan' scheme in the presentation. The complications in the love story might be thought to owe as much to the reckless attitudes of Catullus, whom Willy and Pierce read aloud in the novel, as to Shakespearean comedy. The niceness of Octavian and Kate, rich, clever, powerful, loving and loved, conducting a splendidly hedonistic existence surrounded by a 'court' of less well-adjusted people who depend on them, is perhaps one type of paganism, unworried by God, sexually fulfilled, tolerant, civilised. John Ducane, the puritan and scholar, anxious to be 'good', could represent a disciplined, virtuous, pagan life. Jessica is said to be an 'untainted pagan', to whom Christ and Apollo are equally meaningless myths; she believes only in her youth. (Iris Murdoch has elsewhere compared the decline of belief in the Graeco-Roman gods with the decline of Christianity today.) This neo-Roman freedom in the characters from traditional (Christian) English beliefs is matched by a posing of ultimate questions, especially about the problem of pain in relation to love and death, outside the traditional English frame of reference. The Classical, like the Shakespearean, was seen in Victorian literature as a quite separate element in literary culture from the Novel, which was sometimes said to be 'for our day' what Shakespeare or Virgil had been for earlier epochs. Contemporary novelists lack such confidence in their own medium; they are encouraged by critics like Scholes and Kellogg (in *The Nature of Narrative*) to stop thinking of the Victorian novel as the sole model available, and to look on it as part of a much older tradition of prose narrative including Renaissance novellas, medieval romances and ancient 'novels' like Petronius's. The classical allusions running through *The Nice and the Good* might be regarded as a rejection of the sort of approach which expects Iris Murdoch to be like George Eliot, a reminder that life can no longer be made full sense of by the means of Victorian fiction.

Reading along these lines, one would be checked by the title itself, which suggests a Victorian and especially a Jamesian moral distinction; the comic relationships which develop around the figure of the allegedly 'good' man, John Ducane, and the self-consciously generous couple, Kate and Octavian, provide the conditions for a sceptical appraisal of this difficult pair of words which may be familiar to the reader in the context of novels like *The Spoils of Poynton* (where 'nice' and 'good' are particularly frequent in combination); to the author herself no doubt familiar as terms needing almost demoralising reserves of philosophical caution. But the title's connotations in nineteenth-century fiction are often evoked, in the relationship between Ducane and Jessica, for example: Ducane shocked by her 'paganism' and keen for her to work in a permanent artistic medium instead of creating beautiful 'objects' only to destroy them; she regarding him as 'infinitely old'. Jessica is seen as having broken free from traditional social and cultural bonds; 'she kept her world denuded out of fear of convention'; she is 'to an extent which even John Ducane did not fully appreciate, entirely outside Christianity'; 'her integrity took the form of contempt for the fixed, the permanent, the solid' (Chapter 11). In contrast to her bare, existentialist condition, Ducane, with his private income derived from trade, and his puritanism, his dutiful, although Godless wish to be a good man, seems almost Victorian. He uses the term 'gentleman' in talking to the amoral Biranne with an air of relying on its authority which in the context makes him seem outside his proper period.[11] A. S. Byatt found the novel morally serious and moving, and it is affecting, despite the incongruity of manner and the literary games, for there is a pleasure in the story and a moral interest in the characters' behaviour which makes comparison with George Eliot a possibility but which will not satisfy readers who take such a comparison for granted, or resist the admittedly disturbing effect produced by varying the narrative style.

Another mode is that of Sartre. As Octavian contemplates the corpse in Chapter 1, the detective story tone changes: 'Here were the assembled parts of a human being . . . The mystery appalled him . . . parts, pieces, stuff.' Iris Murdoch's *Sartre: Romantic Rationalist* begins with an account of *La Nausée* (*Nausea*) which she calls 'a philosophical myth' and she quotes Roquentin's feeling of horror at the sight of pebbles on the beach which leads him to a revelation: 'I understood that there was no middle way between non-existence and this swooning abundance.' She comments: 'The doubter sees the world of everyday reality as a fallen and bedraggled place — fallen out of the realm of being into the realm of existence . . . What does exist is brute and nameless . . .'

The Nice and the Good is one of several novels with the sea as background and the stones of the shore are given a prominence which recalls Roquentin's reaction to them. Paula Biranne's children collect them delightedly, valuing each individual stone and wanting to find a place for them all. Octavian's brother Theo shares Roquentin's feeling:

> These stones, which brought such pleasure to the twins, were a nightmare to Theo. Their multiplicity and randomness appalled him. The intention of God could reach only a little way through the opacity of matter, and where it failed to penetrate there was just jumble and desolation . . . Does nature suffer here, in her extremities, Theo wondered, or is all dead here? . . . Yet was not . . . he himself as meaningless as these stones, since in real truth there was no God? [Chapter 18]

Noticing this parallel, one sees that Uncle Theo belongs to a different, Sartrean or Beckettian, fictional world from the Jamesian Octavian and Ducane, much less 'nice' than theirs. Iris Murdoch observes that Sartre finds a positive value in being outside society and in being without human dignity, and she sometimes finds the same. That is true of almost all her novels, although her outsiders and undignified people seem very varied, even if we think of only a few: Jake and Finn in *Under the Net*; and (at the end) Michael in *The Bell*; Tallis in *A Fairly Honourable Defeat* who, asked why, *in extremis*, he does not appeal to the local Samaritans, replies that he *is* the local Samaritans; and Uncle Theo as well. He is like Roquentin placed among a self-satisfied bourgeoisie who live in hope of 'adventures'. '*Salauds*' says Roquentin and so, in other words, does Uncle Theo. Like some Beckett characters, he spends much of his time in bed, is dirty, and is regarded as less than a man. He withdrew long ago from the world of British India into a Buddhist monastery but was expelled after an incident with a boy-novice. His 'goodness' does not amount to much — comforting the twins or drowning an injured bird — but it is plausible, and so (just) is his ambition to resume a religious life. 'A lonely, anguished being', his presence gives the novel a seriousness which balances the comic adventures and the whimsy.

So, in a different way, does the sea. In the first chapter of her

Sartre, Iris Murdoch quotes from the English text of *Nausea*: 'the real sea is cold and black and full of creatures; it crawls beneath that thin green film that is made to cheat us' and she comments: 'the vision of the phenomenologist has something in common with that of the poet and the painter'. The brilliant surfaces of the sea, close to their Dorset house, are enjoyed as a background by the characters of *The Nice and the Good*; its cold and deadliness are discovered in the episode at the end when Ducane rescues Pierce from death in the seacaves. It is because the sea is beyond the power of our minds to grasp that it attracts Iris Murdoch and Sartre; like reality, it is 'more and other than our descriptions of it'. It provides images too; the novel, she says, defining Sartre's limits as a novelist in the last chapter of *Sartre* is an 'art of image rather than of analysis'. The images of Theo among the stones of the shore, or drowning the bird in the shallows, and of Ducane and Pierce pressed against the ceiling of the cave as the sea rises, belong to the art in her novel which she owes to Sartre and which, in B. S. Johnson's terms, recognises 'the chaos and mess' of existence.[12]

Throughout the novel the Biranne children — twins — claim to see flying saucers (they subscribe to a flying saucer journal). At the very end of the novel they are watching a 'beautiful flying saucer' hovering on the edge of their (our) world. This is being 'playful' with the novel and risking attack as 'silly'. It is mixing genres, and slighting the traditional reader; or perhaps admitting to him that he has been asked to adapt to a degree of scepticism about the solid world of the conventional novel. Certainly the practical men, Octavian and Ducane, belong there; and although she knows the arguments which threaten to discredit their system of values, it is a world Iris Murdoch sympathises with. Alain Robbe-Grillet says that two *systèmes de vérite* are better than one. Certainly it is wrong to look for unity and plausibility in a novel like this, as if Iris Murdoch were, in B. S. Johnson's phrase, 'imitating the act of being' George Eliot — and also wrong to ignore the consciously Victorian features. Given the disparity of outlooks encompassed in the novel it is impressive how 'Murdochian' it all remains.

Fantasy, the testing of ideas, naturalism, scenes of low life, bold invention, ultimate questions, scandal, mixing of genres, varying of styles and registers, topicality and intellectual fun: Mikhail Bakhtin's characteristics of the menippea fit *The Nice and the Good* very neatly, which makes it pleasing to remember the powers of renewal in literature he claims for it. Iris Murdoch's *The Fire and the*

Sun, based on the Romanes Lecture for 1976, is an explanation of
'why Plato banished the Artists', an account of Plato's thought, and
a defence of the artist's role today. She writes in her conclusion:

> The spiritual ambiguity of art, its connection with the 'limitless'
> unconscious, its use of irony, its interest in evil, worried Plato. But
> the very ambiguity and voracious ubiquitousness of art is its
> characteristic freedom. Art, especially literature, is a great hall of
> reflection where we can all meet and where everything under the
> sun can be examined and considered. For this reason it is feared
> and attacked by dictators, and by authoritarian moralists like the
> one under discussion. The artist is a great informant, at least a
> gossip, at best a sage . . . [p. 86]

Menippean art was the sort Plato would be most concerned to
banish; Iris Murdoch's definition of the artist, since she obviously
has her own sort in mind, helps to place the modern novelist in a
larger context than the immediate post-Victorian predicament.

The Fire and the Sun is a statement, not always direct, of Iris
Murdoch's position as philosopher and novelist. She has often told
us not to use her philosophy to decode her novels. She is keen at the
end of her essay to answer Plato by asserting the power of art:
'perhaps art proves more than philosophy can' (p. 83); bad art is a
lie; good art can clarify evil and remind us of the 'hardness' of truth.
'Of course art is huge and European philosophy is strangely small,
so that Whitehead scarcely exaggerates in calling it all footnotes to
Plato' (p. 78). This long and large view of the situation of the writer
is refreshing after the insistence on present-day quandaries in
'Against Dryness'.

The human condition (as she says in that essay) is the business of
the novelist today, and it is hers too, as philosopher and novelist. 'Of
course the Greeks in general always took a fairly grim view of the
human situation' (p. 13) is typically laconic; she repeatedly cites
Plato's feeling that life is not 'anything much', and her summary of
him — 'human affairs are not serious though they have to be taken
seriously' (p. 13) — seems a view she shares. She is not a religious
believer, nor a Marxist. She declines, as an artist, to 'serve society',
in its own interest; though she believes in art, she does not devote
enough time to writing any one novel to create a single
masterpiece, but produces (almost) a book a year, indifferent to
polishing: these are both unVictorian contradictions. She can unite

moral seriousness and a spirit of fun in a way they couldn't. Bernard
Bergonzi suggests that 'Molloy and Malone are gay!' (after Yeats's
line)[13] and something like that twentieth-century bravery of Beckett
is present in Iris Murdoch's work too.

There is much in the mentality behind her work which is in touch
with the Victorians, even so, and hence the peculiarly rich composition of the Murdoch world. Most significant in her 'traditional' sensibility is her sense of the decline — as A. S. Byatt
has noted — of Christianity and what it means. Finn in *Under
the Net* talks of going back to Ireland where they've still got religion.
In one of the most recent novels, *Henry and Cato* (1976), written when
Iris Murdoch was preparing *The Fire and the Sun*, there is a debate
about Christian belief (and Platonism) against a background in
which our cultural disarray is viewed, as so often in her earlier
novels, in contrast to what survives of Victorian England. Henry
and Cato have known each other since schooldays, though they are
far apart when the novel begins. Henry has fled from the country
house and estate presided over by a hated elder brother and his ally
their mother, to the Mid-West of America where he lives a new style
of life, abetted by a West Coast couple, as a college professor (in the
history of art), unmarried, unbelieving, unsuccessful and happy.
Cato has fled from his austerely atheistic and radical father, John
Forbes (a real university teacher), into a Roman Catholic order
(which seems to be the Jesuits), breaking his father's heart. One day
in St Louis, Henry reads in a discarded London paper of his
brother's death, and he flies home, as the novel begins, to cope with
his inheritance. The priest Cato has become infatuated with a
teenage boy, whose revolver he is dropping in the Thames in
Chapter 1. Henry and Cato are going to have to abandon their new
lives; the blurb on the jacket of the first edition called them 'prodigal
sons'. D. A. N. Jones mentioned this, which he thought was
'doubtless drafted by the author' in his *Times Literary Supplement*
review (24 September 1976), and mentioned also the titles of the
book's two Parts: 'Rites of Passage' and 'The Great Teacher':
'Presumably, the earlier chapters are describing what her "prodigal
sons" are doomed to experience, as they are tested by life, and the
latter half of the book shows them learning, through suffering, how
to be happy and/or Christian.'

It is not surprising that the same review compares the effect of the
interweaving of the Henry and Cato stories to 'that of the
alternating chapters in *The Old Curiosity Shop*'; Dickens had a

'demonic involvement' with Quilp, and Iris Murdoch is more committed to Cato. This is a fair point but the instinct to refer to Dickens suggests that Iris Murdoch is still being read as though she were a Victorian novelist. The review ends by finding the presumed meanings of 'Rites of Passage' and the 'The Great Teacher' less interesting than 'the discussions between priests about faith and life's absurdity', which shows a natural preference for a more up-to-date style of making us think. At the end of *Henry and Cato*, during one of these discussions, the philosopher–priest Brendan says that thinking is 'a matter of keeping oneself from slipping back into all sorts of illusions, it's a way of keeping near the truth, even when, especially when, the truth cannot be formulated' (Panther edition, 1977, p. 350; subsequent page references are to this edition). There is a wide variety of illusions among the novel's characters but Brendan's intellectual approach to problems of character and illusion is distinctly more contemporary than the terminology of the blurb and the section titles, which seem almost provocatively old-fashioned. 'The Great Teacher' turns out to be a poem that Brendan can hardly remember, read when a child: 'I can just sort of conjure up the atmosphere,' he says (p. 352). Traditional concepts and modern minds are uneasily related in the priests' discussions as in the format and, indeed, throughout the novel.

The story is assembled from a number of traditional types of fictional conflict: between the younger son and the heir to an estate; between the new heir and the dowager; between feudal duties and radical conscience; between a 'worthy' father and a 'worthless' ('prodigal') son; between sacred and profane love; and between indulgence and duty at many levels. A summary of the situation in the early chapters could well make it seem like a nineteenth-century novel. Coming home to inherit, Henry is awaited by his mother who is brooding over what sort of marriage he is going to make and what will become of the estate. The oak meadow has been sold to neighbouring John Forbes: what will Henry think of that? When Henry decides to sell everything and use the money to help the village, the claims of social justice compete with those of the estate and its odd retainers, his mother and her 'companion', the whisky-drinking, ageing poet Lucius. John Forbes meanwhile is fretting over his children; not only has Cato deserted him for the Roman priesthood — his daughter Colette is refusing to be educated and threatens to marry the wastrel Henry.

But if this creates the impression that English life as reflected in fiction has continued unchanged since 1914, other features of the story sharply remind us of the changes. Cato is considering leaving the priesthood out of love for the young gangster Joe. Henry's attempt to renounce his inheritance in the cause of freedom is checked when he meets a girl who claims to have been his brother's mistress. In fact there seems to be a deliberate counterpointing, characteristic of Iris Murdoch, of a settled England repeatedly presented in connection with great country houses and chaotic influences from outside; a deliberate emphasis on the disintegration of patterns of community life on which older fiction depended.

'There is still a country house,' Raymond Williams writes, discussing 'bearings after Lawrence' in his *The English Novel From Dickens to Lawrence*, 'and there've been a few surprising new tenants, going steadily up in the world, whose names I've forgotten';[14] the implication of irrelevance misses the point of how old novel-conventions like those of the country house can be used with new effect in a modern novel. A house like Henry's would have seemed 'rather run down since the War' in Evelyn Waugh. In the context of Henry's return from America to claim his inheritance, it seems as anachronistic as his old friend Cato Forbes's conversion to Catholicism and the priesthood seems to Henry: 'like a visit to the past'. The resulting incongruities can be amusing: though London is only forty miles away by Volvo, Henry's mother behaves 'as if Laxlinden still had to be reached over a bad road by a carriage and horses' (p. 189). The discordancy extends into other areas of the story: Henry's arrival at his brother's secret London flat and his discovery of Stephanie in residence is an awkward moment for both of them, but the air of social uncertainty is created by their meeting in roles — 'my brother's heir' and 'your brother's mistress' — which used to be incompatible at the level of formal relations. Henry is determined to be polite, though excited by the idea of inheriting Stephanie. The pitch of social embarrassment they achieve is worthy of Michael Frayn. The sexual frankness of the comedy startles throughout the book by being so closely connected with conventional manners. After his engagement to Stephanie, Henry chats with Cato: ' "I hear you're marrying some whore." "Yes," said Henry, "I am" ' (p.306). The psychological frankness can be as disconcerting as the reappraisal of sanctimonious Victorian social roles in Evelyn Waugh and Ivy Compton Burnett. There is something too of the jolt in the discarding of a traditional reticence which Fowles uses in *The French Lieutenant's Woman*, as in this statement of a younger son's jealousy of the heir: 'Henry, soon made aware that Sandy owned everything down to the very earth that tolerated Henry stood upon, used to pray daily for his brother's death' (p. 16). The balancing of the whole apparatus of a great estate against an individual's momentary act of decision is viewed with a clarity derived from existentialism: when Henry is choosing what to do with his inheritance, the reader is shown how illusory the great certainties about Hall and Estate and Heir were, but also sees their value in the ensuing vacuum: 'I'm nothing,' Henry tells Cato, who is urging him to keep the estate. That, says Cato, is the beginning of wisdom. Henry replies: 'Your wisdom, not mine. I'm like the chap in Dostoevsky who said "If there's no God, how can I be a captain?" And I'm not even a captain' (p. 75).

A moment later he feels startled when the teenage thug, 'Beautiful Joe', calls him 'Sir'. This lack of social conviction is later exploited by Joe, after Cato, infatuated with him, has lost his faith and given up the priesthood. He kidnaps Cato, extracts money from Henry, and bullies Cato into writing a plea for his sister Colette to surrender as a hostage. Cato eventually attacks Joe as he is attempting to rape Colette; Joe is killed and Colette is permanently scarred. Cato and Colette's father, the upright John Forbes, is shocked by Cato's 'unofficerlike' conduct as a captive, a concept that seems meaningless to Colette. D. A. N. Jones in his *TLS* review rightly remarks that this adventurous part of the story seems 'absurd and dream-like' and cannot be read as one reads a thriller. There is a sense of unreality here, perhaps because the concepts, which thrillers still depend on, of 'gentleman' and 'cad', have been subverted by the sense of historical perspective in the novel's social comedy; but in the semantic vacuum, without God, it seems to be suggested, and without captains, the feeling of chaos and evil in Joe's almost frivolous assumption of terrorism is real and frightening.

Brendan interprets Plato for Cato's benefit at the end in words which Iris Murdoch also uses in *The Fire and the Sun*: 'Human affairs are not serious, but they have to be taken seriously' (p. 350).[15] Henry marries Colette and keeps Laxlinden more or less intact; we are given a partial Victorian happy ending. But human affairs are seen in a complex, shifting perspective. Henry has gained the whole world, Bredan has renounced it for a mission in Calcutta; Cato and Stephanie have to try to live in disconnected conditions, neither of them with a proper role. Present-day images convey a tawdry quality: Stephanie, in possession of her old flat and the ransom money, fills in a computer-dating form, analysing herself by selecting her favourite colour. The suggested meagreness of modern life is contrasted with richer images through which a traditional order of instinctive values can be sensed, as when Cato disposes of his cassock in a rubbish tip and feels afterwards 'wicked and relieved, as if he had been burying a dead baby' — then watches a kestrel swooping on a mouse; or when Henry returns to Laxlinden from the Mid-West by starlight, climbing in over the gate and pausing in the grounds to see himself observed by a fox. Such incidents recall the imaginative truth to life of the best Victorian fiction and so — above all — does the novel's narrative drive. 'It is the exceptional novelist today,' Lionel Trilling writes in *Sincerity and Authenticity*, 'who would say of himself, as Henry James did, that he "loved the story as story"' (p. 134). Iris Murdoch can say so, and her enthusiasm for a story, whether or not philosophically reckless, is stronger than ever in the most recent novels. But it is not founded on a naïve authenticity. What Brendan says about taking human affairs seriously is based on her reading of Plato and is the best clue to her characteristic adjustments between closeness to life and intellectual detachment. Brendan has a set of Nietzsche on his shelves. Nietzsche feared that the death of God would remove all significant 'weight' from human affairs. Iris Murdoch's role has been to create significance despite the bare humanism of philosophy after Nietzsche. It has not meant trying to write fiction like the Victorians, but dealing with what she finds usable in the older novel to create her own imaginative version of our world.

4 Angus Wilson: *No Laughing Matter*

More than any other postwar novelist, Angus Wilson has been acknowledged, with praise or blame according to critical credo, as a successor to the great Victorians. Bernard Bergonzi, for example, approaching him cautiously, calls him 'a distinguished practitioner in the tradition of George Eliot' (*The Situation of the Novel*, p. 152). He suggests that Wilson's liberal creativity and liberal beliefs may come to be equally out of date in a totalitarian future and cites B. S. Johnson's disapproval as evidence of the way things are going: 'I'm sure social historians in the future will look to Angus Wilson and say, "Yes, that's what it must have been like to live then." But the actual methods he uses are those of Dickens . . .'

N. H. Reeve, contributing 'Reflections on "Fictionality"' to *The Contemporary English Novel* (ed. Bradbury and Palmer), observes that Johnson's remarks on literary theory are not sophisticated (p. 123), and by current academic standards this is true; but what he says is clear and may reflect a common experience of Wilson's work among readers who are not concerned to distinguish precisely between his 'actual methods' and those of Dickens. But Johnson is misleading. When he says, elsewhere, that praise is bestowed on 'neo-Dickensian' novelists, elevated to Chairs of English Literature in consequence, the slight is ill-judged in view of Angus Wilson's academic achievements as a critic and a Dickens scholar.[1] Wilson has himself written about the influence of Dickens on his own imagination. But to call him 'neo-Dickensian', except as a slogan of rejection or esteem, raises all sorts of critical problems.

A new Dickens or a new George Eliot would quickly outgrow the influence of Dickens or George Eliot. For Wilson to be truly Dickensian would involve the presence of Wilsonian qualities strong and original enough to make us forget what was owed to the past. No contemporary novelist has been able to renew the novel in quite that way; even Powell, though so uninhibited by his knowledge of other people's novels, is far more aware of past achievements than

Dickens was or needed to be. The strong nineteenth-century ambience in Wilson's earlier novels, reported by all critics, whether they admire the power to revitalise or allege that the methods are secondhand, is an imitative, literary quality, present in most of our fiction, and distinguishing it from what went before. Wilson has always seemed qualified by experience and interests to produce a panoramic 'portrait of our age' in the Victorian manner. He was on the staff of what is now the British Library when he wrote his first stories in the 1940s and published a collection of them, *The Wrong Set*, in 1949, and he knows officialdom (at least the cultural kind) at first hand; in his books he has combined a satirical scrutiny of the ruling classes with an awareness of the ramifications of the middle class and with a knowledge of underground and especially homosexual milieux. This social range has been seen by many critics as a Victorian strength in Wilson. Wilson's moral approach to social criticism, his scepticism about liberal values as understood and practised by responsible modern Englishmen, his power to record and ridicule social life and language, his fascination with middle-class family behaviour and with childhood, his sympathy with the figure of the nonconformist within the 'Establishment' — all make him, one might imagine, if not our Dickens, then perhaps our Thackeray.

The will has been present, also, to create a major fictional study of modern society. Although repeatedly using what seemed slight topics, the new social use to be found for a country house in *Hemlock and After* (1952), the concocting of an archaeological fraud in *Anglo-Saxon Attitudes* (1956), a widow's readjustment to life in *The Middle Age of Mrs Eliot* (1958), family readjustments in a New Town in *Late Call* (1964), Wilson builds up the novels with workmanlike devices like subplot and mystery, and ambitiously undertakes problems of validity, integrity and purpose for responsible people today. In the best known of the first five novels, *The Old Men at the Zoo* (1961), Wilson uses the administration of a zoo as another means of surveying modern society (this time set, ahead, in the 1970s) and as a fable about the will to power and the prospect of a collapse of our unsatisfactory liberal system into a worse, dictatorial alternative.

Each of these novels is entertaining and rewarding, but none of them does Wilson full justice. It became customary to say that Wilson was happier with the short story, that his talents, though brilliant, were unequal to larger schemes. He was thought, furthermore, in spite of his commitment to realism, to be giving in to the temptations of fantasy, macabre and horrific, and escaping into surrealism: the black comedy of certain scenes involving wild animals in *The Old Man at the Zoo*, in particular, was regarded as a breakdown of the traditionally responsible novelist's role Wilson was supposed to have adopted.

In 1967 the sixth novel, *No Laughing Matter*, came out and, for the most part, reviewers agreed that he had succeeded as a novelist at last. Here was the great panorama of English life in the twentieth century against a background of world events, in which Wilson's inventiveness and energy hardly flagged and all his abilities were brought to bear. What dissent there was attached to the book's departures from orthodox novel practice: dramatic scenes interposed without being justified in the narrative; parody of Ibsen, Shaw, Chekhov, Beckett. Such elements were found clever but disturbing. *As If By Magic* (1973) is a more blatant departure from the manner of the earlier books. A. S. Byatt discussing it in a recent essay calls it 'nihilistic . . . reducing everything to the ridiculous. It is like an onion, consisting of allusion, parody, interpretation, misinterpretation, imitative plot and trumped up analogy'.[2] Parody has become an end in itself. In the course of the 1970s *No Laughing Matter* came to be seen as a key work. It was discussed by Malcolm Bradbury in *Possibilities* and by Robert Burden in *The Contemporary English Novel*, in an essay based on Bradbury's, as a 'fabulation' written by a master of the old, realist novel. The 'subverting' of the realism by techniques which stress its artificial composition, Bradbury says, raises questions about social and individual being. His essay is a dazzling account, but one which leaves the impression of a novel exasperatingly difficult to interpret correctly: the opposite effect of what B. S. Johnson found in the earlier novels, perhaps because too much present-day reality has seeped in.

One aspect of the 'Dickensian' which retains a vital importance in current critical thought about Dickens, preserving him from becoming merely a great symbolist or profound social satirist, and linking him with Shakespeare, is the power to entertain. 'Fictive', 'fabulatory' and 'playful' novels do not necessarily achieve this; some readers are likely to feel that *As If By Magic* becomes tedious through excessive 'playfulness'. But *No Laughing Matter* upholds, as Iris Murdoch, Amis, Powell and, at his best, John Fowles can do, the power of the novel to entertain, and that, in the present age of doubt, seems a good certainty to hold on to. The most solid achievement of Dickens studies has been to restore the proper value of the word 'entertainment'. Novelists in Britain in the same period have kept it alive. We have seen how a contrast developed between separate styles of fiction in the highly individual imaginative world of Iris Murdoch's novels. It is unlikely that she influenced Wilson, but *No Laughing Matter*, though a different sort of novel, achieves a comparable effect of consciously maintaining creative relations with the nineteenth-century novel. Both writers are gifted entertainers; they also share a moral sense which turns them naturally to the example of the Victorians; in the present state of fiction, that example offers them something even more basic to the novel than moral interest: a relationship with the reader who wants to be entertained.

The ambitious scope of *No Laughing Matter* is proclaimed by its format: five books (subdivided into 'years') deal with periods starting 'before the first War' and finishing with 1967; these fifty-five years span five generations of an upper-middle-class family with business roots in Victorian England. The principal characters belong in the third generation: the six talented Matthews children who become more or less grown-up at the end of the first War, and whose stories furnish the bulk of the novel. Growing up is stimulated and stunted for all of them by characterful parents. William and Clara Matthews conceive of themselves theatrically: 'the Billy Pop' is a lazy, selfish, second-rate Edwardian man of letters; Clara 'the Countess' is an overbearing mixture of the seven deadly sins, slightly held in check by wit, vulgarity and a sense of occasion. Their characters together express many of the strengths and weaknesses of their period, and after the War they feel helplessly out of date. Assailed as they are by wilfully irresponsible parents, Quentin, Gladys, Rupert, Margaret, Sukey and Marcus develop sturdy personalities in self-defence. They inherit a flair for drama and produce a ritual 'Game' based on sending up their elders: grandmother and great-aunt; Regan the (drunken) Cook; Billy Pop and the Countess. The adults are so close to caricature in conducting their real lives that the Game breeds a lasting doubt in each of the children about how far life is or isn't a laughing matter.

The novel opens with a brilliant piece of Joycean prose-writing which has already attracted much critical attention. The reader's first impression is one of bewildered excitement: the family's outing to the Wild West Exhibition of 1912 is conveyed through a mock version of stream of consciousness and we undergo a sort of brief deluge in the various Matthews personalities. On a second reading of the novel the bearings are clearer, and various future themes can be made out. But the first Book remains, even after analysis, linguistically inexhaustible and psychologically true. It deserves to be famous: Wilson's technical resourcefulness creates a unique effect of encountering excited, vividly crowded minds.

In the second Book, '1919', language and style are again used very inventively, but characters, setting and situation are seen increasingly clearly and this introduces the dual method, involving realism and parody, and the difficulty of discovering how to read, how to place the narrator, and how to relate to the world of the novel.

The reader looks for a theme and finds the conventional opposition of generations, attached at this point in history to 'before' and 'after' the war, with the determination of the children, in rejecting their 'impossible' parents, to reject the culture, ethos, style, even perhaps social structure of the era the war seems to have ended. Billy and Clara, at least, appear discredited, his manuscripts coming back from publishers, she consoling American officers in return for dinners at 'the Piccahdillah'. The organising principle is rebellion on the younger Matthewses' part against various Victorian aspects of their unsatisfactory parents.

Billy Pop and Clara have been rebels themselves when it has suited them. Quentin, the eldest son, who has come back from the trenches a hero and a Marxist, admits this when he sums up the case against Billy and Clara. He in fact grew up mostly at his grandmother's house, stifled, he says, by 'dividends, roast beef and the Great British Empire'. But he sees his parents' attempt at revolt as a failure, condemns the two older generations together on Marxist grounds, and takes the role, in the Game, of 'Justice Scales', in order to judge them and all they stand for. Relying on his wound, his rank as acting major, his place at London University and his socialist conviction, he sums up with confidence:

'I thought when I retired that I should have to condemn you as a generation, or rather as two generations, indeed as all the older generations, perhaps as the embodiment of accumulated history. You are, after all, all we know of the past. It's you who've put us in the soup and don't seem prepared to help us out of it for fear of scalding your fingers. Not to put any pretence upon it, you are a guilty lot. But as in my moments of retirement I reflected, I soon saw that this business of generations just would not do. Here we have a system and a class in decay. Granny, you with your large annuity, your servants, your house property . . .' [Book 2]

So he goes on, denouncing much-travelled Aunt Mouse for her gilt-edged securities and the 'dear parents . . . destroyed . . . by the system in which they have been brought up'. He does so of course as a character in the Game and he is addressing his brothers and sisters, the youngest, fifteen-year-old Marcus, playing the Countess, Rupert playing the Billy Pop, the others: 'Granny Sukey', 'Margaret Mouse' and 'Regan the Podge' (overweight Gladys).

A young reader in the late sixties might well have felt unsure where the satire is directed. When Quentin 'preaches', in the term he later comes to use, his creed to the others in their own persons telling them that the old (class) system won't work decently for them, they listen because they are impressed by his aura of heroism ('eight millions were killed'); but, although they all want to escape everything they 'know of the past', none of them pays real attention; all are habitually absorbed in alternative new versions of the world.

One of the girls, Sukey, withdraws from the squalor of home into a daydream of a clean, comfortable, middle-class family life, attended by a 'faithful parlourmaid' who is meant to exorcise Regan and all she stands for; she turns making the system work decently into an act of faith and lives the rest of her life enclosed in the soppy mentality of the women's magazine type of story which she later writes, with immense success, for the BBC. Margaret her twin uses fiction another way, reverting to a pre-Victorian model in the detachment of Jane Austen. She teaches herself irony and turns Matthews family life into the 'Carmichael' stories, technically deft and sarcastically anti-Victorian, which make her reputation in the 1920s. Dickens is the one writer she can't bear. Where Sukey evolves a make-believe, mythic version of nineteenth-century life, Margaret is like Gladys and her brothers in choosing a course based on a sharp rejection of 'the Victorian'.

Resistance to home influence takes a feminist pattern in Gladys: she 'thought of the new world lying open to girls . . . [that] she would open to them in her brand new employment agency . . .' (Book 2). Her mother shrieks at her, 'marry well!'; instead, she takes up with an ungentlemanly, already-married lover and business-partner.

Rupert, plucking up the nerve needed to go on the stage, broods about a new theatre, looking on Beerbohm Tree as Margaret looks on Dickens, and Quentin on capitalistic Grandfather Matthews, all three of them set on 'rejecting all old sticks bad or good'. Through the swarm of styles, registers and private languages in the novel's opening phases there emerges a stern, modernist determination to get away from the nineteenth century at any cost; it is presented ambiguously on the whole, with many doubts implied about the possible cost. Marcus, a born rebel, cheerfully accepts his homosexuality, despite Rupert's orthodox warnings about foulness leading to the loony bin, and dreams of the Russian ballet, Bakst, arabesques and luxuries of form and colour, blotting out with erotic drawings and dress designs the familiar ugliness of the house in Fulham. He concentrates his hatred of home on a particular Victorian screen and develops in protest the taste which later inspires his collection of Kandinskis and Klees.

It is one of the ironies of the novel that none of the characters really outgrows the Victorianism they fight against, so that Marcus, for example, ends up — at least as Quentin sees him — as a practical philanthropist of the Robert Owen school, and, on a second reading, we cannot escape seeing, in the young Quentin's earnestness, in Margaret's lady-novelist priggishness and in Marcus's Arabian Nights fantasies, characteristics of the culture they all grew up in. In the Game they enact their elders' roles:

MARCUS THE COUNTESS: How inexpressibly vulgah you are deah boy. It must have taken generations of Matthews trade to produce such vulgarity . . .

RUPERT THE BILLY POP: Only . . . by trade, England is great, her coffers full.

MARCUS THE COUNTESS: And by arms has that greatness been preserved, the dear King sent victorious . . . [Book 2]

This leads to a scrap between them, and so to Quentin's intervention as Justice Scales, reminding them that professions and trades have merged in that great middle class on which everything worthwhile rests. Rupert paternally, and Marcus glamorously bare-shouldered 'with feather duster egret in her hair . . . join in happy duet — I brought the breeding and you brought the dough'. Although Billy, Clara, Mouse, Granny and Regan represent only a shabby outer edge of their age, they supply roles in which concepts of the past can be parodied. The Game shows the beginning of Victorian myths which were to develop with the century. Billy and Clara become more Victorian as time goes by; Billy is singing 1850s patriotic songs on the eve of the Second World War. The Game-players 'cultivate a sense of the past', in a phrase Rupert mockingly borrows from the Countess, and it stays with them even though they lampoon it.

The Game conveys their sense of the past with fragments of quotation and allusion intended to evoke the nineteenth century as it survives in popular awareness. John Fowles noted, referring to the problem of dialogue for *The French Lieutenant's Woman*, that language actually used in 1867 was insufficiently differentiated to be true to our preconceptions. Wilson's players have keen ears for what is distinctive: 'A young gel of beauty, attainments and breeding,' cries Margaret, lamenting her mother's marriage in the idiom of her great aunt. 'She's not been unwilling to grant her favours elsewhere if these terrible stories are true' groans Sukey as Granny Matthews. Gladys as Regan urges the children to avoid 'muck' and get to know 'the upper tens'. 'I was poor but I was honest', she sings (Book 2). The parents lapse from respectability into the pungent diction of a Victorian underworld: 'MARCUS THE COUNTESS sprang away . . . "Your breath smells, Billah," she said, "Oh God! You've let yourself go to pieces." "Come to that," said her ex-partner ungallantly, "you stink like a whore's knocking shop"' (Book 2).

Considered as 'real' children and young people, the Matthewses are struggling for independence and maturity: 'O, for God's sake get out of our lives,' shouts Rupert at his father (Book 2). Marcus never 'grows away' from the Countess. Rupert later 'becomes' Billy in order to portray Andrey Prozorhov in *The Three Sisters* and to seduce the elderly leading lady who helps his career. But looked at as novel characters, their interchangeability with their elders is critically disconcerting. This is what causes Malcolm Bradbury's query about the novel's formal capacity to deal with the problems it raises of social and personal authenticity. The narrator seems not unlike his characters in his ambivalent relation to established modes of proceeding. But the effect is exhilarating, and Mikhail Bakhtin's concept of the menippean, carnival species of literature with its clashes of genre and changes of tone, in a spirit of intellectual riot, seems more appropriate than anxious coping with philosophic problems of integrity.

'Camp' is an anarchic weapon with which Wilson and his creation Marcus are expert. Marcus, worst bullied by the Countess, stars in the Game as MARCUS THE COUNTESS; though he is more defiant than the others of Victorian absolutes, in rejecting manliness, he becomes more involved than they do in the old 'society' world of army officers and duchesses. The narrator's voice joins easily with his in a common tone: ' "I want fun," she added, "gaiety, laughter. I want to dance round the clock." And so she did in the arms of RUPERT THE BILLY POP' (Book 2). Marcus's demand contradicts the title and so does his approach to life throughout. Even his anti-intellectualism seems endorsed by a sneaking irresponsibility in the novel, as if too academic an approach to it would be unrewarding: 'Are you *all* at the University?' Marcus asks at the end, confronted with the younger generation in 1967. 'New University? Whatever's that? Surely they have enough of them already with their old Oxford and Cambridge — terrible old things bathing naked . . .' (Book 5). Marcus embodies a blend of vivacity and nonconformism which is close to the book's meaning or, in a fashionable phrase, its 'authentic register'. It is a powerful agent, perhaps as potent an affront to past codes of seemliness, in 1919, as Quentin's Marxism, and, arguably, more subversive a force today.

Bradbury compares the theatricality of *No Laughing Matter* to that of Dickens: 'this sense of personal fragility, awareness of society not as a solid substance but as a seeming, is in Wilson's writing too, and, as in Dickens, it poses strange problems of control . . . The result is a novelist who is less a controlling artist capable of moral poise than one acting vigorously as an inventor' (*Possibilities*, p. 217). This is true; but Wilson's interest in 'control' is not like a nineteenth-century novelist's. The 'Dickensian' in his work is meant to be seen and used as a means of interpretation. By Dickens's criteria, Marcus's theatricality is abnormal: 'MARCUS THE COUNTESS lay back against the nursery table . . . "Don't force it Billah, for God's sake don't force it," she shrieked . . . RUPERT THE BILLY POP said sadly, bewilderedly, "I don't know of any other way of doing it, my dear" ' (Book 2). Yet by criteria Marcus and Rupert share, the asexuality of Dickens's characters is abnormal. Explaining his mother's title of Countess, Rupert suggests it may be a 'genteelism' 'established for the benefit of the nursery'. Quentin's horror when Gladys flushes reminds us how close 1919 was to the laws about respecting the Cheek of the Young Person. If moral poise is lacking as a control, there is design in the counterbalancing of literary modes.

In Powell's *The Kindly Ones* (1962) the narrator comments on the performances of Magnus Donners's dinner guests as Deadly Sins: 'here before us . . . was displayed the nursery and playroom life of generations of "great houses": the abounding physical vitality of big, aristocratic families, their absolute disregard for physical dignity in uninhibited delight in "dressing up" . . .' (Chapter 2). Even among the bourgeois Matthewses the spirit of uninhibited play can be seen as a healthy feature of family life in a pre-Freudian era. The conditions of a Dickens novel made it impossible to show such theatricality as that of Rupert and Marcus; we are meant to realise that and at the same time to sense how Dickensian the absurdity becomes; Rupert enacts his father with the exuberance and nonchalance all the players share: ' "I am an old man," RUPERT THE BILLY POP said, "a very old man, my lord, a very old writing man. I played for Thirsty Scribblers against the Cheshire Cheese Chaps . . . in '06. Even then I was out for a duck" ' (Book 2).

We are expected to keep in mind the ambiguity of the title. The sexual nature of Rupert and Marcus shows through the comedy, where Dickens would have had to cover up with whimsy; but, turning to our own stuffiness, Freudian crudities are dispelled in a true gaiety which Wilson fully shares, at best, with Dickens.

Even granted the healthy influence of the menippean spirit, what, it may be asked, becomes of Wilson's liberal commitments, his ability to say something valid in our age of atrocities? Bernard Bergonzi contrasts Wilson with writers like Camus, Pasternak and Gunter Grass who deal with 'experience of a different order' from 'those reflected by someone like Angus Wilson', and he refers to 'torture, deportation, arbitrary power' as horrors which paralyse the nerve of English literary intellectuals. Bergonzi regrets the absence in *No Laughing Matter*, despite the historic perspective, 'of ideas . . . as a significant dimension in the narrative' (*The Situation of the Novel*, pp. 153, 161).

The last point might be a Frenchman's objection to Dickens and is part of the feeling of impatience in Bernard Bergonzi's book with certain aspects of what he sees as English ideology. The question of 'order of experience' is difficult. At the end of the Game in *No Laughing Matter* Wilson uses the death of some kittens, destroyed in the previous section on the Countess's orders, as a domestic correlative to the larger concerns which occupy Quentin: the war with eight million killed, the end of a social system. Marcus shrieks, 'The kittens are dead!' and falls into a screaming fit, though recovering quite soon, sufficiently to congratulate Quentin on the 'stronger brew' of his sense of humour. The incident of the killing of the kittens and its connection with the background of war and atrocity is Wilson's attempt to focus on the modern experience of evil. Like Quentin's memories of the trenches, it hovers in the background of the exuberant performances in the Game.

Although the 'Family Sunday Play' is a burlesque of Ibsen, the action could have come from a Victorian farce or have featured in *Sketches by Boz*. Quentin has been planning to coax Granny and Aunt Mouse into saving the younger Matthewses from the results of their parents' misappropriation of funds: Marcus about to be sent home from school with unpaid fees, and so forth. Two battles go on: one between parents and children for the old women's money; the other between the Matthewses' kittens and the guests' pets, a lapdog and a parrot, in the kitchen. Granny and aunt depart, angrily demanding the kittens' execution. Billy and the Countess produce champagne and dispose of the kittens while the children are under its influence. This nauseating incident is juxtaposed with images of the war — 'Harrison's guts all spewed against the wire' — and with horrors to come — ' "Burying it! I've never heard such nonsense. What's wrong with the ovens?" The Countess spoke prophetically . . .' (Book 2) — and past callousness recalled by Margaret:'. . . *false* moralising, Aunt Mouse. Weeping over little Nell and then letting little match-sellers die. Like Grandfather's generation' (Book 2).

The third Book, itself the length of a novel, treats the period between the wars with a stress on the more dismal aspects of public events. We see the attempts of Margaret's generation, keen to do *better*, to find adequate responses to Hitler, the Stalinist purges, the Spanish Civil War, and violence in London. Events in Bermondsey, in Germany and in Moscow extend into a chaotic world implications lightly touched by the mock tragedy of Book 2. Billy Pop was squeamish at the time and reminded of his soldier father: 'Anybody could massacre Afghans or Zulus. I don't suppose his duties often called on him to drown kittens' (Book 2). He had his say after the event, telling his children that 'life *is* unjust. The Countess and I today have only been dusty instruments' (Book 2); he left for his club, amidst an aroma of cigar smoke, with a tag about *la comédie humaine*, escaping from his children's contempt.

The younger Matthewses live through the crises of the next twenty years with a commitment — which varies in the form it takes in their different lives and personalities — which is an understandable reaction to their parents' amused detachment. It is not surprising that they associate callousness and mess with their parents' and grandparents' generations, whether bad writing, bad art, false morals or mistaken politics. The success with which Wilson creates his Matthews family, however conventional such an achievement, is what makes the episode of the kittens effective as a figuring of evil, blending ruthless action, indifference to feelings, and economic interest; and it supplies an artistic reply to Nathalie Sarraute's question of how an invented story could rival those of the concentration camps: something closer to our experience which brings those stories home to us. Billy Pop's 'life *is* unjust', in the narrative context, shows a callousness equal to condoning the horrors which seemed to be outside Wilson's scope. We understand the older Matthewses and realise the meaning of Quentin's objection to them: 'you are a guilty lot'. But Wilson uses the fifty years' perspective to distance the youthful indignation of Quentin and the others, whose private hopes are set in relation to their historical moment, so that we sympathise with them, although we see that evil can't be left behind in the nineteenth century.

The private lives and public setting are successfully related, and this gives *No Laughing Matter* a traditional kind of effectiveness which must be due to artistic control though it remains difficult to identify; the narrator cannot be detected, nor, ideologically speaking, can his position. Reflecting on the novel, we may find the result unsatisfactory. But in reading we form an idea of the narrator, or 'impresario', or 'Angus Wilson', in literary terms; he is our contemporary, he belongs to a culture distinct from Billy's or Margaret's in time, though encompassing both. Literary style and method become a significant dimension in the narrative, helping us interpret and judge.

In the third Book, the six Matthewses become scattered, so that parallel stories develop, and a special interest attaches to scenes which bring the strands together. Rupert, Margaret, Quentin and Marcus attend an anti-Fascist protest meeting in 1937. Quentin is notorious as a brilliant left-wing journalist (Q. J. Matthews) currently out of favour with the Party (because anti-Stanlist) and seeing editors reluctant to take his 'disloyal' articles. He finds himself amused at the political innocence of his brother and sister on the platform: Margaret, as a distinguished novelist and 'new Jane Austen', talks about 'the irony of history which will defeat Hitler'; Rupert, equally successful as an actor, offers readings from Milton, Shakespeare, the Romantic poets and Abraham Lincoln. A children's writer from Germany speaks of 'the spirit of creation never vanquished', and disgusts Quentin, though moving Rupert close to tears. 'Better to hear the Comrades spout the Gospel than all this liberal rubbish,' Quentin tells himself. Margaret and Rupert are equally distressed by what they take as the shortcomings of each other's performances, but Quentin's outlook seems abrasively modern, not so much because of his political journalist's thoughts as because of his idiom: ' ". . . invincible human imagination" blaa, blaa, blaa . . . Rupert and Shelley — God help us! He'd seen some of the Comrades' faces, they were paying hard for their solidarity with the intellectuals. Serve them bloody well right. He picked out a young blonde, fresh-faced girl, following the line of her neck, he let his hand take her firm breast . . .' (Book 3, Part 3). Wilson takes advantage, in passages like this, of the contemporary novelist's opportunity to shift the style of narrative or dialogue from one generation to another in the history of the novel.

The Billy Pop's attitude to life is inseparable from the literary style he has learnt from 'important chaps like Gosse and Q'. Other literary styles are associated with liberal heroism or liberal inadequacy in the minds of the characters. Wilson conveys the impatience with what was so strongly felt in the 1930s to be 'bygone tradition' in culture and society. The period when the authority of Milton and Shakespeare was taken for granted is felt to be over; but the conflicting ideologies, and literary styles, of 1937 are themselves seen, like the Comrades' urgency and illiberalism, in perspective.

As in previous Wilson novels, much in the narrative method of the third Book seems traditional. Wilson cannot resist devising little ironies. Quentin is first denounced by Party members as a traitor, then beaten up outside by Irish drunks as a 'dirty Red'. But even after the Communist hecklers at the meeting have been silenced by a Party boss, the cry of 'traitor' is continued, from the back of the hall, by Marcus. Nowadays he spends most of his time building up an art collection for his friend Jack, a Jewish millionaire. Anti-Semitism has recently made him aware of politics and he barracks Quentin jealously ('he *would* be a Trotskyist!'), but gets himself thrown out sooner than obey orders to stop shouting. Anthony Powell could scarcley have contrived a more incongruous example of the bizarre alignments and hostilities of the period. 'Committed' readers are always likely to be put off somewhat by a politically irresponsible comic spirit in both writers, which they share with Dickens.

It seems to come alive especially in connection with speechmaking, as though detecting some absurdity there, lodged irredeemably in human nature. Even Quentin, himself addicted to speeches, is struck by thoughts like this at a conference in Moscow: 'The long eighteenth-century gallery with its baroque carving, its mirrors and chandeliers, was like the scene of some Victorian academic banquet' (Book 3, Part 2). He goes on to imagine 'a Victorian mixed bag of worthies' — Carlyle, Tennyson, Miss Nightingale, Arnold, George Eliot — pontificating in such a place, and the passage of rather Victorian rhetoric ends with the notion of Soviet officialdom as a 'Lytton Strachey sketch' for a circle in hell. Perhaps Quentin's resentment of home life with his grandmother survives in this Stracheyan mixture of intimacy and malice in thinking about the Victorians; the prose rhythms and mannerisms (Book 3, Part 2) mimic the English past as he begins to turn against the Soviet present.

Angus Wilson uses the fact that his characters' minds are saturated with nineteenth-century life, particularly as it is known from novels. They see their own lives in relation to the books they grew up with; their 1920s and 1930s are coloured by stories and images from the previous age. This is realistic, of course, though the technique — which makes the reader's mind boggle if he reflects on the complexity with which it twines fiction and life together — is new. Wilson makes the history of the Novel serve his history.

The story of Gladys's downfall, one of six parallel narratives in the multi-plotted Book 3, illustrates the counterpointing involved. Now a hardworking and fairly successful business-girl, she is persuaded by her Alfred to give up the employment agency and go into antiques. She learns her new trade. In 1937 we find her planning to surprise two elderly refugees with the news that their canvas is a Grünewald. Gladys appears through the novelist's eyes of Margaret at a business-women's talk where Gladys speaks emotionally on behalf of Basque children. Margaret is put off by her style which suggests 'those awful horrors that made Dickens so impossible to read' (Book 3, Part 3). She interprets Gladys's scheme of giving the old couple a happy surprise as 'sentimentality': the old gentleman's face bursting into happiness: 'That awful Dickens again'

(Book 3, Part 3). The Wilson reader of 1967 is certainly meant to see through Margaret's false 1937 version of Dickens, whose reputation was never lower than in the 1930s, never higher than in the 1960s. But the Dickensian aspect of the situation works out unexpectedly. Alfred borrows the Grünewald money and cannot repay in time. Gladys takes the blame for him — a heroic gesture that upsets the sentimental conception of roles: the kind-hearted lady is forced into the part of a thief, the nice old gentleman into an angry Jew.

'I don't *want* . . . storytelling powers,' Margaret reflects about her own modernist art (Book 3, Part 3). Wilson's own instinct for how to tell a story is especially strong in this section, but he has absorbed the scepticism of the modernists and there is nothing naïve about his narrative. He implies that the Dickens world is in fact unequal to historical upheaval on the scale which displaces Gladys's Herr Ahrend. The old refugee's bearded face switches from one Dickens stereotype to another in the characters' minds, becoming Fagin-like as he reacts to the pressure of anti-Semitism and exile. There is no happy ending for Gladys after the sentiment and suspense, but prison. She is sentenced just before Munich; the sense that something has gone drastically wrong is conveyed in this contrast with the decorum of Dickens's novels, where the moral confidence of the author is so sure. Both sisters are revealed in relation to Dickens. To divert attention from Alf's guilt, Gladys fools around and yarns with a vulgarity that disconcerts Margaret sitting in court. Then, seeing the dignity Gladys summons to meet her sentence of four years' penal servitude, Margaret makes a note for her current work in progress.

Praising Wilson at the close of his book *The English Novel From Dickens to Lawrence* (1970), Raymond Williams calls him 'a continually experimenting' writer, and adds: 'It can't be done, that exploration, in a single ratifying, explaining voice. In so profound and so difficult a multipersonal reality, the shapes of observation can seem to turn to shadows, and the grammar of presentation, of contemporary presentation, is very difficult to learn' (p. 152). One of the ways in which Wilson experiments with presentation is connected with Raymond Williams's theme, in *The English Novel*, that traditional novelists worked with concepts of community. While the traditional novel used subplots and parallel stories to convey the feeling of social solidity, Wilson uses the alternating strands of his six stories to illustrate the disintegrating condition of twentieth-century English society. This need not be less serious for being done with a lightness of touch: Marcus shouting 'traitor' at Quentin; Margaret taking notes on Gladys going to jail. And even beneath the weakening of social ties in a big, prosperous, bourgeois family like this one, Wilson suggests a malfunctioning of basic family relationships.

Marcus is the Matthews who seems early on in the novel the most tenuously linked to his culture. He starts life on leaving school as a male prostitute and even when 'established' in life with Jack and a figure in Mayfair, he gravitates to the fringes of society, turning up in one scene at a Fascist luncheon, in another getting arrested as an anti-Fascist demonstrator. His social mobility and unconventionality are likely to seem attractive as a way of life in the contrast, which the novel emphasises, with that of his sister, Sukey. She has cut herself off from brothers and sisters, as being all more or less disreputable, and leads an outwardly model life as the wife of a headmaster, in the country. Dedicated as she is to middle-class Anglican motherhood, she provides Wilson the satirist with his favourite sort of target. She might seem hardly worth the trouble of setting up, but in relation to the nonconformity not only of Marcus but of the other Matthewses too, the attack on her complacency is significant. It is a sign of Wilson's competence in this line of satire that Sukey's obsessive maternal love for P. S., her youngest son, does come across as unhealthy, even as a kind of perversion, while Marcus's interest in boys does not. The relationships between Gladys and Alf and Marcus and Jack are stronger than Sukey's weird private religion of family. The agreement she makes with God before 1939, sacrificing in her own mind her elder sons to preserve the youngest, almost seems to invite its outcome when P. S. is killed in Palestine while the others survive. The superficially traditional appearance of the framework only stresses how weak the old sanctities of mother and son, Anglican faith and England can be made to look; and everything 'Dickensian' in the novel's method and the characters' minds becomes disturbing, in the same way that Iris Murdoch's work can disturb. Both remind us of how misleading the appearances of continuity with tradition in present-day life often are, and how unlike a fragment of the nineteenth century much of England really is.

Iris Murdoch's 'Against Dryness', which ends by advocating 'the destructive power of character' as a means of puncturing myth and as an alternative to becoming mesmerised by form, directs us to a paradox in *No Laughing Matter* where the characters are so vivid and memorable, yet not 'there' in the Jamesian sense since the technique plays too many tricks with them. Billy Pop and Clara are perhaps most likely of all to be remembered, yet they appear as characters in an amazing variety of styles drawn from other novels and plays including Jane Austen and Samuel Beckett. They are killed by the bomb which falls on their hotel in the persons of 'Pop' and 'Motor' ('Pop' swathed like a mummy) in a brief 'dramatic catastrophe'. But this disregard for their integrity as characters scarcely matters when we remember them; many couples in orthodox Edwardian novels are far less vivid, and less convincing in the sense of what works. The attraction of character and story are so strong, perhaps, that the mind will adjust to any technique while they remain interesting, yet reject realism as unreal once that interest is lost. This might explain the disappointment some 'orthodox' novel readers feel with the brief and straightforward last two Books, full of significance regarding modern life as they are.

One significant point is that the family, so rooted in England at the turn of the century, is now widely dispersed and mostly abroad. These last two Books, covering 1946, 1956 and 1967, are rather like the Epilogue in some Victorian novels (*Middlemarch*, for example) which explains what happened afterwards, and this innocent old convention might be seen here as a sarcastic reflection on the story of England, now at the same stage. The young Matthewses of 1967, in the last Book, visit Gladys, living among expatriate Britons in Portugal, and Marcus, still rich after Jack's death, and surrounded by servants in a grand house on the coast of Morocco. Quentin, a disillusioned television pundit, is doing a documentary on the Moroccans, 'Should they Emerge?'; he and Margaret, another guest, are unimpressed by Marcus's good cause, a scent factory to create work; and they do not understand the Moroccans. The Moroccans' thoughts about the Matthewses remind us at the very end, although this too is ironically undermined, that the English world of the Matthews family (like the English novel) has only ever been a part of the whole.

To the youngest generation, in Book 5, their grandparents seem perhaps even more alien, belonging to an utterly bygone civilisation, hardly to be distinguished from any other. The subtle and precise interest in the gradations of recent history which the whole novel takes for granted is submitted to mocking hints about how quickly the 'modern' ceases to be new. Even so the presentation in *No Laughing Matter* of layers of Matthews generations, and the layers of fictional procedure, let us see how inseparably interknit our present culture is with the past. Jake's view in *Under the Net* about how historical perspective paralyses (especially in literature) was fashionable in the sixties, but this novel deserves to survive them because it makes that perspective so creative and able to renew.

5 Kingsley Amis

An excellence in the writing, an insistence on 'Englishness' and an aggressive concern with values are three points on which all critics of Amis seem to agree. Amis's own kind of verbal sprightliness has been generally recognised and praised. From the opening pages of *Lucky Jim* (1954) onwards, his prose has been for many of his readers the language of contemporary common sense; it is a style that has contributed to the way educated English is used today. His 'Englishness' on the other hand has been seen as regrettably insular and irrelevant in terms of world literature, reactionary in technique, averse to experiment. The best summing up of Amis's commitment to received values is that of W. W. Robson who sees 'an effort to recreate the idea of the gentleman in an age when this idea has lost its religious, social and moral basis, to become the vaguely regretted anachronism that it is for the hero of Amis's *Take a Girl Like You*'.[1]

Jean-Paul Sartre's denial that prose can be an imaginative medium has become notorious. Iris Murdoch comments on it in 'Against Dryness' that 'most modern novels are not *written*'.[2] Amis's books are, though without the baroque effects of many contemporary stylists. His work has consistently followed the objectives declared by John Fowles for *Daniel Martin*: he is 'unfashionably' concerned with humanism and with 'what it is to be English'; his novels are in themselves something of an affront to more pretentious experimental ventures in fiction. But, however tiresome it may have been for those who like to put novelists in categories, Amis's writing has always been original, and subversive of stale and secondhand language and opinion; it constitutes a refutation of Sartre's opinion about prose fiction. And whereas Sartre abandoned the novel as a medium unequal to his own needs, Amis has written entertaining fiction for twenty-five years without repeating himself and without losing interest in the technical side of imaginative prose.

For although he has appeared superficially as the most blatant instance of a gifted writer rejecting innovation, Amis has been experimenting with exceptional subtlety, though within the 'limits' of story, character and, above all, dialogue; more than most novelists of any time he is aware of how story and character can be found in the way people talk. Much attention has been paid to the novel in recent years by professional scholars in linguistics, and they have tended to find in Amis the most intriguing illustrations of what creative language can do when fully stretched artistically and still faithful to natural speech. It is this power, above all, which keeps Amis in touch with the novel of the past; his originality has been achieved through creative relations with various traditions, including that of Dickens, whom, so he has said, he cannot swallow; that of Jane Austen, of whom he claims he morally disapproves; and that of Fielding, whom he has praised most generously. Yet to try to account for him as a traditionalist would be absurd; the contemporary tone of his work is the creation of a mind which understands how and why Fielding belongs to a culture quite unlike our own. He resembles Fielding, Jane Austen and Dickens, not because he clings to a type of novel which was appropriate to their times and not to ours, but because he shares with them an acute sense of the contemporary in relation to the past, especially in language, and in spoken language most of all. It is here that he has been, as they were, an innovator.

Like most English novelists, Amis is a satirist. One aspect of his work is a power of vituperation which has been compared with that of the *flyters* of medieval and ancient literature — the poets of spleen like Dunbar in fifteenth-century Scotland and Martial in first-century Rome who railed against the times and jeered at their enemies in lists:

> Here they come — tramp, tramp, tramp — all those characters you thought were discredited, or had never read, or (if you were like me) had never heard of: Barbusse, Sartre, Camus, Kierkegaard, Nietzsche, Hermann Hesse, Hemingway, Van Gogh, Nijinsky, Tolstoy, Dostoievsky, George Fox, Blake, Sri Ramakrishna, George Gurdjieff, T. E. Hulme and a large number of bit-players. The Legion of the Lost, they call us, the Legion of the Lost are we, as the old song has it. Marching on to hell with the drum playing — pick up the step there!

This maliciously assembled catalogue comes from the opening

paragraph of 'The Legion of the Lost', Amis's review of Colin Wilson's *The Outsider* (1956), and is reprinted in his collection of essays and reviews, *What Became of Jane Austen?* (1970). Amis praises Colin Wilson for being readable, clear and unpretentious — consistently-held Amis values — and regrets only the need for such a book: 'One of the prime indications of the sickness of mankind in the mid-twentieth century is that so much excited attention is paid to books about the sickness of mankind in the mid-twentieth century.' The review is a cheerful satire on, or *flyting* of, the 'Outsider' — the *legionnaires'* 'collective label' — and, as clearly as any of his occasional writings, it indicates the intellectual stance and tone this very intellectual writer has preserved — despite shifts away from progressive political views held in the fifties, and despite continual new directions in the novels themselves — in the more than a dozen books since *Lucky Jim* came out in 1954. The 'Outsider' is, Amis says, more sick of self-love, adolescent, anti-rational, anti-humanist and arrogant than Childe Harold, and lazier, sillier and more pretentious. In terms of literary status several of the names obviously belong in better company and there only at their most foolish: we all, he says, have adolescent moments. It is the amoral and anti-social influence of the concept that is deplored and the encouragement offered to a minority to feel superior to *us*, that is to those of us for whom reality is not unreal and who don't feel inclined to question our identity or our existence. 'How am I to live?' is a reasonable question. 'Who am I?' is not. Amis concludes:

> A case could be made out for people shouldering the burden of their own nastiness, enduring their boredom and depression, without finding it necessary to blame someone or something — Perhaps there are curative properties in the notion that ordering up another bottle, attending a jam session, or getting introduced to a young lady, while they may solve no problems at all, are yet not necessarily without dignity . . .

That 1956 optimism is qualified in *What Became of Jane Austen?* by a postscript conceding that Colin Wilson was partly right about the key influence of the Outsider figure and reflecting that society is partly sick as a result.

The position defended here is anti-modernist. Blake, Dostoevsky and Tolstoy are cited because of their appeal to modernist writers who in Amis's view take their literary, philosophical and political radicalism too seriously at the expense of good sense and good writing and because, in 1956, Amis was at the height of his early reputation as an Angry Young Man, and cultural debunking, associated with *Lucky Jim*, was expected of him. Throughout the early novels, major literary figures, from Henry James back to Cicero, are treated with thoughtful disrespect. Amis was also an English don in 1956 and he remained a central figure in the British literary scene, as a critic, reviewer, editor and general emitter of opinion. Academic scruple has always been combined in his work, on the other hand, with an openness to popular contemporary genres which have received almost no serious critical attention in English from anyone else. The counterpart of his sniping at the reputations of James, Dickens and Jane Austen can be seen in his studies of science fiction, detective fiction and the spy story. His views on science fiction offer a significant contrast to those of Michel Butor (both have written on Jules Verne). Butor considers science fiction '*une mythologie en poussière*', unequal to present literary wants.[3] Amis judges science fiction stories and films on their merits. Reporting his attendance at an SF Exhibition where a bad film won a prize, he wrote: 'My American colleague thought it was rubbish too, but the French and Italian majority went on about its relation to the contemporary consciousness, I believe it was.'[4] The scorn for French and European intellectual modishness comes across with a slightly self-conscious English bluffness, but in Amis the 'English Ideology' has its most trenchant, combative and creative writer.

David Lodge points out, in his article 'The Modern, the Contemporary and the Importance of Being Amis' (in *Language of Fiction*), how the 'contemporary' and 'anti-modern' approach to fiction does not prevent 'Amis's use of language [from being] as inextricably part of his importance as Henry James's was of his or Joyce's was of his'. This makes him an ideal example among recent novelists of Lodge's thesis in *Language of Fiction* that novels must be read as closely as poetry; reading Amis's novels beside his verse reveals how highly crafted both are and how keen the ear for language is in both. As David Lodge demonstrates, finding examples in his own speech habits, certain Amis locutions have helped to create the idiom and tone of current English style. He goes on to argue that the neglected third novel, *I Like It Here*, is a modern British example of a novel 'turned inward upon literary art' like *Tristram Shandy* or *Pale Fire*. David Lodge is right to remind us that there can be subtleties of technique in novels which do not advertise their own experimental status, and to stress that it is, even so, the quality of the writing which gives his work its edge. Amis has become increasingly more adventurous with form and technique since 1966, when *Language of Fiction* was published, and the literary playfulness observed then has been developed in a number of ways in recent books, but the novels have remained inveterately realist in their use of English; in spite of excursions into fantasy or surrealism, the writing has never lost touch with the way his readers find words for themselves.

It could be objected that Amis stands outside my thesis that modern English novelists conceive their work in relation to Victorian novels because he has identified himself with eighteenth-century novelists and especially with Fielding. *I Like It Here* included a eulogy of Fielding (in the context of a visit to his grave in Lisbon) which has become famous: 'Perhaps it was worth dying in your forties if two hundred years later you were the only non-contemporary novelist who could be read with unaffected and whole-hearted interest . . . [having achieved] a moral seriousness that could be made apparent without evangelical puffing and blowing' (Chapter 15). Bernard Bergonzi, for example, has linked Amis with eighteenth-century 'robustness and moral simplicity' rather than with 'the high Victorian seriousness admired and to some extent imitated by Snow or Wilson'.[5] Elsewhere, Amis has praised the 'invigorating coldness' of the pre-Victorian novel — in his 1957 'Jane Austen' article attacking *Mansfield Park*, where he praises it in her.

Garnet Bowen's praise of Fielding in *I Like It Here* is an anti-Victorian outburst; Bowen is a typical early (1950s) Amis character in this distaste for aspects of life that seem hangovers from some sort of Victorianism. Patrick Standish in *Take a Girl* is struggling to free himself from toils of hypocrisy and cant belonging to the previous century. But despite the adjustments made by Patrick, Bowen or Jim Dixon to the far greater mobility and flexibility of their own society, the values which inform the novels are directly inherited from the nineteenth century. Martin Green in an article called 'British Decency' in the *Kenyon Review* in 1959 suggested Amis as the heir of Lawrence, Leavis and Orwell. That is company he might well disdain but the comparisons do indicate the continuity from, not so much high Victorian seriousness as the moral values of the Victorian middle class. Albert Smith, author of *The Scattergood*

Family — whom Dickens defended in the Garrick Club quarrel and whom Thackeray despised as a Bohemian — is the kind of mid-Victorian novelist and essayist — though much less talented — with whom he might be linked. The more positive values of the lower-middle class, whom the Victorians never permitted (except in the case of Dickens whom the 'high' Victorians never came to terms with) to speak with authority, have found a cultivated, intelligent, bigoted but humane voice in Kingsley Amis. His work is more balanced, has a broader appeal, and may turn out to last longer than that of Lawrence, Leavis or Orwell.

British Decency does not seem much, George Steiner thinks, to set against the Holocaust.[6] In the year following Martin Green's article, Amis published *Take a Girl Like You* (1960), his most ambitious attempt up to then at a conventional novel of the times, and the result suggested that even British decency could no longer be relied on. At one point in the hero's drunkenness he feels himself to be living in the disordered world of some French experimental work. With its story and dialogue, its moral issue and topical themes, its characters' inner life 'shown' and not 'told', *Take a Girl Like You* is a work of exemplary technical flair within the limits of conventional fiction, and it is not surprising that Roger Fowler in his *Linguistics and the Novel* (1977) uses a sample from this novel, set beside a passage from Thackeray's *Vanity Fair* (1848), to illustrate from a linguist's point of view what can be done with imaginative prose. This might have produced what was needed to refute French theorists, supposing that anyone could. In fact, *Take a Girl* turned out to be something different: a brilliant and important failure.

The novel is dominated by the relationship between the two central characters, Patrick Standish and Jenny Bunn — by his pursuit of her. Almost all critics who mention the book see it as a modern *Clarissa* though it has very little in common with Richardson's psychological epic except for the strategy of 'procrastinated rape', the hero's attack on marriage and the issue of what it means to behave like a gentleman. Patrick teaches Latin in a good school; he has limited private means, though these came from his mother's shop, and a smart flat and large car, though these are shared with a colleague, Graham. He is socially adaptable ('classless' in the 1960s term): at ease with Jenny's father, a hearse driver (a typically awkward Amis touch), and more or less at ease with Lord Edgerstoune when dining at the latter's country place. He sees himself, although a shade ironically, as a 'progressive intellectual' and up against forces of reaction, at least in his private life, in people like Charlton the school's secretary, who tells him that masters are meant to behave like gentlemen. He takes himself to be basically 'decent', and Amis shows that he can behave with moral generosity, but he drinks too much, drives too fast, dreads the future and senility, tries to 'think about sex most of the time', pursues women, avoids marriage, and hopes for the best. Most of all this depends on the decline of Victorian standards in his local community — as Charlton points out — and he is more than ready for the permissiveness of the 1960s. Asked when it was he first came to the school, he underlines this impatience: '1857, I mean 1957.'

Jenny has 'come down' from the North of England, which the other characters regard as an utterly remote industrial waste locked in the grip of Primitive Methodism. She teaches at a local infants' school and reads *Woman's Domain*. She is hoping for permissiveness in moderation, symbolised for her by the image of scarlet jeans, but stopping short of premarital intercourse, and she wants to marry Patrick.

The conflict of interests here is resolved only at the end of the novel where Patrick 'rapes' Jenny when she is drunk, acting with a lack of decency about which the novel is morally vague. 'He'll marry her and bugger off,' Amis told Clive James in an interview which James wrote up for the *New Review*, and this is implied, though not said, at the close:

> 'Well, those old Bible-class ideas have certainly taken a knocking, haven't they?'
> 'They were bound to, you know, darling, with a girl like you. It was inevitable.'
> 'I expect it was. But I can't help feeling it's rather a pity.'

These are the last words on the matter; the novel attempts no more than to reveal the moral crisis of the society it portrays, caught as Patrick's 1857–1957 remark suggests between two centuries, between the contemporary London West End and Jenny's perhaps exaggeratedly out-of-date Industrial North. Jenny asks another — London — girl about virginity, at the party where she loses hers, and the question is shrugged off as if possessing only historical interest: ' "I thought it was all to do with arranged marriages and betrothals and dowries and purdah and all that. I thought the whole

thing had more or less blown over" ' (Chapter 26). Bernard
Bergonzi considers the novel morally 'annoying', and David Lodge
argues that Amis's anti-metaphysical, British empirical limitations
create dissonances in what the comedy ought to have developed into
a happy ending. Both accounts are perceptive and sympathetic and
both recognise the social accuracy with which Amis captures a
phase of the country's transition. Neither of them goes as far as
suggesting what seems, from the way Amis's subsequent novels have
developed, to be the case with *Take a Girl Like You*: that Amis
reached his own limits here in writing straight, conventional fiction
and arguably (since no one has proved better at it than Amis)
reached the limits of what is at present possible. In that case, *Clarissa*
could be seen as a most appropriate comparison, since it was one of
the first great novels of moral character and social conduct, and
Take a Girl would be one of the last attempts by a really talented
novelist to work straightforwardly in the same tradition. It fails, and
Amis has never written this sort of novel since; when he has come
close to doing so, as in *Girl, 20*, the moral vacuum W. W. Robson
referred to is much more warily allowed for by the method, as we
shall see.

    Take a Girl Like You alternates between recording what Roger
Fowler calls the 'mind styles' of Jenny and Patrick, and does each
with a brilliance which Fowler illustrates from a 'Jenny passage'
where her *Woman's Domain* diction and phrasing are contrasted
with the more mature verbal resources of the prose narrative.
Unfortunately this method for getting the character into perspective works less well with Patrick since his 'mind style' appears to be
so close to that of the author. Jenny's intellectual and moral position
tends to be absorbed by that of Patrick and any possibility of judging
either of them by the way the language works, normally the surest
guide in Amis, fails. Here is Patrick explaining to Jenny that her
idea of the gentleman is out of date:

> 'There used to be a third sort, admitted. The sort that could, but
> didn't . . . not with the girl he was going to marry anyway.
> You'd have liked him all right though, and he wouldn't have
> given you any trouble trying to get you into bed before the day.
> The snag about him is he's dead. He died in 1914 or thereabouts.
> He isn't ever going to turn up, Jenny, that bloke with the manners
> and the respect and the honour and the bunches of flowers *and* the
> attraction.' [Chapter 13]

Amis has in a sense defeated himself by creating a character in Patrick whose personal blend of gentlemanliness and caddishness is hard to place, in a narrative which is ambiguous about the significance of both concepts and pervaded by the character's own brilliant but muddled thinking as well. Patrick observes the quaint way of life of a surviving country house with amused tolerance. Before 1914, even before 1945, the country house would have served as a milieu in which to place him socially and perhaps morally, but it can no longer do so. At the book's other social extreme, Jenny's Bible-class upbringing is dismissed with 'rather a pity'. The novel is so good — the visit of Patrick and Julian to Archie Edgerstoune's place is a masterpiece of social observation — that we are made aware of what Robson means by 'social vacuum' in the context of a rich but precarious prose narrative which demonstrates the real impossibility of writing a novel as if the conditions of 1857 still obtained. *Take a Girl Like You* is an important failure because it brings out so clearly and completely the absence for a novelist today of standards held in common with his characters or with his reader.

In his next book, *One Fat Englishman* (1963), Amis exaggerates the most unpleasant features of the 'gentleman' and combines them with the lust, greed, egoism and irritability of Patrick Standish developed to a grotesque degree in the person of his new character, Roger Micheldene — a figure of an allegorically conceived monstrosity that Dickens might have baulked at. Roger possesses an old-fashioned gusto, slightly reminiscent of Peacock's Dr Folliott. His awful Englishness, snobbish and carping, is opposed to the awfulness — as he sees it — of America, in an unresolvable dialectic not unlike that of a Peacock debate; this allows Amis a good deal of satire on modern America, foisted on to an irresponsible English protagonist. Satirical caricature, which remained in the background of *Take a Girl*, becomes the gist of *One Fat Englishman*, but even more significantly the menippean features which David Lodge notes in *I Like It Here* are given a central importance. Parody, verbal and literary games, stylised farce, weird connections between the abstractly intellectual and the vulgarly physical fill the work with a carnival air (and the grotesque cover design used by Penguin seems much more suitable for this novel than for *Take a Girl Like You*). Roger quoting lines of the *Aeneid* for staying-power on top of the story's Danish heroine, Mrs Bang; Roger hammering on the wrong door in quest of his American confessor in the middle of the night: 'Come down at once you long-frocked clown . . . Let me in this instant you spiritual dentist . . .' (Chapter 13), and later immersing Father Colgate in a fish tank or rescuing (by stealing) a Swinburne manuscript from American hands — this is not a figure we are meant to take as seriously as we take Jim Dixon; nor does he belong to the same sort of novel.

But *One Fat Englishman* does remain firmly within the limits of conventional fiction; it uses Roger's reflections on the excesses of what is allegedly the now American mode to define its own conventionality: 'the expected paraplegic necrophiles, hippoerotic jockeys, exhibitionistic castrates, coprophagic pig-farmers, armless flagellationists and the rest of the bunch' (Chapter 7) are kept out of the work of the young American writer, Macher, and out of Amis's book too, except that the zealous cataloguing of these curiosities contributes to the total effect. In this, the traditional culture so appallingly represented by Micheldene is seen for the first time in Amis, despite the frequent swipes at it taken by Jim and Patrick, as a threatened, and possibly dispensable achievement. The novels that followed have opposed the traditional culture both to social development, chiefly in England, and to a glumly observed indifference or hostility on the part of the universe.

What emerges in the novels of the late 1960s and 1970s is a new style in Amis's fiction. In many of the books he uses popular genres to introduce a new perspective on the traditional social and psychological concerns of the novel. In *The Anti-Death League* (1966) he abandoned comedy altogether and devised an Amis version of the spy story in what could be described as a meditation on death, or as an attack (as Amis is reported to have said) on 'God' in the sense of 'the way things are'. *The Green Man* (1969) is more entertaining and more ambitious as an experiment with genres and an assault on the ways of God to man. Both books confront the problem of evil with an anti-theological fervour which is conceived of in popular terms. *The Green Man* creates a sense of desperation and horror at the presence of evil; this is conveyed through the person of a very credible character as the narrator, who offsets the effects of fantasy, and through a forceful and natural prose which gives a unity to the complex manipulation of genres. The result is a *tour de force* composed of ghost story, science fiction, historical pastiche and the species of philosophical whimsy which Michael Frayn has created in novels like *Sweet Dreams* (1973); these elements are combined with Amisian social and sexual comedy.

> Nevertheless, I was sure she was going to yïeld that afternoon when she was ready to, and this time understood at the same moment why I was sure. By opening her legs to me today of all days, she would be being strangely responsive to my strange need, finding herself strangely in tune with this strange man—in other words she could represent herself as an interesting person. But before she got on to being strangely responsive, she was going to exact her full toll by making me put up with her questioning patiently enough, and long enough, for it seems that I agreed she was an interesting person. Seeming, luckily for me, was all that was going to be required, since she needed no confirmation of her view of herself . . . [Chapter 2]

Maurice Allington, innkeeper of the Green Man, is taking Diana, the wife of his friend Jack Maybury, out to the woods for the afternoon following (and hence the 'strangeness') his father's death the night before. The passage is immediately recognisable as a piece of Amis prose: it combines fluency with the convolutions and repetitions that arise in speech; and it achieves a modulated control of the sentence and of variation in registers between his—slangy and blunt: 'opening her legs'—and hers, influenced by the Women's Page of the *Guardian* (which she carries with her to hide behind from passers-by) in phrases like 'strangely responsive to my strange need'. The rhythms are true to what could actually be said (Amis reprints in *What Became of Jane Austen?* a review faulting Wesker for failing to achieve this). At the same time he constantly turns his own deftness with language against language itself—an effect described by David Lodge in the essay on Amis in his *Language of Fiction*. The effect can be seen here even though Maurice is expressing himself with such aggressive panache, asserting himself and scoffing at female affectation. The reiteration of 'strange' queries a banal mental convention and also ridicules our whimsical uses of the word, a touch of satire reinforced in a few pages' time by the presence of a prehistoric tree-devil. The reflection that 'seeming, luckily for me, was all that was going to be required' echoes Jim Dixon, but does so only faintly. Not only is Maurice's attitude to women, implied in every sentence of this passage, more ruthless and competent than Jim's; he exists as a character in a different kind of relationship to the novel he is in.

In a straightforward, old-fashioned mimetic novel it would be a mistake to allow a first-person narrator to discuss the novel as a literary form — Maurice, however, is allowed to do so. He despises, he tells us, novels altogether, preferring poetry and painting. Even at the best, in Proust or Stendhal, he finds 'theirs a puny and piffling art', quite incapable of doing justice to the way things are. Lyric verse, he adds, 'is equidistant from fiction and life, and is autonomous' (Chapter 2). These views jolt us into seeing the narrator for the convention he is, and that makes us wonder about his relation to the author. The fantasy and pastiche elements which Amis is handling, we might decide, move the novel closer to an autonomous status like that of a lyric poem. In a Joycean work like Flann O'Brien's *At Swim-Two-Birds*, the different and conflicting levels of meaning disrupt the illusory power of the fiction; we are delighted and amused, but there is no question of suspending our disbelief. Amis contrives to unsettle the conventional components of his novel, the relationship of narrator to narration, for example, or of realistic and supernatural narrative tones, without disturbing the coherence or the compulsion of the story. He gives us the pleasure of the 'fabulation' and that of reading a traditional novel.

Sexual comedy is of course a type of fiction which, by virtue of the incongruities discussed in Chapters 1 and 7, automatically evokes the Victorian novel when it involves a comedy of manners as it often does in Iris Murdoch and Angus Wilson. In this passage and in all such scenes, any concern with the question of the hero's status as a gentleman is at its most critical. Maurice is planning to get Diana and his own wife into the same bed. When, eventually, he succeeds, they turn out to be more interested in each other. Amis claimed in his essay 'No More Parades' (in *What Became of Jane Austen?*) about his time in Cambridge that 'an eminent member of the English faculty' had said that Peterhouse (Amis's college) could no longer be taken seriously since they had elected a pornographer. This rather Victorian reaction does show how unVictorian this aspect of one of our most firmly Establishment novelists has, fairly recently, been able to appear. Amis commented that 'Cambridge is the least damaging place in England in which not to be found funny'. The sexual scenes in *The Green Man* are funny and also cruel:

'Maurice . . . don't you think sexual attraction is the most

peculiar and unpredictable and simply *mad* thing in the world?'
    At this, I cheered up a little. Either Diana was semi-consciously
groping for the sixty-four-cent question, the ultimate bit of balls
which I would pass the test by letting her get away with, or she
was just running out of material. 'I've never understood it,' I said
humbly. [Chapter 2]

A line in one of Amis's poems says that 'Women are really much
nicer than men'; their shortcomings are nonetheless as closely
observed as their attractions by male characters in the novels:
Patrick Standish, Max Hunter (in *The Anti-Death League*), Jake (in
Jake's Thing) flout the old convention of delicacy to ladies though,
like Maurice, they try to preserve a conventional politeness if only,
with Patrick and Jake, as part of the game. A Roman or, perhaps,
eighteenth-century exasperation with women is worked into Kingsley Amis's vision of what girls are like. But this anti-chivalrous
slant, which can be seen as anti-Victorian, does not affect the
basically decent standard which the central character respects. A
Catullus or a real Lovelace of the 1740s would disgust any Amis
hero and Dr Underhill, the Green Man's ghost, disgusts Maurice.
    Underhill unites (or united) two Amis *bêtes noires*, pedantry and a
preference for 'nymphets'. The fact of his being, as a ghost,
inhuman, is somehow combined with the implication that he is not a
gentleman, at least not by the standards of modern Cambridge
where Maurice goes to research the ghost's background: the
civilised politeness of his academic contacts there seems a reflection
not just on the uncouther, younger Cambridge elements, but also on
Underhill, who is an impressively individual ghost. The seventeenth-century prose of his papers helps to make him seem real:
'April 29th 1686: Must cast aside fleshy delights, and all such
concerns (for the moment)'. The way his dead lusts have survived
and seem to parallel, in his schemes to satisfy them, Maurice's own,
generates an aura of evil, as something alien and distorted, in
Underhill's existence. Meanwhile decent Maurice's susceptibilities
are attacked on a grander scale in another area of the fantasy. Max
Beerbohm in 'Enoch Soames' decides that the devil is not a
gentleman. Maurice has this feeling about God, with whom he takes
a glass of whisky in Chapter 4.
    Any of the earlier Amis heroes might have enjoyed such a
conversation, 'man to man', in the form of daydream or semi-
intoxicated fantasy. Allington is closer to alcoholism than any of

them, but the novel makes it clear that he is not suffering an hallucination, and is not an 'unreliable' narrator. Amis's God, like his ghost, is interesting as a social being and the crucial judgement on him is made at this level of social behaviour, as is proper in a novel. Theologically, this God is crudely conceived, differing from the Miltonic account (which he commends) chiefly in lacking foreknowledge and in containing Satan as a part of his own nature. In his 1962 essay about the character of Christ, 'On Christ's Nature' (in *What Became of Jane Austen?*), Amis said that he agreed with William Empson about the wickedness of God, and that is a major theme of *The Anti-Death League*. Maurice's visitor possesses a cool indifference to suffering but he works by 'rules of the game' in the Miltonic fashion and the limits to his omniscience might make him seem more sympathetic to a post-Christian reader than God is in Empson's *Milton's God*.

On this occasion he has made himself humanly presentable in the guise of a sprucely turned out, articulate young man, with well-polished shoes, sufficiently distinct from the detestable Cambridge sociology dons who frequent the Green Man to be acceptable to Maurice as a guest. There is something in his manner, however, in his 'not very trustworthy face' and in the hint of 'vexation' in his voice when Maurice spots an inconsistency in the physical arrangements made to isolate their meeting which suggest what is unsatisfactory in his nature at the level of a character appearing in a novel. These traits are accompanied by a streak of vulgarity, of bad manners in an ostentatious show of power. As Maurice offers whisky, the hand prepared to take it momentarily putrefies: ' "That was unnecessary," I said, sitting down again. "Don't you believe it, old boy. Puts things on the right footing between us. This isn't just a social call, you know. Cheers" ' (Chapter 4). The dialogue here presents the visitor for assessment as if he were, for example, director of a brewery which has bought up the inn. Maurice afterwards retains an impression of 'triviality'; if he isn't impressed it is because, behind the brusque and slightly bullying manner, there is callousness. God says about suffering, 'it's purely and simply the run of the play. No malice in the world . . .'

In 1957 Amis attacked Jane Austen's reputation as a novelist in 'What Became of Jane Austen?' But in his satirical portraits of the egotistical and pretentious academics and intellectuals of the novels, Bertram and Professor Welch, Dick and Charlton, Micheldene, Dr Best, even Dr Underhill, the buffoons, pseuds and shits from

Lucky Jim onwards, he is attacking the same refusal to be aware of other people's feelings which she attacked. Amis is of course outside the religion she took for granted but he judges by the standard which she created for the English novel and finds that his God is not a gentleman.

Nor is the parson whom Maurice calls in to exorcise Underhill. A trendy disbeliever, the Reverend Tom Rodney Sonnenschein, Rector of St James's, Fareham has exchanged religious dogma for a vaguely liberal 'concern'. Although he belongs to the real social world of the book, he has so much less weight than the figures of fantasy that his explanations about Victorian superstition appear doubly comic: ' "Immortality's just a passing phase. Basically, it was thought up by the Victorians, especially the early Victorians, as a sort of guilt thing. They'd created the evils of the Industrial Revolution . . . and the only refuge from hell on earth they could think of was a new life away from the smoke . . ." ' (Chapter 4). The rural background of rectory and parish duties adds to the incongruity of the Reverend Rodney. He has to be lured into agreeing to do the exorcism through his own social ambition and spite. The change in social and doctrinal standards is matched, it is implied, by moral decay. The pseudo-journalese opinion and knowingness — 'especially the early Victorians' — undermined by so astonishing an historical ignorance suggest the tradition of dramatic comedy from Jonson to Fielding rather than satire in traditional fiction, and *The Green Man* takes the clergyman more seriously as a sign of the times than Firbank or Waugh would have done.

The novel ends, all the same, with more good humour than any of the previous books since *Lucky Jim*. Sonnenschein performs, although unbelievingly, the rituals needed to dispose of Underhill and the ghastly primeval Green Man, so that the fantasy meshes neatly with the social satire. Maurice rescues his daughter, withdrawn during most of the novel into a teenage sulk, from the monsters, and she turns out a dutiful support to him when his wife leaves with Diana. At the very end Maurice is contemplating his prospects, in Eternity and in the more immediate evening's duty-round; he fortifies himself with a stiff scotch. Amis has taken risks with the sort of novel he writes. His liberties with the novelist's absolute power to concoct illusions would have taken him outside the limits of a story with a happy ending if the management of tone in Maurice's narration had been less brilliantly done. In *Take a Girl Like You* Amis reached the end of one line of development when he took his characters' moral world for granted and then lost touch with them in the novel's crisis. In *The Green Man*, he shuffles conventions with the adroitness of a John Barth or a Flann O'Brien, exploiting uncertainties in the reader about the rules of what is real in a story to impose his own convictions in the ensuing hesitation about what is humanly right and proper and what is outrageous. Maurice himself is one of Amis's greatest successes: a tough landlord and a reader of poetry; a man with lusts and sympathies, a heart and a very strong head; we feel he deserves to chat with God. He and the unfailingly appropriate words he is given hold the work together. Amis has produced in this book as elegant a 'fabulation' as Robert Scholes could hope for, and he has preserved and reasserted the humanist conviction and hope of the traditional novel.

In his novels of the 1970s, Amis has continued to experiment with genre, creating his own style of detective story in *The Riverside Villas Murder* (1973) and producing in *The Alteration* (1976) an alternative version of the 1970s following science-fiction schemes of parallel universes and the idea if not the example of Nabokov's 1969 novel *Ada*, in which our world is not quite the real world. *Russian Hide and Seek* (1980) is set in a twenty-first-century England under Russian rule. In the twentieth century of *The Alteration* the Reformation has never taken place and the Catholic Church (with a Yorkshireman as Pope) holds science and progress at bay. *Ending up* (1974) is a meditation on senility and an exercise in horror. But Amis remains a satirist of the English social scene which in the 1970s has seemed increasingly in disarray. If good feeling and good writing are not enough to combat the postculture which George Steiner envisages, at least — as he says in *In Bluebeard's Castle* — we need to retain the power to be shocked. That could be seen as the justification of *Girl, 20* (1971), published the same year as Steiner's book, in the mood of apocalyptic gloom in which the 1970s began.

Douglas Yandell, a music critic, is a thoroughly decent and therefore (it seems) out-of-date hero. Appalled by pop and postmodernism in general, he struggles amidst almost Bunyanesque discouragements, including the teenaged mistress of his principal crony, who sees him as the incarnation of what's wrong with traditional culture:

'What makes you such a howling bitch?' [he asks her]

'I expect it's the same thing as makes you a top-heavy red-haired four-eyes who's never had anything to come up to being tossed off by the Captain of Boats and impotent and likes bloody symphonies and fugues and the first variation comes before the statement of the theme and give me a decent glass of British beer and dash it all Carruthers I don't know what young people are coming to these days and a scrounger and an old woman and a failure and a hanger-on and a prig and terrified and a shower and a brisk rub down every morning and you can't throw yourself away on a little trollop like that Roy you must think of your wife Roy old boy and I'll come along but I don't say I approve and bloody dead. Please delete the terms in the above that do not apply. If any.'

Yandell recovers from this with his own rhetorical resources, appraising her performance in the register of one of his own reviews: 'This was delivered at top speed and without solicitude of any kind. Her upper lip was thinned to vanishing point and remained so while she stared silently at me. I found myself much impressed by the width of her vocabulary and social grasp' (Chapter 3). There is probably no more concise or forceful attack on the phenomenon of the gentleman in modern English. The implied author of an Amis novel, as we have seen, tends to preside in a close relation to the protagonist, whose personality can often be seen as a projection or exaggeration of his. On the whole, one has to assume the heroes are far lazier and more self-indulgent than the real author. Roger Micheldene is clearly further from the disapproving authorial centre, and more the object of it, in *One Fat Englishman* than Maurice Allington is in *The Green Man*; a certain leeway seems appropriate in the scope provided here for competent readings; in reading about Micheldene one does not imagine his creator to be an Americanophile total abstainer. In *Girl, 20* the bad faith and outmoded stuffiness imputed to the narrator's pose of neutrality by the Girl's 'bloody dead' tirade have just enough justification in his cautious, professional musician's make-up to give us a sense of distance between narrator and final judgement.

This kind of 'allowance' in a satirical narrative, which one finds in Waugh and in Thackeray, depends on a traditional narrative structure. Yandell as story-teller is entirely suited to such a role and function; as we see when he is unimpressed by the writer, Gilbert, for example, who believes he has outlived the novel:

'A novel?' I asked.

'No, no. The culture that produced it is dying. Something much freer from narrow traditions, more adventurous altogether in form. It bears analogies to music and the visual arts. I've got into the habit of thinking of it as my *London Suite* in three movements and three colours.'

This, if indeed an ingrained habit, was one I considered he should set about breaking while there was still time, but did not like to say so.

The pedantic, slightly fussy tone — 'if indeed' — exactly suits what Yandell is meant to be. But a moment later Yandell's comment on Gilbert sounds rather like Amis's own manner: ' "Story. Rhythm. Characters. Plasticity. Shape. Melody. Frame. Plot," said Gilbert, so oratorically that I could not tell whether he was ridiculing these concepts or claiming that *London Suite* had as much of all of them as anybody could possibly want' (Chapter 1). Nor, presumably can the reader, but *Girl, 20* has equivalents to them which would presumably strike Gilbert as 'narrow'. There is a certain defiance, in view of the attitudes satirised, about the novel's technical brilliance, as there is, in effect, in the scene late in the story where Sir Roy Vandervane, famous conductor and left-wing TV pundit, performs a composition of his own at a pop concert. His virtuosity bores the audience and enrages a section of it whose members smash his Stradivarius in response. Short of this extreme attitude, even readers much more tolerant than Yandell or Amis towards the 1970 London scene are likely to have been moved by the writing. Without speculating about Plasticity or Shape, one can feel that the quality of control in the planning and composition of the novel are a plea for sanity and proportion. 'Imperialist Racist Fascist' is the title of the first chapter and while Douglas Yandell's newspaper editor in the book seems to be all three, the reckless use of the slogan is made to seem not only dangerous, but humourless too. Two opposed cultural worlds are critically in conflict in the story, Vandervane grotesquely attempting to belong to both in his pursuit of Girl, 20 (now actually girl, 17); most of the characters are bewildered and at a loss. Vandervane's marriage and household break up at the end; his daughter takes to heroin and so to suicide. The moral is implied by Yandell, but the author's vision seems more inspired by a Roman satirist's contemplation of the human scene (perhaps Martial's) rather than by the humanist position of Thackeray. But the final guide is the prose, which has a power no Latin writer ever had: to blend a quick sympathy and appreciation of people (like Yandell's girl-friend Vivienne and her father) with the sensual, irritable human norm, to which Amis is invariably loyal. That power derives from two centuries of the novel and is the best reason for not abandoning its narrowness in favour of *London Suites* or anything else.

Amis's willingness to accept risk has always been one of the most attractive features of his work. It leaves his work wide open to attack. A Marxist critic would find him a good example of what happens to an able bourgeois writer 'under late Capitalism' who won't accept reality. Finding himself lacking the necessary supporting apparatus of middle-class morality, he has deserted the traditional (Richardsonian, money–marriage–morality) system of writing a novel after *Take a Girl* for a species of prose satire pervasively bitter and polemical in tone; using a large admixture of fantasy, he tends to dwell on features of his society which seem closest to fantasy; undertaking empty exercises in minor genres; attacking traditional beliefs and hankering at the same time after the social order and dignity they represented. And this would lead steadily away from what the novels are really like; from their constant obsession with society in man; and with living through moral choices, even without guidance.

Jake's Thing (1978) returns to the university background used by *Lucky Jim*, though this time to Oxford and a sixty-year-old academic nonconformist. Jake is a classics don and wine-connoisseur whom Amis has provided with the conventional trappings of a gentleman as carefully as he deprived Jim of them in 1954. But this divergence hardly matters in comparison with the horror they share at what life can be like; and at how many people are set on making it worse. One feels surprised at times in *Lucky Jim* at what Jim expects of the Welches, and astonished in *Jake's Thing* that someone of Jake's intelligence and age should retain any faith in psychiatry, which is the object of so much of the satire. Both heroes share an engaging mixture of innocence and rage which comes to alert even the most complacent reader to the world about him.

Jake's Thing produces a strong sense of bafflement, but that has been a side-product of most major satire. In the 1957 Jane Austen article Amis complained of the certainties behind Fanny Price's role in *Mansfield Park*: 'She is ashamed of her own home in Portsmouth where there is much "error" and she finds "everybody underbred" ': alien concepts, it's implied, belonging to long ago. In the disapproval developed in *Jake's Thing*, Amis is closer to such certainties and ashamed, as it were, of his own home. Even in Harley Street and at Oxford, upbringing has not been doing its job and there is much error. In Swift and Pope a horror develops as the satirist matures which can at its intensest recall the impact of tragedy. Amis has a control of language which makes that kind of comparison conceivable and also a common sense that guards his work from the pretentiousness afflicting some writers of black comedy in France and America. As always it is the prose that enables him to say something new; increasingly, it is also something unwelcome and widely acknowledged only because so well said. Such an achievement is always traditional and up to date.

6 Anthony Powell's
A Dance to the Music of Time

'The most important effort in fiction since the war' (Kingsley Amis); 'the finest long comic novel that England has produced this century' (Anthony Burgess); 'if they are not "great", these beautiful books are as near it as makes no difference for their contemporary readers' (Roy Fuller); 'a joy to all' (Philip Larkin); 'a literary mansion' (William Trevor); 'a comic masterpiece' (Bernard Bergonzi): the paperbacks of Powell's books proclaim his achievement. It is a feature of the literary scene that extravagant claims are constantly made for individual novelists by the same critical community which urges that the novel is over and done with. Allowing for reviewers who overpraise, this sample, — which includes the opinions of writers not given to gushing, — shows the scale of Powell's success with *A Dance to the Music of Time*.

Here, it might be hoped, is a single achievement to refute the view that we live in an age of 'craftsmen' at the best, that there are many minor talents and that 'greatness' is not to be looked for. It is a term Roy Fuller is cautious about using, implying that past standards cannot apply or future standards be guessed: perhaps 'uniqueness' is a more meaningful claim today.

James Tucker, the author of the first full-length study of the whole of *Music of Time*, is cautious about the question of status, which does seem to arise with Powell more than with other contemporary novelists: we want to compare him with Joyce, with Proust, with Stendhal. Tucker admits what is most likely to put English readers off: the absence of the social world most readers will be familiar with, 'that poorer, duller, grubbier world most of us inhabit'; and the distance preserved from emotions, especially 'the emotional lives of women'. 'A largely humane point of view', 'a powerful sense of life through character' and technical originality (with the first-person narrative in particular) are the essence of his case for Powell.[1] It is a modest but firm assessment. Other critics are likely to stress the comic and mythopoeic vision (as Arthur Mizener

and Frederick R. Karl do, for example).[2] But postmodernist taste
may cause the richness of allusion and imagery, of pattern and
design, of repetition and counterpoint — the formal beauty which
offers such scope for being analysed (though my present chapter
neglects it) — to distract attention from Powell's genius for people,
which it is good to see asserted in this first critical book. Powell's full
achievement is beyond what any one critic is likely to say; in this
respect he can be compared with the great Victorians.

James Tucker is right to consider *Music of Time* as one novel,
composed of twelve books. Nearly three thousand pages long, it
requires to be read as a single work as none of the Victorian novel
sequences does, and unlike Richardson's *Clarissa* or Proust's *A la
recherche du temps perdu*, it is easily accessible and can be read through
in about a week. No other English novel of this scope and quality is
so consistently enjoyable; it is a challenge to Barthes's ideas about
degrees of pleasure in reading a text which is either *lisible* or *scriptible*.
The novel is unfailingly readable and would exhaust any structuralist *système*, of the sort devised by Genette for Proust, intended to
explain it; as is recognised by the *Guardian* reviewer who says that
'Mr Powell has created a world as rich as Joyce's . . . or
P. G. Wodehouse's'. The prose-writing provides unity and
continuity; it can accommodate passages from Proust or Robert
Burton, Welsh hymns and 1920s night-club songs: no intrusion is too
rich. Powell's grand style has astonishing staying powers; it only
rarely nods. *Music of Time* can be seen as an epic of twentieth-
century England; or as a vast assembly of anecdotes; as the ultimate
version of a crafted text, or a fictional masquerade; or as a great
comic novel, a reassertion of humanist literature. Its being grandly
conceived helps to explain the enthusiasm of American reviewers;
and it is very original, which could explain a certain critical
uneasiness. *Music of Time* is an embarrassment to pessimistic
generalisations about the feebleness of fiction after James, after
Lawrence or after Joyce; he makes 'classical modernism' seem less
closed-off and remote.

Given the novel's size and the variety of narrative modes it
uses, some principle is needed to guide the reader through. The
figures of the 'hero', Nicholas Jenkins, and the 'villain', Kenneth
Widmerpool, who haunts his course through life, have been taken to
provide the most meaningful contrast, and so they do. But because
Nick Jenkins, Powell's narrator, grows up as a modernist, intrigued
by but separate from the world of before 1914, and because so many

of the characters — General Conyers, Mr Deacon, St John Clarke, Uncle Giles and 'my father', Le Bas and Sillery — are survivors from that world, making the best of 'modern' conditions, this familiar contrast between Victorian and Moderns becomes a pervasive feature of the comedy and a means of remembering and interpreting as we read on. Jenkins and Widmerpool themselves, as our knowledge of them extends over many volumes and as they grow and ramify as characters, adapting and reconciling themselves to changes in time, come to encompass both worlds.

That may be the reason why Powell is often wrongly identified as a 'thirties' novelist. He published five short novels in the 1930s, and did not publish another until 1951, the year when the first volume of *Music of Time*, *A Question of Upbringing*, came out. Bernard Bergonzi has compared the Powell of *Afternoon Men* (1931) with Hemingway, Waugh and Eliot.[3] *At Lady Molly's* (1957), *Casanova's Chinese Restaurant* (1960) and *The Kindly Ones* (1962) constitute a second 'trilogy' which re-creates the atmosphere of thirties life in upper-class and intellectual circles in London. But in these books, and throughout the novel, we are conscious of the differentiations of period among the characters, the different decades which decisively influenced them or whose style they have adopted. Earlier novelists observed such effects, but the twentieth century has accelerated the change; 'the most changeful half a century in history', Leo reflects in the Epilogue of *The Go-Between*. Powell observes acutely how individuals adjust, and the curious historical anomalies contribute to his narrator's highly developed sense of the bizarre.

The novel deals directly with Nick Jenkins's lifetime between 1914 when he is about eight and the 1960s; but Nick (we are presumably on Christian name terms with a first-person narrator) is aware of and keenly interested in his elders and the scenes he selects from his own youth are dominated by characters who belong substantially to the nineteenth century. Some retain more of the past than others. The way different eras can coexist in the same social group, the same family and even the same individual, is a frequent source of comedy in Powell.

The historical manoeuvrability in the method is plain to see in the story of Kenneth Widmerpool's courtship in *At Lady Molly's*. The book begins with one of the novel's fittest survivors and one of its oldest, Aylmer Conyers:

We had known General Conyers immemorially not because my

father had ever served under him but through some long-forgotten connexion with my mother's parents, to one or other of whom he may even have been distantly related. In any case, he was on record as having frequented their house in an era so remote and legendary that, if commission was no longer by purchase, regiments of the line were still designated by a number instead of the name of a county. In spite of belonging to this dim, archaic period, traces of which were sometimes revealed in his dress and speech — he was, for example, one of the last to my knowledge to speak of the Household Cavalry as 'the Plungers' — his place in family myth was established not only as a soldier with interests beyond his profession, but even as a man of the world always 'abreast of the times'. This taste for being in the fashion and giving his opinion on every subject was held against him by some people, notably Uncle Giles, no friend of up-to-date thought, and on principle suspicious of worldly success, however mild.

The subjective historical outlook which creates family legends and myth is treated with sympathetic amusement, as is the very idea of being 'abreast of the times'. The late nineteenth century in which General Conyers made his career seems fabulous to Nicholas and he collects anecdotes which support this impression: his interest in General Conyers is connected with the romantic attraction he finds in military lore. Uncle Giles has provided a story about Conyers in South Africa, getting involved in the charge of a whole cavalry division, 'after French moved over the Modder River' in 1900. Nicholas pictures 'the dusty squadrons wheeling from column into line' and is always hoping for a chance to ask about it. More recently, in 1914, in an episode during the narrator's childhood recounted in *The Kindly Ones*, the general intervened decisively, saving the situation at the Jenkins's bungalow, when the housemaid Billson came naked into the drawing-room to give notice. This action has added to his 'mythic' status in the family.

At the time at which *At Lady Molly's* is set, General Conyers is nearly eighty. His fabled past, and remoteness from ordinary preoccupations of the early 1930s, make him an improbable brother-in-law for Nick's contemporary Widmerpool. Mrs Conyers's younger sister, Mildred, is a widow with a 'fast' reputation on the French Riviera. Widmerpool is a businessman, physically awkward, humourless and unimaginative, absolutely dedicated to succeeding in the world, and with enough practical intelligence and will-power to do so. The reader can, by the fourth volume, summarise Widmerpool in terms like these, but Nicholas can't. General Conyers has heard bad reports of Widmerpool's ruthlessness and wants to know what he is 'really like'. The disparity of age is at first a point hard to grasp:

'. . . Much younger than her, isn't he?'
　'I was at school with him. He must be about — '
　'Nonsense,' said the General. 'You can't have been *at school* with him . . . No, no, you couldn't have been at school with him.'
　Mrs Conyers, too, now shook her head in support of her husband. This claim to have been at school with Widmerpool was something not to be credited . . . [*A.L.M.*, Chapter 2]

Nicholas turns out to be incapable of giving an account of Widmerpool's character. The scale on which he is unsuitable as a husband for Mildred is difficult to convey in words, and the book makes an elaborate comedy out of their incompatibility.

Nicholas's connection with General Conyers and Widmerpool emphasises the difference of generations and this introduces an absurdity into Widmerpool's Victorian stuffiness as a suitor, in contrast to the dashing Mildred, and into Nicholas's slowness, though a novelist and scriptwriter, to make sense of Widmerpool, and his lagging behind the General in psychoanalytical expertise. Mildred is said to have 'slept with every old timer between Cannes and St Tropez' (Chapter 5). Widmerpool is unsure about *l'usage du monde*, and consults Nick, over lunch at his club, as one who mixes with artists, 'whose morals are proverbial'. Later, incapacitated by jaundice, Widmerpool has to abandon Mildred to one of her old flames at a night-club. It is from Conyers that Nick learns that Widmerpool has failed to satisfy Mildred, and the engagement has been ended. Nicholas, himself about to marry, is struck by the old man's detachment: 'neither shocked, facetious, nor caustic'. Abreast of the time as usual, General Conyers has been reading Freud. 'For my own part, I felt a twinge of compassion for Widmerpool in his disaster, even though I was unable to rise to the General's heights of scientific detachment . . . ' Conyers speculates: ' "typical intuitive extrovert — classical case, almost. Cold blooded . . ."; ". . . a touch of exaggerated narcissism?" ' Is his mother domineering? What did his father do? ' "Manufactured artificial manure, I believe." "Did he . . ." said the General. "Did he . . ." There was a pause while he thought over this information. It was undeniable that he had been setting the pace. I felt that I must look to my psycho-analytical laurels . . . "Do you think it was fear of castration?" I asked' (Chapter 5). After this discussion of Widmerpool, Nick asks about the charge at the Modder River: Conyers recalls that he hadn't a proper mount and couldn't get his pony out of a trot. They reflect on the cause of Nick's interest: ' "Infantilism perhaps. A primordial image." The General agreed, cordially.' Conyers places Nick as an 'introverted intuitive type'.

The individual tone General Conyers achieves dignifies his terminology with the scientific humanism of an earlier age. It is customary for novelists to make fun of Freudian jargon. Powell's approach is more complex and thoughtful. Obviously Widmerpool's egotism, urge for power and total lack of interest in people — the characteristics which disconcert Nick Jenkins — may be capable of clinical explanation. But the concepts and vocabulary of psychoanalysis seem unpromising, a dubious modern development which Nick, a young scriptwriter, finds strange in such a man as Conyers who represents for him traditional commonsense at its most reliable. His own association of the general with a romantic military past is undermined by the real, unglamorous half-forgotten story: 'later on in the day I shot a Boer in the shin'. Nick himself is made to seem tied to the past. The comic possibilities are pleasantly brought out as the old Victorian soldier goes into the subconscious workings of sexual maladjustment, and the young intellectual of the 1930s, about to be married, tries to get on to the subject of old campaigns. Stereotyped simplifications — and therefore all hope of scientifically accounting for Widmerpool, we are made to feel — are abandoned and the comedy creates a strong sense of the unpredictability of human nature.

Another character who appeals as General Conyers does to the narrator's imagination is St John Clarke. In the early books he is talked about as an ageing novelist still popular though no longer fashionable. Nick meets him only once, in *Casanova's Chinese Restaurant*, and although he dies not long afterwards, this hardly matters since he lives on in talk and memory. The titles of his works are a joke that recurs when copies are found from time to time, or when they are mentioned by other characters in conversation: *Match Me Such Marvel*, *Dust Thou Art*, *E'en the Longest River*, *The Heart is Highland, Fields of Amaranth*. As a modernist Nick disapproves of them: 'briefly they seemed to me trivial, unreal, vulgar, badly put together, odiously phrased, and "insincere" ' (*C.C.R.*, Chapter 2). But, like most of his generation, he has enjoyed them in his teens.

Clarke's rehabilitation is attempted in *The Acceptance World* (1955) by Mark Members, a young man of letters in touch with new bearings on the continent, who becomes his secretary. The process of re-education passes out of Members's control however when a more ruthless young writer, J. G. Quiggin, converts the old man to Marxism. Members describes to Nick how the term 'bourgeois' began to crop up in St John Clarke's comments on life: hats, pudding forks, the Ritz, Lady Huntercombe and Cézanne are 'bourgeois'. Members is misled at first by the fact that Clarke considers himself a natural aristocrat and likes to mix with real ones. Quiggin soon afterwards takes St John Clarke over, becoming secretary in place of Members who is presumably considered 'bourgeois', in the Marxist sense, himself.

It is through the medium of Mark Members's anecdotes, though, that Nick is able to build up an elaborate comic portrait of Clarke. Members describes his envy of the knighthood offered to his contemporary, the portraitist Isbister, even more mediocre as a painter, Nick considers, than Clarke is as a writer; Isbister refused, 'to spite his wife' in Clarke's view, though 'that didn't prevent him telling everyone': ' "Isbister was beloved of the gods, Mark," he had cried aloud, looking up with a haggard face from *The Times* of New Year's Day . . . "R.A. before he was forty-five" . . .' (Chapter 4).

When he is getting to know the impecunious novelist, Trapnel, in *Books Do Furnish a Room*, Nick compares him as a borrower of money with the old acquaintances who used to try to borrow from Clarke in Members's stories: 'somewhere between men of letters and blackmailers, a largely forgotten type'. Trapnel himself, Nick reflects, is 'no professional sponge in the manner of characters often depicted in nineteenth-century novels . . .' (Chapter 4); he pictures Trapnel applying his twentieth-century style of borrowing to St John Clarke — perhaps succeeding by quoting aptly from some appalling passage in one of the romantic novels. The literary period evoked by this style conflicts with Clarke's anti-bourgeois mode developed by Quiggin. Quiggin's obituary for his old employer mentions 'bewildered' sympathy for the Workers' Cause; other papers 'spoke only of his deep love for the Peter Pan statue in Kensington Gardens and his contributions to Queen Mary's Gift Book' (*C.C.R.*, Chapter 4).

Soon after coming under Quiggin's control, St John Clarke is to be seen in political demonstrations, pushed by his secretary in a wheelchair, his white hair impressive in the wind. He thus passes from one fashionable manner to another: from the secondhand romanticism suggested by the titles of his works to the equally unreal parlour socialism which Powell captures in other titles: *The Pistons of Our Locomotives Sing the Songs of Our Workers.* Adaptability enables him to survive in the world of society hostesses. Nick's meeting with him is at a luncheon party where the old man explains why he no longer writes and gives examples of his two incompatible manners:

'To tell the truth, Lady Warminster, I get more pleasure from watching the confabulation of sparrows in their parliament on the roof-tops opposite my study window, or from seeing the clouds scudding over the Serpentine in windy weather, than I do from covering sheets of foolscap with spidery script that only a few sympathetic souls, some now passed on to the Great Unknown, would ever care to read.

No sparrow on any roof was ever lonely

As I am, nor any animal untamed.

Doesn't Petrarch say that somewhere? He is a great stay to me. Childish pleasures you may tell me, Lady Warminster, but I answer you that growing old consists abundantly in growing young.'

He realises at this point that he has relapsed absent-mindedly into his 'outdated, even decadent state of mind, wholly inconsistent with political regeneration', and he corrects himself:

'I meant to imply that, when there are so many causes to claim one's attention, it seems a waste of time to write about the trivial encounters of an individual like myself, who has spent so much of his time pursuing selfish, and I fear, often frivolous aims. We shall have to learn to live more collectively, Lady Warminster. There is no doubt about it.' [*C.C.R.*, Chapter 2]

This might seem to illustrate what Philippe Sollers means by saying that one either writes or is written.[4] But Powell has a classical belief that human nature is constant. Each of the two styles which coexist in St John Clarke is absurdly affected; they are grotesquely comic when combined. The anomalies in the man reflect the instability of the period. The man himself would be absurd in any period and, the narrator thinks, sinister.

'Something about St John Clarke put him in the category — of which Widmerpool was another example — of persons at once absurd and threatening' (*C.C.R.*, Chapter 2). What makes them threatening is that they are power-seekers. They tend to be seen as tragi-comic and that is the tendency of the novel as a whole. Nicholas's friend Hugh Moreland, on his deathbed, in *Temporary Kings*, refers to a title he always enjoys: *Cambises, King of Percia: a Lamentable Tragedy, mixed full of Pleasant Mirth*: 'not particularly exciting, but it does summarise life' (Chapter 6). It summarise's *Music of Time* as well.

The tragi-comedy of Widmerpool dominates the novel. He is a character on the scale of Rastignac, Oblomov, Becky Sharpe or Charlus, and more dangerous in what he represents to modern societies than any of them. Powell's presentation of him as a villain in contrast to Nick the 'decent' hero is one of his most remarkable achievements.

The risk is that the contrast will appear complacent or even smug, that readers habituated to anti-heroes will side with Widmerpool, perhaps pity him as a victim of society. General Conyers's account of the fiasco which ends his courtship of Mildred, and the pointed contrast in *At Lady Molly's* of his failure as a suitor and Nick's success, illustrates this danger. But Widmerpool seen against the background of the 1930s is hard to like. He is, he explains, 'with' the National Socialists in Germany, 'in so far as they believe in planning', at the same time as he is 'moving steadily to the left'. Powell satirises in Widmerpool a sinister use of language, officially impersonal, totally false, inelegant and ruthless: ' "I quite see that there are aspects of Hitler's programme to which objection may most legitimately be taken" '(*A.L.M.*, Chapter 2). Widmerpool's stupidity as a lover is connected with the implicit point that if he were a German he would be rising complacently under Hitler.

Nick meets his wife at Thrubworth Park, a country house where Erridge, 'the red earl', lives in one room, surrounded by left-wing tracts and bound copies of the *Boy's Own Paper*. The leather-jacketed journalist Quiggin has 'got hold of' him for the time being. But the earl is mean and slightly deranged and when he goes off to China with Quiggin's girl-friend we feel there is some justice in this thwarting of at least one adventurer. The mild Jenkins, in such company, seems to deserve the best prize, Erridge's sister Isobel.

Powell rightly makes her a very marginal character and leaves their happy marriage out of the novel. Nick's satisfaction in the 'social' aspect of his marriage is just visible; he carries it off with a sense of decorum that is lacking elsewhere. The august Lady Warminster, his mother-in-law, receives him into 'the family' amidst its disarray and that of the whole 1930s world, as if they were both living a hundred years previously. An essential part of the comedy of *At Lady Molly's* is the novel's long perspective which sees how weirdly historical periods overlap.

'Great changes' in the world, and his own role in consequence of them, is a favourite theme of Widmerpool's. 'Men like myself will be needed,' he explains to Nick in 1945. ' "If they are to be found." He clapped me on the back. "No flattery," he said. "No flattery, but I sometimes wonder whether you're not right." ' This conversation takes place in *The Military Philosophers* (1968), at the stage in the novel where the full evil of Widmerpool is apparent for the first time. He has ended the war as a full colonel with a post not far from the centre of power.

> 'I have come to the conclusion that I enjoy power,' said Widmerpool. 'That is something the war has taught me. In this connexion, it has more than once occurred to me that I might like governing . . .'
> He brought his lips together, then parted them. This contortion formed a phrase, but, the words inaudible, its sense escaped me.
> 'Governing whom?'
> Leaning forward and smiling, Widmerpool repeated the movement of his lips. This time although he spoke only in a whisper, the two words were intelligible.
> 'Black men . . .' [Chapter 5]

The American critic, Arthur Mizener, considers that Widmerpool's nature is a peculiarly twentieth-century phenomenon.[5] Obviously men like this, thick-skinned, humourless power-seekers, have advanced themselves in the most stable societies in the past, and the richest cultures have made little impression on them. The dialogue in this passage could be paralleled from seventeenth-century drama, especially the 'no flattery' exchange. 'To those familiar with the rhythm of living there are few surprises in this world,' says the occult scholar Canon

Fenneau, in *Hearing Secret Harmonies* (Chapter 4) and though his phrasing would cause Nick Jenkins to raise his eyebrows, he would presumably endorse it as a mystical version of the lesson, to be found in Ben Jonson, that human nature never changes. But Mizener is right that the present era, in Powell's view, provides Widmerpool with very favourable opportunities. Jenkins is struck by how he differs from the 'public man' of the last century.

It would have pleased many critics better if Widmerpool had been made a success at Eton. But Powell is using the public school background accurately. Widmerpool is the schoolmaster's ideal, an indefatigable trier and a conformist, but his awkwardness, ugliness and poor performance at games make him unpopular. Nick forms a false assessment of him, as a ludicrous nonentity, in *A Question of Upbringing*, where he himself is a very conventional 1920s public schoolboy. His friends, Charles Stringham and Peter Templar, possess in different ways the qualities he expects to lead to success in life; in particular, they pretend to an effortless superiority which is the opposite to Widmerpool's style. When Nick meets him at a house in Touraine where they have both gone to improve their French, Widmerpool wants them to talk French together. '*Oui*, Widmerpool' would sound flippant, Nick reflects. Shameless effort is combined with a tone-deafness in social relations which isolates him like a 'grotesque' character in Dickens. His determination takes him to high army rank and into the Attlee government. 'I don't set up as an expert,' Conyers says about psychoanalysis, though he clearly is one. Widmerpool flagrantly contradicts this older ideal of brilliant dabbling; his is the new type of professionalism; seen in contrast to a nineteenth-century norm, it is efficient and chilling. In 1939 (in *The Kindly Ones*, 1962) Nick rings him up:

> They put me through to a secretary.
> 'Captain Widmerpool is embodied,' she said in an unfriendly voice.
> I could tell from her tone, efficient, charmless, unimaginative, that she had been given special instructions by Widmerpool himself to use the term 'embodied' in describing his military condition. [Chapter 4]

Bernard Bergonzi comments on the presentation of Widmerpool as a 'cold-blooded' type of modern soldier, that Jenkins 'the cool observer of a comic order' has nothing to oppose to Widmerpool's ruthlessness (which has sent Stringham and Templer to their deaths) since he does not really believe in the ideal of the gentlemanly officer which inspires Guy Crouchback in Evelyn Waugh's trilogy of war novels.[6] But whereas the threatening absurdity of Widmerpool, to be felt here in his use of military jargon, derives from the complete isolation from literary culture which makes him unable to hear what is wrong with 'embodied', the narrator's power to observe what makes him comic is asserted as a vitally sane resource in a mad world.

Throughout the three novels which deal with the war (*The Valley of Bones*, 1964; *The Soldier's Art*, 1966; *The Military Philosophers*, 1968), Powell stresses the links between English and French culture and Nick's admiration for both. Trollope and Balzac are just names to Widmerpool: possibly generals. We are clearly meant to see the narrator as a civilised man. Nick's attitude to modern life can be seen most clearly in his friendship with the composer Moreland who replaces Stringham, when he retires into alcoholism, and whose friendship is an antithesis to the prolonged acquaintance with Widmerpool. They share not so much a social background — Moreland was not even at Eton — as a sense of the value of the arts combined with a sense of humour. The pleasure of conversation and especially of anecdote becomes, in a world ruled by Widmerpools, a subversive activity. In one of their last meetings, when Moreland is dying, in *Temporary Kings*, he tells the story of Sir Magnus Donners, the great industrialist (known to them both), when he thought himself 'on the brink of eternity' — told by his doctors he had only a year to live. Donners retired to a cottage to read (in his own words) 'the best — only the best — of all literatures' and in between books listened to the best ('only the best') music.

'In the end did all this culture bring about a cure?'

'It wasn't the culture. The medicos made a mistake . . . Everything with Donners was right as rain. After spending a month or two at his dream cottage, he went back to making money, governing the country, achieving all time records in utterance of conversational clichés . . .'

'Also, if one may say so, without showing much outward sign of having concentrated on the best literature of half-a-dozen nations.' [Chapter 6]

After leaving Moreland for the last time, Nick meets Widmerpool, now a life-peer and on his way to the Lords; he has recently just managed to survive politically a scandal about his dealings with an east European country. He talks grandiloquently about his own case: ' "Fortunately I was in a position to rebut my accusers. In the Upper House, wherever else I am called upon to serve the purposes of political truth, I shall contrive to assail the limitations of contemporary empiricism, and expose the bankruptcy of cold-war propagandists." He sounded more than a little unhinged' (*T.K.*, Chapter 6).

The last trilogy as a whole deals with Widmerpool Unhinged — and, throughout these books, a powerful public figure. The Jenkins–Moreland response to Donners and Widmerpool is as powerless to change their world as European culture is to affect Donners or come to Widmerpool's notice. But Moreland's last days in *Temporary Kings*, in contrast to Widmerpool's end in the next book, are dignified by the intelligent, brave humour which Bergonzi praises in Beckett. How to live, given conditions of life which are characteristically bizarre or horrible, is a question Powell takes as seriously as any novelist today.

Widmerpool claims to have rebutted his accusers. In fact he has escaped disgrace and prosecution only by betraying espionage 'contacts'. Power has corrupted the cautious respectability of his early days in *A Buyer's Market* (1952) when he was nervously involved in 'finding a doctor' for the 'left-wing nymph', Gypsy Jones. But he is, as Nick says when someone suggests that Widmerpool might like to run a Communist *apparat*, 'the greatest bourgeois who ever lived' (*T.K.*, Chapter 1). There is an incongruity about the Communist leanings of this massively pompous British Establishment figure which recalls that of Quentin Matthews's vision of the Moscow apparatchiks as eminent Victorians in *No Laughing Matter* (see above, Chapter 4). Despite the many distinctly contemporary aspects of Widmerpool's career, his mannerisms and habits of mind often recall, as Nick's comment suggests, a nineteenth-century middle-class stolidity. In the early books, his ponderous formality of speech and outlook seem old-fashioned: 'You don't suppose I have the money to marry, do you?' (*B.M.*, Chapter 1). He issues invitations to meet 'my lady mother', and his insensitivity to nuance makes it hard for him to grasp how, by the 1920s, the tone of 'society' has changed since his mother knew it: ' "I am dining with Lady Augusta Cutts for the Drum-Clinton dance," said Widmerpool. "One eats well at Lady Augusta's. But I feel annoyed — even a little hurt — about Mrs Soundness . . ." "The card may have gone astray in the post" ' (*B.M.*, Chapter 1). He would have sounded stilted and over-earnest as a young man in 'society' in the 1880s.

Throughout the novel his way of speechmaking in conversation recalls pontificators in Victorian novels, which makes his increasing hostility to all bourgeois norms seem doubly ludicrous. The Lord Widmerpool of *Hearing Secret Harmonies*, as head of a new university, becomes a champion of student opinion and alternative life-styles in the late 1960s. At a literary dinner he introduces two students who are the twin daughters of J. G. Quiggin: ' "They are the couple who threw paint over me in my capacity as university chancellor. It was the right thing to do. It was the only thing to do . . . I am now eternally glad that I did not avoid that. I learnt a lesson. Even now, there are marks of red paint on my body that may remain until my dying day, as memorial to a weak spirit" ' (Chapter 3). Widmerpool has shown signs of masochism in the past. The present dinner, in honour of a biography of the novelist Trapnel, for whom Widmerpool's demonic wife Pamela left him twenty years earlier in *Books Do Furnish a Room*, gives him the chance to publicise his earlier humiliations:

> 'I go further than merely proclaiming that fact to you of Pamela's affair with Trapnel. I take pride in ridiculing what is — or rather was — absurdly called honour, respectability, law, order, obedience, custom, rule, hierarchy, precept, regulation, all that is insidiously imposed by the morally, ideologically and spiritually naked, and politically bankrupt, on those they have oppressed and do oppress.'

Despite the modishness of this position in the 1960s, the rhetorical structure and rhythms are antiquated. The Quiggin girls throw a stink bomb. Widmerpool goes off to join a mystical group of (mostly) young people dedicated to Harmony, Power and Death, and dies on one of the group's naked runs by night, still struggling to get ahead.

Intermittently throughout *Music of Time*, Nick has been intrigued by the activities of various occultists, who deal in lore deriving ultimately from sources such as Hermes Trismegistus, but more immediately from the vogue for magic at the turn of the century. As a child, in *The Kindly Ones*, Nick first observes their leader, the sinister Dr Trelawney, taking his scantily-dressed followers for country runs, before 1914. The 1960s drop-out, Scorpio Murtlock, claims to be the reincarnation of Trelawney. Both, certainly, are in love with power. The spiritualist concept of return and renewal appeals to the narrator as expressing metaphorically the tendency of things to recur. The end of the novel stresses the reappearance in the 1960s of fashions that had seemed out of date a generation earlier: the 'rediscovery' of bad Victorian paintings, especially the huge, clumsily executed male nudes (in the manner of Simeon Solomon) done by Edgar Deacon, whom Nick knew in the 1920s; the renewal of interest in St John Clarke; the revival of Trelawneyism. These anomalous bits of the past, appearing in the new life-style of the 1960s, make a suitable background for the discordant figure of Widmerpool.

If Widmerpool represents Powell's idea of how not to live in any era, Nick is a character whose sense of proportion we are meant to admire. He is also a novelist–narrator, presumably now recounting his memoirs after a career — occasionally mentioned — of 'creating characters' in fiction of his own. He is Powell's contemporary, born about 1905, at Oxford about 1924, writing in the 1930s, and he sees himself as a modern, one who cannot get on with the Victorians. At the heart of the novel, in one of its funniest scenes, he makes a declaration of literary taste and, in awkward circumstances, denounces Trollope to a Trollope-reading senior officer during the war. General Liddament in *The Soldier's Art* is astounded that a 'book-reader' should find Trollope hard-going:

> '*You've never found Trollope easy to read?*'
> 'No, sir.'
> He was clearly unable to credit my words. This was an unhappy situation. There was a long pause while he glared at me.
> 'Why not?' he asked at last. [Chapter 1]

Nick attempts a reply: 'a few worn shreds of long-forgotten literary criticism', he says, and provides phrases suggesting that Trollope is inartistic and conventional, though impressive as 'a picture of the times'. '"Rubbish," said General Liddament.' Nick fears he may be put under arrest. Asked what he does like, he thinks of Laclos, Lermontov and Svevo, but declares for Balzac.

Distaste for Trollope (many of Powell's readers today would agree with General Liddament) is an accurate feature of the portrayal, in the narrator, of a literary man of the period. Laclos, Lermontov and Svevo are authors who were especially admired in the 1930s, partly because so unlike Victorian novelists. Svevo's handling of the comic incident in the first person, in *The Confessions of Zeno*, is perhaps an influence on Jenkins's narrative. But the author he might have named — though unsuitable in conversation with a British general — is Proust, who is providing his evening reading, we are told, in *The Military Philosophers*. The question of how far *Music of Time* compares with *A la recherche du temps perdu* has been gone into by many critics; Powell himself has emphasised the differences. But Proust represents the deliberately non-Victorian part of Nicholas Jenkins's mind and so does his love of French civilisation (in spite of difficulties with French). The isolation of Victorian literature is sometimes exaggerated; not only James, Arnold and Swinburne, but Thackeray and Dickens were in close touch with France. But the importance of France for Nick does correspond to a development of English culture which took place early this century: a new degree of tolerance and flexibility, which we can see in him, in his affection for Mr Deacon for example.

Yet although Powell as a novelist in the 1930s was, like almost all novelists between the wars, in revolt against Trollope, by the time of writing *A Dance to the Music of Time* he could see that Nicholas Jenkins grows up in a world which is still thoroughly Victorian in its institutions, and in its most interesting people. Not only General Conyers and St John Clarke but the narrator's family, his house-master and Oxford tutor, servants, early acquaintances among people known to his parents, derive from and still essentially belong to the social world Trollope knew. Powell observes this Victorian world with a modernist's eye. He can see signs of both eras in his narrator who is fully aware of modern literature, but in many ways is a conservative character out of his element in modern life.

Nick makes his strongest impression in the early novels by what he leaves out of his account of school, university and early life in London. He departs from the tradition of the 'confessional' novel which from *David Copperfield* to *Daniel Martin* has been one strong line of continuity with Victorian fiction. *A Question of Upbringing* uses a series of anecdotes to portray an introductory assortment of characters, but the private sufferings and excitements of a tradi-tional English education, gone into by novelists more thoroughly in

this century than in the last, are coolly left out, as is most of the 1920s
Oxford of Evelyn Waugh and Christopher Sykes. Nick deals with
his friend Stringham's boredom at Oxford but hardly deigns to
mention his own. Most of what we can make out behind the 'I' is
implied: he is modest, reticent and — as he does tell us, quite
unnecessarily, later on — fascinated by the details of other people's
lives.

The selective, detached method of artistic recall creates characters very vividly, in the first two books, most impressive being that of
the Eton housemaster, Le Bas, a type peculiar to England and to this
period: an athlete and a scholar who has been turned by school
routine into a grotesquely neurotic figure, ludicrous to his pupils
and cut off from ordinary life. Sillery, Uncle Giles, Sunny
Farebrother and Mr Deacon are other cases of weird, self-sufficient
individuals, who attract Nick's attention and interest. All are
recorded with a scrupulous refusal, on the narrator's part, to treat
them as 'characters', though they appear to be acting eccentric
character parts: Sillery with his quaint speech-habits, dress,
mannerisms, diet, using the role of eccentric don to amuse the
undergraduates among whom he searches for gossip and 'influence';
Uncle Giles and Farebrother assuming 'characters' partly as
camouflage for financial activities; Mr Deacon the homosexual
painter, an acquaintance of Nick's parents, a mixture of oddity and
principles, is perhaps the most genuinely eccentric, and is treated by
Nick and by others with some respect. As 'characters' they all seem
Victorian. Allowing for their academic or professional status, they
belong to Dickens's class of 'shabby-genteel' people, and to the
richly contradictory, misleading and ramshackle hierarchy of
English society before 1914; the opportunities it offered for creative
compromises between private maladjustments and public roles in
society have never existed since in the same degree. These figures
make us think of Dickens because they come from his world.
Observed by Nick, and by other young intellectuals like Barnby and
Moreland, they seem archaic, although the novel puts that point of
view in its own historical setting, and shows how the 'Victorian' and
'modernist' are merged.

It is worth noting that none of them is strikingly aristocratic or
exotic in origin; some critics imply that Nick's interest in people
extends only to these two groups, which is untrue. But Powell makes
his narrator unashamedly pukka. 'Why are you so stuck up?' the
farouche agitator, Gypsy Jones, demands of him in *A Buyer's Market*.

'I'm just made that way,' he tells her (Chapter 4). Gypsy thinks he should 'fight it' for the sake of the social revolution. Nick does mellow as the books go by, dealing easily with all sorts, but hauteur remains natural to him; how far author and reader share a point of view on it is not an easy question; it arises because the fastidious, modernist narrator does not assume the Victorian novel's broadly middle-class relationship with the reader.

Nick is a broadly sympathetic and attractive character because his interest in people takes him so far into society, and because his sense of reality lets him turn his own social predilections into a part of the comedy. Brooding about how to place Widmerpool, Nick daydreams 'a soothing picture of generations of Widmerpools in a rural setting: an ancient if dilapidated manor house: Widmerpool tombs in the churchyard: tankards of ale at the Widmerpool Arms' (*A. L. M.*, Chapter 2). No such Trollopian social order has much meaning any more, but Nick's liking for such an orderly, aesthetically pleasing imaginative world — knowing it to be fanciful — does not distract his attention from the real social world he lives in (or the real Widmerpool), though it encourages the play of fancy.

His own background, glimpsed in the first section of *The Kindly Ones* where he recalls the Billson incident from his own childhood, is a sufficiently odd mixture of the military and the supernatural to help explain his liking for the traditional and fanciful. Such a blend appears, for example, later in the same book when he sorts out the effects of the deceased Uncle Giles, always a suspicious, unreliable character in a shady business world, and finds his army commission: 'VICTORIA . . . To our Trusty and well-beloved *Giles Delahey Jenkins, Gentleman,* Greeting. We, reposing especial Trust and Confidence in your Loyalty, Courage and good Conduct, do by these Presents Constitute and Appoint you to be an Officer in Our Land Forces . . .' (Chapter 3). 'The Queen's faith in human nature appeared boundless,' he says, remembering Giles. 'His Conduct, in the army or out of it, could not possibly be described as Good . . .' The lengthy meditation which takes place here on Victoria and her misplaced confidence is a good example of the narrator's mind playing with discrepancies between a literary, idealised world — that implied by the language of the Commission — and the intractable facts of life.

The next item from Uncle Giles's remains is a translation of *The Perfumed Garden* (Cosmopoli, 1886), the English version of a French officer's translation.

I pictured this French staff officer sitting at his desk. The sun was streaming into the room through green latticed windows of Moorish design, an oil sketch by Fromentin or J. F. Lewis. Dressed in a light-blue frogged coatee and scarlet peg-topped trousers buttoning under the boot, he wore a pointed moustache and imperial . . . He was absolutely detached, a man who had tasted the sensual pleasures of the Second Empire and Third Republic to their dregs, indeed, come to North Africa to escape such insistent banalities. Now he was examining their qualities and defects in absolute calm. Here with the parched wind blowing in from the desert he found a kindred spirit in the Sheik Nefzaoui, to whose sixteenth-century Arabic he was determined to do justice in the language of Racine and Voltaire . . . [K. O., Chapter 3]

'Absolutely detached', 'dregs', 'absolute calm' — the mockery, given the subject matter, is reminiscent of Proust. But a moment later Nick gets on with the job of burying Uncle Giles. 'I put the volume aside to reconsider. There was work to be done.' *The Kindly Ones*, which begins in 1914 and closes in 1939, treats twentieth-century Furies (conceived of as suffragettes in section I) and modern war. Nick has always been drawn by romantic images of soldiering, but although he starts his time in the army with Lyautey's rule in mind that 'an officer should be gay', he is not surprised to find himself the comrade of Bithel, and aide to Widmerpool.

Bithel is an even less well-qualified officer than Uncle Giles: a drunk, a fraud and figure of fun. Even the mobile laundry is a command that is beyond his powers. Widmerpool has him expelled from the army; he leaves in tears, his dreams shattered, as complete a contrast as could be looked for to the ideals of a Victorian commission or that of Lyautey, or to Nick's mental sketch of the French scholar-officer, 'absolutely detached'. Yet Nick accepts him, while he lasts, as a comrade-in-arms and as a sort of fellow-intellectual — he likes St John Clarke — among the Welsh Bank-employees who surround them. His sense of the remoteness from these ideals of the whole modern army admittedly reinforces Nick's patience with Bithel. Widmerpool is indignant on finding out that 'Bith' is not a VC's brother after all. Nick reflects that 'there seemed no reason why a VC's younger brother should not fall short in commanding a mobile laundry' (*S. A.*, Chapter 1). But a fellow-sympathy with Bithel survives all the ironies; they share the boredom, fear and misery of duty in Northern Ireland and Nick is recalling something unknown to Widmerpool when he finds Bithel thirty years later, still drunk and attached to Scorp Murtlock's 'Harmony' group in *Hearing Secret Harmonies* and speaks of their having 'soldiered together'.

Nick develops, beside the formidable polite disapproval which James Hall has written about,[7] an attitude to life that is close to Terence's line that 'nothing human is alien to me', a state of mind that matures from sympathetic curiosity towards an intelligently sceptical humanism in the course of the books about the war.

Stephen Wall has suggested that Stendhal is more a model for Powell than Proust.[8] Nick often thinks in Stendhalian terms which are part of his modernist re-education: military ambition, in Roland Gwatkin for instance, reminds him of Stendhal's heroes' romantic aspirations; the '*voie oblique*' in Powell, the political scepticism, the love of anecdote, the power to search out indignity: these could all be related to Stendhal, who could be particularly brought to mind by the comic sequences of *The Military Philosophers*. The seventeenth century as a literary period was another 'discovery' of Nick's generation, and his enthusiasm for it — and for Robert Burton especially, a counterpart to Powell's work on Aubrey — is another reaction against the taste in which he was educated. Le Bas considers Burton 'morbid' (preferring Lord de Tabley and Andrew Lang). The Proustian influence, already mentioned, especially explicit in *The Military Philosophers* where Nick spends a night in Cabourg, Proust's Balbec, is also apparent in Nick's reluctance to analyse — or sum up in simple terms — anybody's 'character'. He was unable to explain Widmerpool to General Conyers, and, although considering himself 'something of an expert' on St John Clarke, cannot say, in *Casanova's Chinese Restaurant*, 'what sort of a man' Clarke was. The 'one single, brief, brilliant epigram' to contain him does not form itself; the angle from which to attempt him is hard to find (*C. C. R.*, Chapter 4). Bithel, too, is elusive; the narrator's amused hesitancy grows into a positive respect for the difference of others.

It is the narrator's increasingly thoughtful interest in character which gives the novel its unity. If the third trilogy invites comparison with Evelyn Waugh, the last three books, more complex in plotting, more mannered, involved, and grotesque than before, are closer to Iris Murdoch. But the narrative remains completely in control, and is always entertaining. Nick's academic work on Robert Burton provides him, in the seventeenth-century science of melancholy, with a richer and less mechanical approach than Freud's to human oddity, especially at its extremes as in Erridge. But the Freudian General Conyers has provided him with the revealing concept of a 'personal myth'.

The most potent of such myths is to be found in the person of Trapnel who extends Nick's thinking about character by his opinions and behaviour. The novel's background is haunted by the sad figure of the old novelist St John Clarke. The final volumes are dominated by Trapnel, a Durrellesque figure with dyed service greatcoat, tropical suit and death's head swordstick, and with his romanticism, his faith in 'the writer' and his opposition to naturalism as a theory. 'Looking round and shoving it all down', he says, is as artificial as if the characters were kings and queens and speaking in blank verse (*B. D. F. R.*, Chapter 5). Role-playing, Nick comes to see, can confuse even the players. A Burtonian list is needed for Trapnel's roles; he wants to be 'a writer, a dandy, a lover, a comrade, an eccentric, a sage, a virtuoso, a good chap, a man of honour, a hard case, a spendthrift, an opportunist . . .' 'among other things' (*B. D. F. R.*, Chapter 4).

Trapnel is a dedicated neo-modernist of the Durrell/Lowry generation, and knowing him allows the modernist Nick to distance himself from the phase of literature to which he belongs. *Profiles in String*, Trapnel's great work, is destroyed by his mistress, Widmerpool's wife, and he dies not long afterwards, survived by his personal myth which attracts the American researcher, Russell Gwinnett, drawn into Trapnel's world (and Pamela Widmerpool's) in *Temporary Kings*. Living into the 1960s, Nick seems increasingly to reflect on how life is basically unchanging; *Hearing Secret Harmonies* ends with a catalogue from Burton, a torrent of human activities thought of at a far remove. He thinks of Trapnel in relation to Cyrano de Bergerac, Ariosto and Petronius.

Some people (Philippe Sollers, for example, and perhaps Roland Barthes) would say that man, being 'social', constantly changes, and possibly has not yet been 'invented'. Powell's novel is sensitive to the changes, decade by decade, in fashion-conscious people like Mark Members and J. G. Quiggin. It records too, more vividly than any modern work, how one period survives in the next, modified and modifying, how Victorian we can be even when rebelling against 'the Victorian'. 'What is your generation?' Le Bas, like Father Time, asks Nick when he revisits school at the end of

Books Do Furnish a Room. The characters seem to live through several generations and to combine different generations in themselves. But, as Nick looks at all this, he hears, among the 'profuse . . . private meanings' (*H. S. H.*, Chapter 2) he enjoys discovering, recurring themes in the music of time.

Bernard Bergonzi writes that Powell's is 'the basic human comedy where, as in Chaucer and Rabelais and Shakespeare, folly and weakness and vice are transformed into an unending comic dance'.[9] For a modern British novelist to qualify for such a comparison might well have seemed absurd in 1951 when Powell began, but there is now growing agreement that he does. Rabelais suggests the menippean sense of humour which is present in Powell's extraordinary power to create comedy from the competing literary modes and styles incorporated on such a large scale into his novel. Parody and pastiche are typical of modern fiction in many parts of the world and they often involve the loss of humanist concern and of intelligibility. Humanism and a shared sense of fun are essential to menippean literature and to Anthony Powell. Equally amused by Victorian and postmodernist trends, *A Dance to the Music of Time*, completed in 1975, makes much of the 'new postmodernist' writing of the seventies seem dull, and irrelevant to the real interest of keeping fiction alive.

Part 2

7 The Reading Community

Pursewarden's 'London publishers' were right in one respect. We like novels to seem transparent — windows on fictional worlds. Trollope's readers enjoy looking in at muddy lanes and well-upholstered rooms, London offices and lodgings, stables, cathedrals and clubs. George Eliot's Middlemarch and Hardy's Wessex, like Barsetshire and the Pallisers' London, remain a satisfaction even after the pleasures of Butor and Barth. The new novelist creates uncertainty or deliberate inconsistency, and we recognise that a text is being manipulated; given the powers of Barth or Butor, this can be intellectually entertaining, but we don't become exclusively 'new' readers — or few of us do. An unraveller of Barth who was conditioned to reject Trollope or Tolstoy would be a weird casualty of the modern mind. In fact there is no interference between different types of reading, and English novels reflect our adaptability.

So does criticism: any anthology of views is likely to include examples from two hundred years of critical opinion. A different sort of book, Roger Fowler's *Linguistics and the Novel* (1977) which is an introduction to structuralist ideas about the novel, talks about the 'community' of readers which fiction presupposes; and about the concept of 'intertextuality' or 'dependence on multiple codes' which are derived from a community and shared by the works it creates.[1] What is remarkable in the novel, as we have seen, is the 'intertextual' overlapping between the nineteenth century and the present day; *Linguistics and the Novel* takes this for granted, offering samples of text from Dickens, Thackeray, Amis and Golding. Fowler notes that the novel evolves, as language does, and rightly assumes that readers will be as much at ease with the older 'fictional languages' as with the older English. Victorian critical debates about the novel which still have life in them today show how extensive the overlapping is. The debate between James and Trollope about narrative interventions is still being pursued, despite Wayne Booth's *The Rhetoric of Fiction* (1961) which sorted out the disagreement.[2] Booth stressed the way 'the "implied author"

123

chooses, consciously or unconsciously, what we read . . . he is the sum of his own choices' (Chapter 3); everything in the novel is 'mediated'. The need for such a demonstration of how novels are 'told' to the reader, and the book's subsequent influence, are signs of the extent to which we remain nineteenth-century readers and perhaps wish to do so.

A significant cause of confusion about the novel is the obvious need we have to emphasise contrasts between 'Victorian' and 'contemporary': our fascination with the 'mental gap' dividing us from them. A distinct and definitive separation, were such a thing possible, would have a strong appeal. This seems to encourage English and American postmodernists into following the French example of rejecting conventional narrative as 'nineteenth-century' — an amusement we should have grown out of. It also means that false contrasts create misinterpretations. Overt novelty, in form or typography, attracts attention; in its absence, originality is overlooked. We can be over eager to find modern meanings, especially at the expense of Victorian myths. Two books which have been very widely discussed illustrate these mistakes: L. P. Hartley's *The Go-Between* (1953) and William Golding's *Lord of the Flies* (1954). In the two following chapters, I suggest how they can be re-read with a larger sense of 'intertextual' possibilities.

How we read has come in recent years to be seen as a serious critical problem. Jonathan Culler concludes his *Structuralist Poetics* (1975) by admitting that, after everything Greimas, Jakobson, Barthes and Kristeva have said, we still don't know much about reading. Interest, though, has steadily grown. Wayne Booth's *The Rhetoric of Fiction* discusses how the novelist 'creates his reader'. Among critics Booth has influenced, John Preston is one of the most interesting. His *The Created Self* (1970) develops the idea of a fictional reader, created by the author, with whom the real reader identifies: he studies how this happens in four eighteenth-century novels. 'I make no attempt to provide a "rhetoric of reading", though no doubt this would be worth doing,' he writes, and he looks forward to 'other more radical enquiries into the nature of the reader's role in fiction' (p. 3). Wolfgang Iser's *The Implied Reader* (1974) is such an enquiry. Approaches to the problem of the reader vary. Roland Barthes, for example, is relatively unconcerned with what an author meant.

There is a tendency for scorn of the common reader to coincide with an elevated concept of *le lecteur* which authorises any interpretation, even misunderstandings. Trollope's respect for his public was based on shared values, which, it is said, no longer exist; the reading public has declined to the point where an artist must write only to satisfy himself. Modernist literature parted company with 'ordinary readers' and with those who wrote for them. In France this has led to a rejection of the passive public in favour of imaginative readers whose efforts are meant to equal the author's own.

Alain Robbe-Grillet published *Les Gommes* (*The Erasers*) in 1953. It is the first of a series of 'new novels' including those of Michel Butor and Claude Simon, published by Les Editions de Minuit in Paris. *Les Gommes* is perhaps the least accessible of all, an anti-novel which enacts the myth of Oedipus within a story contained in the time of a pistol shot. Robbe-Grillet is an able publicist and uses his writing to promote ideas about the death of humanism, the integrity of the physical world and the distorting nature of the mind, which are meant to surprise and disconcert rather than stand up to careful thought. Michel Butor is both more formidable intellectually and more readable in a traditional sense. Butor's early novels are beautifully contrived fictional structures intended to make the reader reflect on the workings of fiction; on how imagination and memory (virtually the same thing in Butor) can cure psychological wounds; on how myth shapes the mind. In *La Modification* (1957), for example, a typewriter-salesman, Leon Delmont, travels from Paris to Rome; on the way he decides not to leave his Parisian wife for his Roman mistress after all. France and Italy, pagan and Christian Rome, wife and mistress, two options in life are formally opposed, and the whole novel is related in the second person to remind us of how Delmont is a stranger to himself (a favourite Butor theme). The novel is remorselessly systematic; Butor's English explicators, among them John Sturrock,[3] tell us that we misread him by looking for a story where the intellectual meaning is what matters. We are certainly required to cooperate in making sense of books like this — as with modernist poetry — and Butor writes well enough to make doing so worth trying. He is said to have read Proust's *A la recherche* many times over; he expects the same dedicated attentiveness for his own work. Many readers will obviously feel that the *nouveau roman* is an intellectual curiosity, worth looking into, but cut off from the novel's wholesome vulgarity.

In an interview for the April 1979 issue of *Lire*, Roland Barthes was asked if he thought Solzhenitsyn a 'good' writer. He replied:

> Solzhenitsyn is not a 'good' writer *for us*: the formal problems he has worked out are a little fossilised with regard to us. Without his being responsible — for a very good reason — there are seventy years of culture which he has not, and we have, lived through. This culture is not necessarily better than his, but it's there and we cannot deny it, deny, that is, everything that has happened in French literature since Mallarmé. And someone writing, let's say like Maupassant or Zola, we can't judge him the same way as one of our own modern writers.

> [*Soljénitsyne n'est pas un 'bon' écrivain pour nous : les problèmes de forme qu'il a résolus sont un peu fossilisés par rapport à nous. Sans qu'il en soit responsable — et pour cause — il y a soixante-dix ans de culture qu'il n'a pas traversés et que nous avons traversés. Cette culture n'est pas forcément meilleure que la sienne, mais elle est là et nous ne pouvons pas la nier, nier par exemple tout ce qui s'est passé dans la littérature française depuis Mallarmé. Et quelqu'un écrivant, disons comme Maupassant ou Zola, nous ne pouvons pas le juger de la même façon que quelqu'un qui soit écrivain maintenant chez nous.*][4]

Barthes went on to admit with typical frankness that he does not know much about — or like — foreign literatures. As usual he puts his case — the 'progressive' view of the novel's history — at its most challenging; the French intellectual's sense of 'everything that happened since Mallarmé' is a revealing contrast to the vaguer state of authors in England (though the achievement of Georges Simenon complicates things in France), as Philip Thody points out in *Roland Barthes: A Conservative Estimate* (1977). Professor Thody observes that in some ways Barthes appears out of date in England and he compares *S/Z* to L. C. Knight's attack on 'the hangover in the England of the 1930s of attitudes towards literature dating back to the Victorian period' (p. 117). Barthes might reasonably have said, if he had known more about foreign literatures, that these Victorian hangovers still persist. Philip Thody's suggestion that P. G. Wodehouse ideally satisfies Barthes's criteria for a 'ludic text' is a pleasing reminder that originality in the modern novel need not mean abandoning the common reader: *Right-Ho, Jeeves*, he points out,

. . . has the infinitely ludic quality praised in the book which carries on after *S/Z—Le Plaisir du Texte*. It is impeccably structured, and yet could be split into an infinite number of what one would have to call *lexias*. It clearly does not contain characters in whom one is expected to believe as real people. It holds the reader at a distance by the infinite circularity of its cultural codes ('You know your Shelley, Bertie'; 'Oh, am I?') and is constantly haunted by the invisible presence and possible return of what *S/Z* would call *'la Femme-Reine . . . le Figure castratrice'* (Aunt Agatha).[5]

In his interview for *Lire*, Barthes admitted that if he were to write a novel he would make it thoroughly classical and said (regretfully) that he would thus fail (for once) to be *avant-garde*; that doesn't necessarily follow. But it is interesting to see him recognise that readability might be attempted again, that writers might be more intelligible (*'moins lutter avec les données sémantiques du langage'*), and that a 'cultural epoch' is made up of many 'concomitant' enterprises.[6] The last discovery was new in Barthes's work. He did not consider the possibility of combining the 'classical' and *avant-garde'* alternatives as so many English novels do. The diversity of concomitant tactics is the strength of our own cultural period, and our fiction is not so remote from the age of 'Maupassant and Zola' as he believed to be the case of the novel in France.

In his 1979 essay 'Beckett, Lowry and the Anti-Novel', Ronald Binns observes that ideas like those of Barthes in the 1960s and early 1970s, publicised in England by Stephen Heath, Jonathan Culler and Christine Brooke-Rose, are 'influential' and 'critically vigorous'. He notes that 'in the context of the recent glut of anti-novelists (Barth, Coover, Brautigan, Vonnegut, Pynchon, B. S. Johnson *et al.*), it is a writer like J. G. Farrell, quite self-consciously reproducing the features of the naturalistic novel, even down to the heresy of omniscient and guiding commentary, who appears startling and inventive'.[7] This is true (Farrell is praised by Bernard Bergonzi for restoring an emphasis on the real),[8] and Binns's essay suggests that 'orthodox' and 'anti-' novels are misleading terms. The remoteness and falseness or irrelevance of the nineteenth century is nonetheless an important tenet for many writers, and Barthes's concept of 'myth' is probably needed to explain it.

In the opening pages of his 'Notes Towards the Re-definition of

Culture', *In Bluebeard's Castle* (1971), George Steiner discusses the way in which present-day Western culture, 'or "post-culture" ', uses its past to identify its own situation. He begins:

> It is not the literal past that rules us, save, possibly in a biological sense. It is images of the past. These are often as highly structured and selective as myths. Images and symbolic constructs of the past are imprinted, almost in the manner of genetic information, on our sensibility. Each new historical era mirrors itself in the picture and active mythology of its past . . .[9]

In our own case, George Steiner maintains, we depend upon 'a myth of the nineteenth century': we connect myths of the Golden Age and the Fall with the hundred years which ended with the outbreak of the First World War, and imagine a past which was peaceful, socially stable, politically progressive, dignified, restrained, devout, scientific, civilised and well-adjusted . . . a happier time than ours. Historical evidence that this 'garden of liberal culture' was based on social and imperial exploitation, on the factories, the slums and the Empire does not effectively disturb the hold of the 'myths' on our imagination.[10] It is true that we use 'Victorian' to emphasise extremes: of comfort and poverty, sentiment and heartlessness, dedication and indolence, innocence and depravity. We contrast the welfare state either with the Victorians' unconcern or with their private responsibility and independence; and, in debates today, we compare our permissiveness with their dignified self-restraint or with their hypocritical prudishness. Their problems are still unsolved; present-day preoccupations influence our reading of Victorian novels and the way we read contemporary fiction is affected by myths about the Victorians.

Another kind of myth and a different view of fiction can be found in Marthe Robert's Freudian study of the nature and history of the novel, *Roman des origines et origines du roman* (1972), which argues that there are two 'basic types' of novel corresponding to the types of story with which a child consoles itself in infancy: the novel of the *enfant trouvé*, or foundling, and the novel of the *bâtard*. The 'bastard' is a realist, seeking like Balzac and his heroes to conquer the world; the *'enfant trouvé'* takes flight from reality in dream worlds of words. The interaction of these types in *Don Quixote* and *Robinson Crusoe*, she thinks, created the novel, and, in the nineteenth century, brought it to what she sees as its fullest development, in Balzac and Flaubert.

The novel as a genre teems with foundlings and bastards because it reflects the '*roman familial*' in which the infant creates a fantasy self with alternative parents. But today the novel, she says, with the *nouveau roman* in mind, is 'free to be no more than a string of phrases' but has lost its power over the stories with which our minds make sense of reality.[11] If Marthe Robert had known more about English fiction, she might have made more of her thesis, which is intriguing: Powell's Widmerpool, for example, is a clear case of a *bâtard*, and Nick Jenkins of an *enfant trouvé* consoling himself with worlds of words. The novel today, according to Marthe Robert, is occupied, at its best, in challenging the 'modes of thought which are now only the stereotypes of a worn-out cultural heritage': '*les façons de penser qui ne sont plus que les steréotypes d'un héritage cultural usé*' (Part 2, Section 2). This cliché of contemporary thought, which comes in her summing up, is unworthy of the vigorous argument of her book as a whole and would not stand up to a view of modern fiction broad enough to take in England.

Hartley's *The Go-Between* and Golding's *Lord of the Flies* are novels which have made a stronger impact than mere '*enfilades de phrases*' are likely to do; and which make creative use of both the recent 'cultural heritage' and older more permanent kinds of narrative interest, of the sort Freudians perhaps cannot explain but which at least they keep us aware of. Instincts as well as fashions go to create the Reading Community.

8 Hartley's *The Go-Between*: Neo-Victorian or New Novel?

The *Go-Between* was published the same year as Alain Robbe-Grillet's *Les Gommes*: 1953. It might seem that here are two extremes in the standard critical contrast between English conservatism and French experiment in the novel in the 1950s. The years 1953–4 saw the appearance of Amis, Murdoch and Golding working in the mode of fiction which has seemed so conventional by contrast with the new developments in France. Hartley was neither young nor new in 1953. He was fifty-eight and had published what many consider his finest achievement, the trilogy of novels known as *Eustace and Hilda*, in the 1940s. He is often regarded as a disciple of Henry James, even of Hawthorne: here, it might be thought, is the arch neo-Victorian. But now that the originality of the *nouveau roman* (no longer so new) can be regarded with a degree of scepticism, and the innovatory character of English fiction recognised, it is interesting to discover, in what is maybe the most widely admired 'conventional' novel of the last thirty years, a parallel with the 'new novel' in France.

Criticism in England has praised Hartley in conventional terms. Some critics, as we shall see, have praised his oblique rendering of twentieth-century horrors, reflected in quiet, domestic scenes. He has been regarded as the most expert of the 'novelists of childhood'. Penguin Books, who have reissued paperback editions of *The Go-Between* constantly throughout the 1960s and 1970s, make this claim for it, and their blurb implies a comfortably traditional method, quoting Sir John Betjeman: 'of all the novels L. P. Hartley has written I think *The Go-Between* is the best . . . it is in what is to me the best tradition of fiction'. He is recommended also as a religious or mystical writer, influenced by Emily Brontë, able to create a sense of spiritual realities. His *Times* obituary (14 December 1972) saw him in all these ways and as an artistic, Jamesian, social historian, recapturing better than anyone country-house life at the turn of the century.

This reflects the way Hartley saw himself. His book of criticism, *The Novelist's Responsibility* (1967), looks back to Jane Austen, Emily Brontë, Hawthorne and James rather than to the modernists — Proust, Mann, Joyce, Kafka, Musil — whom the French new novelists regarded as their predecessors, in so far as they had any. As a reviewer of fiction since the 1920s, on the other hand, Hartley was fully aware of the achievements of modernism. He had a professional understanding of the situation of the novel in the twentieth century. Perhaps his familiarity with excesses and absurdities in writers of the thirties and forties who tried to shock their readers into 'a new consciousness of reality' made him inclined to pose as a traditionalist with a soothing respect for the least adventurous Common Reader. Neither *Possibilities* nor *The Situation of the Novel* mentions *The Go-Between*, perhaps because it was found too lightweight. The following account of the novel looks at it as a work of technical interest, relevant to the present period of fiction, whose traditional appearance is something of a pose.

A summary of the story can be made fairly straightforwardly (which is not the case with any 'new novel'). Indeed, a brief account of the setting and characters might seem like a parody of Betjeman's idea of 'the best tradition of fiction'. If Lawrence Durrell had attempted a burlesque of what Pursewarden's hawk-featured publishers with binoculars were looking out for to supply to their public, he might have tried something like this. An old gentleman is remembering his boyhood visit to a country house: an intrigue develops against a background of bathing parties and picnics, an approaching ball and a cricket match. The marriageable heiress, Marian, is undecided between gallant and gentle Lord Trimingham, recently disfigured in the Boer War, and the virile but socially 'unknowable' local farmer, Ted Burgess. The boy, acting innocently as go-between, arranges her trysts with Burgess. Tension mounts until, in the catastrophe, the lovers are discovered coupling on an outhouse floor. Ted commits suicide; Trimingham marries Marian; Leo's emotional life is arrested by the shock; it is only now, fifty years later, that he begins to remember and understand.

Such an account falsifies, because of the central and pervasive interest of the narrative technique. Yet a summary shows that Hartley was using a very conventional type of story and deliberately evoking an earlier tradition of fiction as if to emphasise that nothing new was to be looked for at that level of interest. It is in the relationship between the conspicuously modernist craftsmanship and the stock, commonplace scenes and characters of the novel that Hartley might be considered as a novelist in the sense defined by Michel Butor in the essay of 1955, 'Le Roman comme recherche':

> Although a true story can always in the last resort be supported by outside evidence, the novel must itself create what it tells us about. That is why it is *the* phenomenological domain, the place above all in which to study how reality appears, or can appear; it is why the novel is the laboratory of narrative.
>
> [*Alors que le récit viridique a toujours l'appui, la ressource d'une évidence extérieure, le roman doit suffire à susciter ce dont il nous entretient. C'est pourquoi il est le domaine phénomenologique par excellence, le lieu par excellence ou étudier de quelle façon la réalité nous apparaît ou peut nous apparaître; c'est pourquoi le roman est le laboratoire du récit.*][1]

Thinking on these lines, one sees that Iris Murdoch's proposal that modern novels be considered under the two heads of 'crystalline' and 'journalistic' suggests a way to link the *Go-Between* with the *nouveau roman*:

> Indeed it [the crystalline novel] *is* Romanticism in a later phase. The pure, clean, self-contained 'symbol' . . . is the analogue of the lonely self-contained individual. It is what is left of the other-worldliness of Romanticism when the 'messy' humanitarian and revolutionary elements have spent their force. The temptation of art, a temptation to which every work of art yields except the greatest ones, is to console. The modern writer, frightened of technology and (in England) abandoned by philosophy and (in France) presented with simplified dramatic theories, attempts to console us by myths or by stories.[2]

Hartley's Christianity and his Herbert Spencerian liberalism failed to provide him with much philosophical support, as is clear from *The Novelist's Responsibility*,[3] and he was certainly dismayed by twentieth-century conditions in general. He readily comes to seem 'crystalline' in disposition. Iris Murdoch does admit that the better modern novelists are of this kind.

Viewing his work in relation to this concept would have the merit of rescuing him to some extent from the labels of Jamesian and Hawthornean. Being post-Symbolist and post-Romantic, he can be seen as the contemporary of Butor and Robbe-Grillet. In the case of *The Go-Between*, symbolism is exactly analogous to the 'lonely self-contained individual' in the appeal it has for the narrator whose lonely and self-contained nature, and need for consolation, are the reason the story is told. For him, as for the figures behind the dream-like constructions of Robbe-Grillet and Butor,[4] narrative has a therapeutic role. Of course this idea can, like most of the principles behind the *nouveau roman*, be found in earlier literature too. Many narrators in past fiction are consoling themselves by telling stories. *The Go-Between* does, certainly, invite symbolic interpretation in the manner of the older (pre-Sartrean) symbolist novel; a somewhat remorseless symbol-mindedness is something that the older Leo has in common with the younger self he 'resurrects', who is conceived in relation to symbols. But this, like everything else in the novel, is subordinated to the method whereby the narrator re-creates his past through the imaginative working of memory, and here, in the Proustian aspect of the book, a comparison with French fiction of the 1950s is revealing. The first sentence of *The Go-Between* is an epigram that has become famous: 'The past is a foreign country: they do things differently there'. That line might serve as a gloss on Michel Butor's linking of Paris and Rome in *La Modification* (1957). Such a parallel helps to set his work in the decade where it belongs.

The 'crystalline' novel is unlike the nineteenth-century novel, Iris Murdoch says, in portraying the human condition 'without characters in the nineteenth-century sense'.[5] In the larger meaning of the word 'symbolism' — 'the sum of the relationships of what the novel describes to the reality we experience', in Michel Butor's definition — Leo's self-discovery through narrative is a process that contains a rich display of old habits of fiction, but then so in their own way do the novels of Michel Butor. 'Characters in the nineteenth-century sense' are an old habit which the new novel claimed to have abandoned, although, as various English critics have pointed out, the reader characterises the anonymous figures in these novels, especially on a second reading. As for *The Go-Between*, its stereotyped characters appear as 'archetypal figures' to Anne Mulkeen in her 1974 study of Hartley, *Wild Thyme, Winter Lightning*. She describes 'strange configurations in *The Go-Between* where the heat, the deadly nightshade, the winning and losing of the cricket match, and the "distant war" (the Boer War) are connected with the central triangle of characters, where there are "strange parallels" between nature and man and history', where 'Marian,

Ted and Hugh are archetypal figures' and the novelist's problem is how to combine the child's spiritual vision and the knowledge of evil in man (p.100). Blake and Emily Brontë, from whose lyrics Hartley took his epigraphs for *The Shrimp and the Anemone* and *The Go-Between*, are the best guides to this kind of understanding of his achievement, which was touched on by *The Times*'s obituary: 'As in *Eustace and Hilda* Hartley delineates in *The Go-Between* the small things of life, the small pleasures and the small miseries with such affectionate precision that one trusts implicitly the vision of the darker things that he sees as lying below, but only just below, the surface of the ordinary.' The Brontë epigraph to *The Go-Between* evokes the poignancy of childhood:

> But, child of dust, the fragrant flowers,
> The bright blue sky and velvet sod
> Were strange conductors to the bowers
> Thy daring footsteps must have trod.

These lines are from an 1837 lyric, 'I saw thee, child, one summer's day', which ends 'And childhood's flower must waste its bloom/ Beneath the shadow of the tomb'. The novel does create brilliantly a sense of the small pleasures and miseries of a child's life, and evokes with a formidable delicacy and elusiveness of touch the presence of darker things. In Leo's watching the monstrous growth induced by the heat on the belladonna, his catching Ted at cricket, his chatting with Lord Trimingham about war, we are given a sense of 'configurations' involving nature, chance and evil. The sexual drama and the destruction of the boy's trust in life are linked especially with the pervasive reminders of 'the distant war'. 'Trying to sneak past in dead ground', Hugh calls after Leo; Hugh with 'his whole face . . . lopsided' from his scar and Leo's boyish dartings about in the gardens merge for a moment with the Boer War Hugh has just come back from. The way the narrator has the two world wars in mind justifies Anne Mulkeen's comment that he is 'the type of Briton stunned, shattered, discouraged by the impact and horror of war' (p. 110).

War, in the present century, has made it more urgent, Iris Murdoch says, for the novelist to try to come to terms with basic human problems of good and evil. But the crystalline novelist tends to take refuge in fantasy, to 'operate . . . with small myths, toys, crystals' and not 'to grapple with reality' or, if at all, only to console.

'Le Roman comme recherche' demanded that the novelist portray the human condition, and 'present reality'. But in France the sense of overwhelming evil in contemporary reality has just as often unnerved the novelist, as it did Nathalie Sarraute: '*Quelle histoire inventée pourrait rivaliser avec . . . les récits des camps de concentration . . .?*'[6] Hartley does take refuge from the horrors of modern existence in fictions which deal artfully with private sorrows. Yet his ability to reflect the conflicts of his age has been recognised by the British critics, Walter Allen and W. W. Robson.

Robson sees in *Eustace and Hilda* 'a more profound study than *Lord of the Flies* of the "impulse to dominate" which has nearly wrecked our world already and may one day succeed in doing so entirely'.[7] Walter Allen has also emphasised Hartley's power to use a limited social world, and one viewed through the medium of childhood, to explore indirectly the twentieth-century experience of evil on a scale beyond the scope of direct treatment in literature. In *Tradition and Dream* he writes: 'Yet though his world is a small one, and apparently demure, the smallness and the demureness are deceptive, for his world can uncannily reflect the violence and the conflicts from which it is seemingly isolated' (p. 254). The opening scene of the *Eustace and Hilda* trilogy has become famous for the image it provides of the helplessness of moral scruple before the natural impulses in marine creatures, and in people too. Eustace, aged nine, peers into a rock pool where an anemone is devouring a shrimp. He ponders each creature's case and the irreconcilable conflict of interests. He calls in Hilda, his elder sister, whose 'ruthless' moral sense grasps 'an evil principle at the back of the anemone affair'. Her intervention is too late to save the shrimp, and the anemone is disembowelled. Hartley develops gradually, in the course of the novel, the ironic relevance of this incident to the relationship of Eustace and Hilda and to the destructive nature of human dependence as a fact of life.

Hartley may be considered as a novelist of our insecure era, without it being taken for granted that he is either a talented survival from an earlier period, as even his admirers imply, or merely a maker of beautiful 'toys'. *The Go-Between* is often regarded this way: as a fine, old-fashioned artefact. It is steeped in Hartley's awareness of novels of the past, but is written nevertheless with a sense of the situation of the novel, in Europe as well as in England, in the age of Robbe-Grillet and Butor.

The narrator of *The Go-Between* is engaged in a peculiarly drastic type of self-appraisal. He is occupied throughout the novel in remembering the events of fifty years ago when, on his thirteenth birthday, he suffered a trauma from which he has never recovered: we share his gradual rediscovery of his earlier self. Although the voice which addresses us is intelligently and pleasingly modulated, the Leo Colston who has existed until now — subject to the block which made him forget what happened in 1900 — is as oddly removed from normal life as a Beckett protagonist.

'All dried up inside' is Marian's impression of him in the Epilogue: the desiccation is Beckettian — no religious beliefs, no friends, no emotional life, no sexual desire, no music, no war-time risks or peace-time pleasures, no creative work, no introspection has until now disturbed Leo's commitment to bibliography (and kindred war-work) for half a century. Bibliography is a fine profession and involves disciplines doubtless beyond the capacity of Murphy and Malone. But its routine and factual character is what attracts Leo: it offers him an escape from life: 'another world came to my aid — the world of facts. I accumulated facts: facts which existed independently of me, facts which my private wishes could not add to or subtract from. Soon I came to regard these facts as truths . . .' (Epilogue). Trapped by routine and obsessed with collecting data, Leo resembles researchers in Robbe-Grillet and Butor. The contribution his skill with facts makes to the narrative is a point in common with their self-analyses, although he is an 'active' conventional narrator.

In view of the relative openness to interpretation of the 'passive' narrative method in the *nouveau roman*, comparison may seem superficial. Leo's retreat from life can be explained conventionally, as it is by Anne Mulkeen. But it is a sexual trauma with Oedipal connotations that has stunned Leo and its connection with a death (Ted's) for which Leo feels guilty provides a theme in common with *Les Gommes* and *Passage de Milan*. Leo is less likely to remind us of the broken-hearted and broken-down characters of Victorian fiction because we aren't shown whatever crabbed external symptoms he may have developed; internal discourse was a mode with which French fiction experimented in the 1950s — often with disabled, implausible figures — and this is the mode of *The Go-Between*. Hartley's being so readable need not oblige us to see him as merely readable, in the derogatory sense propagated by Roland Barthes in the 1960s when promoting the 'new novel' as a 'writerly' or 'open' type of literature. Barthes has since revised his views, attacking, as we have seen in the last chapter, a 'new conformism of the unreadable'.[8] Robbe-Grillet, who used to ignore the existence of English precedents to his own original schemes (as did Barthes), now admits that the Anglo-Saxon tradition in fiction has always been more flexible than the French. Barthes's tendency has been to contrast extremes: Philippe Sollers and Alexandre Dumas. The narrative method of *The Go-Between* can be seen as 'open' and experimental in ways of its own.

It has been a novel often set for examinations, and students frequently object that they don't believe that the shock Leo suffers from the scene in the outhouse would have a permanently disabling psychological effect. Hartley intended to stretch credulity and to stress the damage done to Leo for dramatic and for moral reasons. Harold Pinter has described how he first read the novel, having been commissioned to do the screenplay for Joseph Losey's film version, and was struck by the contrast between the two Leos.[9] A dialogue takes place in the Prologue between these discordant selves: there is an allegorical aspect to it, youth eager and old age disappointed; but the incongruity of the *dédoublements* (or doublings) of the *nouveau roman* is present too, and one might well be reminded of the keen sense in modern French writers of how identity is subject to time.

The relativity in the portrayal of the two Leos is as rigorous as it would be in a French novel influenced by Saussure. Apart from the fragmentary diary entries, the younger Leo is brought into being by the memories of Leo at sixty-five. But there is hardly a sentence of his narrative in which the older Leo is not occupied in thinking about his earlier self. What we encounter, in fact, is a third version of him, since he is bringing himself back to life in the course of explaining himself to us, re-establishing touch with a vitality that was arrested fifty years ago.

First-person narrative has always raised theoretical doubts for readers who let their minds dwell on the method; Henry James had many reservations about it. One can argue that the gentlemanly tone of Pip's narrative throughout *Great Expectations* undermines the novel's satire on the concept of gentleman, which is perhaps why conservative reviewers of 1860 were so unalarmed by what modern critics see as a radically critical and even subversive work. But *The Go-Between* emphasises the curious relationship between the hero and the narrator: each is in a sense the author of the other. Hartley does not allow it to disturb our enjoyment of the story or the human interest, but he sharpens our awareness of the technique and of what is absurd in the powers of a novelist. 'If my twelve-year-old self, of whom I had grown rather fond, thinking about him, were to reproach me: "Why have you grown up such a dull dog . . .?" ' muses Leo in the Prologue. 'Interiority' is a coinage used of various post-Joycean developments in fiction; interiority here allows a constant comic interplay between two stylistic registers, the small boy's and the bibliographer's: on going downstairs, 'I went bumping down the cataract. I was a Red Indian this morning . . .' (Chapter 5); or on sliding down a straw-stack: 'I omitted a necessary and practical precaution always taken, and without loss of face, by experienced straw-stack sliders . . .' (Chapter 7). The tastes of the boy of twelve are recorded in the prim, precise tone of the old man: 'It was true that I hadn't seen the garden properly. Frankly I preferred the rubbish-heap, for there I had a sense of adventure which was absent from the garden' (Chapter 23).

In *Great Expectations*, we take for granted touches of whimsy in the narrator's account of his own childish mind and behaviour. But the older Leo is so absorbed in rediscovering his lost vivacity, and at the same time so bizarrely remote from it, that the two sets of style and taste coexist in his narrative, and an interest in seventeenth-century art and literature is imposed on a relish for haystacks and rubbish-heaps, and scholarly diction is mixed with schoolboy slang. The counterpointing of personas is so systematic that an effect of *dédoublement* arises, in the interaction of raw immediacy and mellow irony, as if events were being relived with a double consciousness.

In a similar way, the reader's attention is drawn to the organisation of time in the novel. The date 1900 has an almost structuralist prominence, because of the diary, and because of Leo's obsession with the turn of the century, and with round numbers generally. Two centuries and two epochs are opposed by the stressing of the year, and so are two contrasted eras in Leo's life, before and after his thirteenth birthday in 1900. A second time-scheme involves the nineteen days of the visit to Brandham Hall, between the ninth and the twenty-seventh of July. The contrast between the long-range view of two centuries and the boy's minute ordering of time into segments during his stay is a conspicuously diagrammatic feature of the novel's design, and helps make the reader more conscious of the problems of time in fiction.

A good incidental feature of Hartley's understanding of child-hood is Leo's power to lose himself in the present even while

fascinated by the measurement of time. We have a vivid impression
of the expanse of his day, with tracts of time between the fixed hours
for meals, and of how the days merged together in experience: three
days, in Chapter 9, are made to seem, in the reading, like a phase of
life, although every detail can be placed in time. The diary (a
typical *nouveau roman* device, incidentally) helps with this and so
does Leo's daily recording of temperatures. His trips as go-between
require timing. The events of the last afternoon are measured by the
clock. One is struck by the significance of time during these nineteen
days which stand out from the vague passage of the subsequent fifty
years. The cricket-match provides examples of the novelist's
control, evoking cricket's delays and suspense, or a moment of
stillness, out of play: 'the ball lay at Mrs Maudsley's feet looking
strangely small and harmless'; and of cricket's suddenness too —
Leo catches Ted in a moment that ends the game. In a rash
moment, a week later, Ted is to shoot himself. *Les Gommes* takes
place within the timespan of a gunshot. Clocks and calendars obsess
the 'new novel' because their writers are intrigued by the illusion of
fictional time and by the gap between time as we know it and time as
we measure it. Hartley intimates a similar awareness, without fuss.

John Barth's 'Life Story' in *Lost in the Funhouse* (1968) includes
some ingenious grumbling about the troubles of being a technician
of the novel: 'Another story about a writer writing a story! Another
regressus in infinitum! Who doesn't prefer art that at least overtly
imitates something other than its own processes? That doesn't
proclaim "Don't forget I'm an artifice!"? That takes for granted its
mimetic nature instead of asserting it in order (not so slyly after all)
to deny it, or vice versa?' Given this kind of awareness of 'fabulation'
in fiction it is increasingly impossible to write with the straightfor-
wardness John Barth is making fun of. Hartley's work does not
proclaim its own artifice, but insinuates it.

While the conventions of first-person narration in Dickens or
Conrad allowed prodigious efforts of recall, Leo reconstructs his
past with the aid of certain figurative devices for which, as Peter
Bien has pointed out, 'symbol' is an inadequate term.[10] The young
Leo, inspired by the zodiac, obviously was inclined to find meaning
in everything around him: to select and order his experience. The
old Leo remembers him this way, with the help of the deadly
nightshade, the heat, the green of his clothes and his bicycle, the
Boers, unlucky thirteen, the fateful catch at cricket. The narrator
finds in them a relevance to events which enables him to assemble a

story. He does so with a studied care which is typical of him, although the result seems implausible to some readers. The cricket-match is less a sporting event than a ritual display of relationships between the teams and among the players. At best, the fusion of memory and meaning is perfect, as when Leo finds an image of Ted's social exclusion and vulnerability in his first appearance at the swimming pool, 'not a weed marred the surface, only one thing broke it: the intruder's bobbing head' (Chapter 4); or remembers the effect of grotesque distortion created by the fully raised seat of the bicycle ready for Marian to ride it at his birthday party. At other times, as with the many omens of Ted's end there is a sense of strain and improbability.

But readers who complain that the novel's proliferation of signs is overdone or 'contrived' are reading within the convention of a first-person narrator's total recall of just what happened. A less conventional response seems called for, which admits the selective, interpretive nature of memory, and sees Leo's contriving of his own story as an aspect of his attempt at self-recovery. The strong Victorian convention of the 'confessional' mode keeps us from confusing Pip or Jane Eyre with novelists, but Leo reshapes his memories with a writer's awareness; to use an educated character as a first-person narrator today makes that almost inevitable, as Fowles's *Daniel Martin*, where narrator becomes novelist, shows. Leo appears at times like a novelist *manqué* who has at last discovered the story he can write.

We are familiar in modern fiction with unreliable, corrupt, unstable and even insane narrators.[11] Leo might be described as an urbane neurotic. Hartley has, like most novelists, fended off suggestions that he was influenced by Freud, and critics have, as usual, offered accounts of his work in Freudian terms nonetheless. Leo's mixture of withdrawal from 'the world of the emotions' and curiosity about it, in the course of his reconstituting of himself through memory, is reminiscent of Michel Butor's more consciously Freudian concern with his characters' mental blocks, probing of the past, and quest for reassurance through ordering material. But Hartley is too conscious of the mystery in what is unique in his character's experience for Freud to be helpful in explaining his work, and that is where he is really unlike the 'new novelists'.

Alain Robbe-Grillet's wish to abolish humanism is connected with his hope of disconnecting the type of novel he inaugurated from literature of the past. Hartley's mildly mystical Christian humanism is deeply attached to the past of English literature and especially to certain nineteenth-century authors: Emily Brontë, Henry James. He was, moreover, personally tied to the world of the country-house — already archaic when he was young in the purity which he pictures in *The Go-Between* — by a feeling which few modern French intellectuals would appreciate. 'That famous cloudless summer of 1914 extends backwards a long way into a world more civil, more confident, more humanely articulate than any we have known since,' writes George Steiner[12] and these words convey the mood of calm conjured up in *The Go-Between*. Steiner is writing about a 'myth of the past'; the popularity of Hartley's novel may be due partly to the strength of the myth. The phrase 'a country house in 1900', is evocative, and mythic, indeed, in Roland Barthes's meaning of the term. Hartley was susceptible to nostalgic imagery, and the Barthes who published *Mythologies* (1954–6, 1957) not long after *The Go-Between* would no doubt have denounced him for indulging bourgeois fantasies, though the later Barthes might well have been more broadminded, less doctrinaire. Like that of all effective novelists, Hartley's work makes creative use of his private mythology; like most intelligent writers, he is aware of it. He is as conscious as Robbe-Grillet or Steiner or Barthes of how we mirror ourselves in versions of the past, and his writing shows an intuitive sympathy with how most of us do so.

The half-century span that Hartley uses allows him, by encompassing everything within the narrator's memory, to evade the problem of point of view which John Fowles exploits so well when he looks back over a century. Memory and a 'mythic' view of the past go naturally together, as Steiner points out. The tranquil country scenes and stable social order which form the background to the characters' lives, the rich harvest and calm, cricketing peasantry illustrate what Steiner means by 'myths of the past that rule us'. Fowles's narrator would be quick to point out the misery — as he does the home circumstances of the servant girl Millie in *The French Lieutenant's Woman* — behind idyllic country appearances. This façade is only one aspect, in *The Go-Between*, of what John Bayley calls 'pastoral'.

Hartley's setting is pastoral in the sense of common usage. John Bayley's concept is much wider, including whatever is 'framed', 'characteristic' or 'proffered': characters determined by their roles are pastoral, in his sense, in a way relevant to *The Go-Between*. 'A coalminer, or a retired colonel in Camberley, are seen as pastoral in

their functions and their characters — the fact that they may not
feel like or be aware of themselves as a coalminer or a colonel cannot
be considered': Bayley is discussing realism in Tolstoy (in *Tolstoy and
the Novel*, Part 3, Section 10) but his discussion (as throughout his
book) ranges over literature and critical ideas: Conrad's *Nostromo* is
pastoral because the state of 'Costaguana holds and determines the
characters': *The Shadow Line* is not, because the sea for Conrad 'is not
a pastoral setting but the natural instructive setting of felt and
experienced life' (Part 3, Section 10). This distinction and the
illustrations which John Bayley draws from life are illuminating: we
adopt a pastoral mode when we buy a new suit or get a new job.
They help to illumine the working of Leo's double-vision — and its
results. The scenes and characters of the novel are conveyed to us
through one determining frame formed by Leo's memory and,
within that, through another formed by the idealising mind of his
twelve-year-old self. After the first few days of his visit (and the gift
of a new suit), Leo remembers he was carried away in his
imagination by the generosity shown to him:

> The expenditure had been godlike; it belonged to another,
> ampler phase of being than the one I was accustomed to. My
> mind could not grasp it but my imagination could make play
> with it, for unlike the mind, which could dismiss what it did not
> understand, my imagination loved to contemplate the incom-
> prehensible and try to express my sense of it by an analogy. And I
> had one ready made. From those resplendent beings, golden with
> sovereigns (and, I suspected, guineas) arriving, staying, leaving
> apparently unaffected by any restrictions of work or family ties,
> citizens of the world who made the world their playground, who
> had it in their power (for I did not forget that) to make me
> miserable with a laugh and happy with a smile — from them it
> was but a short step to the hardly more august and legendary
> figures of the zodiac. [Chapter 4]

This severance of the young Leo from reality is what makes him
vulnerable. The Marian and Trimingham whom the go-between
sees are like creatures in daydreams. Leo likes Trimingham because
he is a ninth viscount; he hardly conceives of a 'Hugh' apart from
that status: he is impressed and pleased by Trimingham's
friendliness — he would have expected, he says, that a lord would be
haughty. At the same level of understanding, Leo registers Marian's

character: she is 'a beauty': ' "My sister is very beautiful," Marcus said to me one day. He announced it quite impersonally, as who should say "Two and two make four", and I received it in the same spirit. It was a fact, like other facts, something to be learned' (Chapter 2). Of course Marian becomes personally important to Leo after her initiative over the new suit, but she remains within the function implied for him by her beauty; he wants her to marry Trimingham because that seems fitting. As for Ted Burgess, his function determines Leo's dealings with him too. When Burgess first discovers Leo on his haystack, he mistakes him for a village boy and threatens him with 'the biggest thrashing you've ever had in your life'. But 'oddly enough this didn't put me against him: I thought it was exactly what an angry farmer ought to say: in a way I should have been disappointed if he had spoken less harshly' (Chapter 5). Despite a mixture of real feelings about Ted, including envy, affection and resentment, Leo never quite grasps that Ted exists separately from the image of an 'angry farmer'.

The adult Leo who recalls this idealising vision he once possessed has the detachment, the moral sense and the feeling of grievance to convey the bewildered desires of Trimingham, Ted Burgess and Marian. All three are types, who think of themselves as such. It is as a working farmer and not a gentleman, as village not Hall, as a man of fields and barns not of sofas and tea-tables, that Ted is conceived as a lover: physically assured and morally uneasy: his 'quick look' when Leo asks politely about his domestic arrangements, 'Do you have a woman every day?': and his angry outburst, 'Clear out of here quick', when pressed to tell about 'spooning', imply a coarseness, a lack of humour and resilience, and of a sense of proportion; and these shortcomings belong with his farmer's role. He is convincing and memorable, but never 'unframed'. Trimingham's blend of simple enthusiasm over being in love with Marian and crisp authority derived from social and military rank are equally stereotyped. Ted might be an Edwardian character sketch of 'The Working Farmer', Trimingham of 'The Gentleman'. Both seem meant to typify what was best in the older order and calmer world before 1914 which George Steiner tells us we dream about. Certainly, such a contrasted pair as Ted and Trimingham, appearing in a novel of 1900, would seem like the products of wishful thinking. But in *The Go-Between*'s scheme of reconstruction of a personal past through memory, they are appropriate; they correspond to our collective notions of what 1900 must have been like. Marian is equally decorous as a heroine: 'there was a sparkle in everything she did'; vivacious, moody, wilful, scheming, she fills the heroine's role in Leo's imagination. Her own memory of her 1900 circumstances, when Leo re-visits her in the 'Epilogue', is trite: 'All those house-parties — people being paired off like animals at stud — it wasn't like that with us. We were made for each other.' Her egotism remains intact. Hartley's subsequent uncertainty about the novel's moral bearing seems irrelevant because she is so true to a nature which we want to bestow on her, as the narrator does: she would have been like that!

The same characteristic, pastoral mode governs the presentation of minor figures like the footman, Henry; and extends to the picnics, the carriage outings among the lanes where the passers-by stare and children scramble for coins the coachman throws them; the cricket with the village side coming up to play at the Hall. Everything is as we would have imagined. It is not unlike the effect of Robbe-Grillet's Hong Kong where the details belong to the Hong Kong which everybody knows and not to the real place, except that here it is the past which is 'the foreign country'.

The characters are miniatures beside the characters of the great nineteenth-century novelists. But the strength of the novel's technique is that it acknowledges their remoteness and mystery; they can be known to us only very indirectly: through the memory of the old Leo, an emotional cripple, who knew them briefly fifty years ago, when he was thirteen and living in a dream. They are, as fictional characters, as remote and touching as people whose pasts have been excavated archaeologically, and we are moved by a similar mixture of intimacy and strangeness by their deaths, when Leo sees Hugh's name on the plaque (in the Epilogue) or hears how 'Marcus was killed in the first war, and Denys too. I forget which went first. Denys, I think . . .'. The vast scale on which lives were lost in the 1914 War, and, later, in the concentration camps, is, as Nathalie Sarraute said, one reason why the artistic portrayal of individual character came to seem inadequate. In the finely attuned setting of Leo's mind the assorted facts about Marcus and Trimingham convey a respect for the individual, however little known or knowable; and the destructiveness of the century is reflected in Hartley's quiet manner as effectively as in novels which deal with war direct.

The Go-Between is equally undemonstrative yet acute in registering social tensions at a distance of fifty years. *Lord of the Flies* is generally seen as a re-interpretation of Victorian 'myths' in *Coral Island*. *The Go-Between* examines a newly invented situation which is intended to strike the reader as characteristically Victorian. The plot and the relationships among the characters are adapted to the way we look at Victorian society. In John Fowles's *The French Lieutenant's Woman* the desire to study and explain the mid-Victorian past is much more explicit, but not necessarily more effective than Hartley's unruffled composure which effaces any hint of its own importance. If the plan of the novel offers a simplified social model of rural England in the nineteenth century — with nobleman, merchant, yeoman, country people and servants — we can share Leo's sense of how 'natural' a 'good match' between Marian and Trimingham seemed then, while remaining aware of how 'social' it seems today. Trimingham's line about Ted's military promise is revealing about late Victorian assumptions: 'A likely man, single — no ties — he'd make a first rate N.C.O.' (Chapter 18). It is Hugh's certainty that Ted couldn't go higher, combined with the lightly stressed irony in 'no ties'—Hugh doesn't know about Ted's tie with Marian — that conveys how incongruous the social arrangements seem now. Such points are not laboured: not even the scene in the outhouse or the appearance of Ted's grandson as eleventh Viscount (in the Epilogue) has the air of scoring a point; but the most delicate hints can have considerable force. Leo asks Hugh his opinion of Ted. ' "Well, he's quite a decent feller" — I remembered he had said this about the Boers — "but he's a bit wild." ' The comment on the Boers came in Chapter 14: ' "The Boer's not a bad feller," said Lord Trimingham tolerantly. "I don't dislike him personally. It's a pity we have to shoot so many of them, but there you are." ' These remarks convey the tone of the English ruling class in the nineteenth century without needing the sort of commentary the narrator of *The French Lieutenant's Woman* supplies.

In another passage, the cricket match creates metaphorically the threat of a Boer victory. When the village side, though not even properly in whites for cricket, seems to be winning:

> Further disasters followed; five wickets down for fifty-six. These Boers in their motley raiment, triumphantly throwing the ball into the air after each kill, how I disliked them! The spectators disposed along the boundary, standing, sitting, lying, or propped against trees, I imagined to be animated by a revolutionary spirit, and revelling in the downfall of their betters. [Chapters 11].

Later, the social panic and hysteria following the discovery of Ted with Marian, and Ted's suicide, are emphasised as agents of Leo's personal breakdown. A cruder art would have shown them as the breakdown of a social system. *The Go-Between*'s best effects are often in what is unsaid, or allowed to remain as nuance, the basic structure being so unmistakable.

The Go-Between, a frankly contrived, mannerist novel, which applies a brilliant technique to a simple story, is perfectly suited to reflect our sense of the Victorian age. If the modern novelist feels inferior as an artist when he looks at the great nineteenth-century novels, he also believes that we *know* more and are able to see through the social façades the Victorian novel took for granted. That belief underlies the 'dismantled' novels in France. Hartley preserves the elements of conventional narrative while showing his reader how selective and inadequate narrative has to be. *The Go-Between* contrives to be intriguing as an exercise in fiction and moving as a novel. We feel how well country-house life before 1914 has been captured: and the illusory nature of any account of the past. Joseph Losey used cinema techniques to evoke the security of the 'more civil, more confident world' before 1914; Harold Pinter's screenplay caught the evanescent and the absurd in Hartley's art. The success of the film is the best evidence of Hartley's place as a new English novelist.

9 Golding's *Lord of the Flies*, Ballantyne's *Coral Island* and the Critics

William Golding's *Lord of the Flies* (1954) must be one of the most taught of all novels. *Pride and Prejudice* and *Great Expectations* presumably lead it among British set books, but not in the world as a whole. Orwell's *Animal Farm* and *1984* are rivals there and Golding's story could be placed with them in a privileged genre of 'fables for our time', but *Lord of the Flies* is more a novel than they are. Like the books which immediately followed it, *The Inheritors* (1955), *Pincher Martin* (1956), *Free Fall* (1959), *The Spire* (1964) and *The Pyramid* (1967), and the more recent *The Scorpion God* (1973) and *Darkness Visible* (1979), it is highly individual, and like them it is an ambitiously conceived literary work. Unlike any of the others, it has proved a popular success, known and discussed far beyond the limits of the normal novel-reading public. As a much studied, widely read work with a reputation for contemporary relevance it has of course acquired numerous critical commentators; Frank Kermode, perhaps its most distinguished critic, has called it 'profoundly attuned to the contemporary sensibility'.[1] In view of this success as a 'novel for our time', it seems significant to find it so often explained as a refutation of 'Victorianism'. Despite its independent status as a modern masterpiece, it is invariably praised in relation to supposed shortcomings in the popular culture of a hundred years earlier; although it is agreed to be a book of adult seriousness, it is constantly contrasted with a Victorian juvenile adventure story.

Its teachability is not accidental; perhaps no novel has ever been composed with the pedagogic aspect of literature so much in mind. It was created in the period after 1945 in which English literature came into its own in universities and schools. In 1945 English began to dominate Arts studies: the (English) 'new criticism', based on close study of texts in the classroom, made the subject teachable at all levels; and in England, America and the anglophone world at

large there was a search for 'relevant' modern works which would
be suitable for analysis by students, and yet not difficult in the ways
that many moderns are. William Golding was teaching English in
the early fifties; in *Lord of the Flies* he produced a novel which
perfectly fitted these requirements.

Such a thing could not be done on purpose, and to suggest that is
to risk denigrating Golding. Few readers, even among those not
entirely convinced by the method, would object to Stevie Smith's
judgement quoted in the Faber edition: 'this beautiful and des-
perate book – something quite out of the ordinary'. All novelists
have critical readers in mind when writing. But Golding was
professionally involved in the close study of literature in schools;
trying to make clear, even to the vaguest pupils, the workings of
symbol and theme, allegory and allusion, ambiguity and counterpoint, levels of meaning, and patterns of imagery. In *Lord of
the Flies* one is impressed by the lucidity and force of literary
meaning, the integration of each episode and even each detail into
an ordered design: the book has an artfulness, even an air of
demonstrating fictional possibilities, which make it eminently
suitable for teaching and which must owe a lot to the well-trained
critical habits of its author.

It is, of course, equally suitable for critical analysis: almost any
passage of the book lends itself to 'appreciation'. The story of the
schoolboys, Ralph and Simon, Piggy and Jack, with the sundry
other 'biguns and littluns' on their island, struggling to be English
and have rules, but increasingly corrupted by hunting and by living
in fear of 'the Beast', has become a part of modern intellectual lore,
and the critical explanations of it are almost as widely diffused as the
novel itself. These all stress the craft and technical effectiveness of
the composition, usually to praise it. 'Almost endlessly the four
major characters are thematically suggestive', says one study.
Leighton Hodson says in his 1969 *William Golding*: 'though to hunt
pedantically for symbols and parallels would be to destroy pleasure
in the book, nevertheless any reader comes upon the rich texture
with delight in its interlocking design where every incident or
description upon reflection illuminates something else'.[2] A hostile
critic, Martin Green, who complains in an article on 'Distaste for
the Contemporary' in *The Nation* (21 May 1960) that Golding
resembles Eliot, Greene and Waugh in 'loading the dice' against
human nature and rejecting progress, holds Golding's 'scrupulous'
craft against him: 'There is no life in his language. It is all ingenuity,

intention and synthetics'. A completely different view can be found in Mark Kinkead-Weekes and Ian Gregor, *William Golding: A Critical Study* (1967): 'A reader can feel that he possesses this novel in an unusually comprehensive way, and that he could give a lucid, even conceptual account of it' (p. 15). It is a commonplace that modern novels are written by English teachers: Angus Wilson, Kingsley Amis, Malcolm Bradbury, David Lodge are a few of the best. But none of them has even tried to concoct so perfect a 'classroom novel' as this first published work of Golding's.

One of the best detailed accounts of the novel is that, just quoted, by Mark Kinkead-Weekes and Ian Gregor: they challenge, through a close reading of the text, what they see as a common first reaction — that it is 'too crystalline, too insistent, too manipulated' a work (p. 15), and they show how the 'circumstantiality' of the method, its 'sense of the real', checks and resists the 'conceptualizing intelligence' (p. 18): how far it is from being a simple *roman a thèse*, how much 'more profound than the thesis we may be tempted to substitute for the experience' (p. 19). Even so, they recognise as all critics do — and as the novel requires — its most remarkable act of 'conceptualizing intelligence' which is the 'refutation' of *Coral Island*. The belief that *Lord of the Flies*, a schoolmaster's novel, has a lesson within it about our own times appears most plainly and interestingly in the discussion of its relations with that earlier book, also much recommended by schoolmasters. The supposed significance of this lesson is what I want to look at more closely, because of what it reveals about the assumptions that lie behind the way we read novels today.

Here is Kinkead-Weekes's and Gregor's statement of how the two books are related:

> Golding reoccupies R. M. Ballantyne's *Coral Island* and declares its portrayal of those idealized British boys, Jack, Ralph and Peterkin in their tropical paradise, to be a fake, since boys are human beings, and human beings are not like that. Or, rather, he does not 'declare', he shows the falsehood by producing an island and boys that are more convincing than Ballantyne's, and then gradually revealing what the difference implies. The structure and technique of *Lord of the Flies* is one of revelation. [pp. 21–2]

This is well put, though it is assumed too readily that a reader will know *Coral Island* well enough to follow Golding's departures from it. His characters do mention it at crucial moments and he uses various details drawn from Ballantyne's book which he discusses in his essay 'Fable' (in *The Hot Gates: and Other Occasional Pieces*). But Golding has even so been forced to protest that 'one work never comes out of another . . . unless it is still born'.[3] Although Kinkead-Weekes and Gregor were able to devote fifty pages to elucidating the novel's texture, most crtics have to summarise it, and, despite the author's warning, there is a strong tendency to oversimplify, and explain it as 'a reversal', 'a refutation', 'a revisiting', 'a reworking', 'a retesting', 'a revision' or 'a correction', or 'an inversion' of *Coral Island*.

'. . . the novel is basically an inverted *Coral Island*', writes John S. Whitley;[4] 'one might say that *Lord of the Flies* is a refutation of *Coral* Island', writes Samuel Hynes.[5] 'Golding reworks Ballantyne's basic situation, setting and narrative episodes . . . to show . . . how inane the nineteenth-century experiment in youthful isolation was', say Oldsey and Weintraub.[6] 'The whole action, moreover, is an ironic reversal of a well-known Victorian boys' book', says Martin Green.[7] 'Golding . . . gives a corrective to Ballantyne's optimism', says Carl Niemeyer.[8]

The year 1958 saw the centenary of *Coral Island* (first published in Edinburgh in 1857; in London in 1858) and two articles appeared in August that year. V. S. Pritchett wrote in the *New Statesman*: 'In *Coral Island* we see the safe community. A century without war and with a settled sense of the human personality has produced it.' On the other hand, he says, Golding's version 'shakes us until we feel in our bones the perennial agony of the species'. In the *Spectator* in the same month, Frank Kermode suggested that '*The Coral Island* could be used in the history of ideas'. 'It belongs to the period preceding the breaking of that great wave of primitivism which has so altered the features of the modern mind . . . Golding had the idea of studying Ralph and Jack against this altered landscape.'[9]

Golding's own image of the relationship between the two books is, as one might expect, the most evocative: *Coral Island* 'rotted to compost' in his mind and in the compost 'the new myth put down roots'. Frank Kermode, who quotes this in a later article, says that Golding's term *myth* 'is the right one; out of the single small seed grows this instrument "for controlling . . . ordering . . . giving a shape and significance to the immense paradox of futility and anarchy, which is contemporary history". These are Mr Eliot's words on Joyce's myth, but they will serve for Golding'.[10]

Thus the establishment of *Lord of the Flies* as a new classic of central relevance in modern culture, exhaustively studied and explicated, has had the very odd incidental result of turning the attention of an academic community, eager to explain 'contemporary sensibility', on a mid-Victorian book for boys. We might recall here Daniel Martin's 'new version of the Midas touch with despair taking the place of gold', among the high caste of intellectuals for whom it is 'offensive to suggest publicly that anything might turn out well in this world'.[11] Given such an outlook, the fascination with 'Ballantyne the Brave' (the title of a recent book on him)[12] becomes more understandable. He is seen as the Victorian counterpart of Golding's wise pessimism. This in turn helps to explain how it happens that *Coral Island* is actually *attacked* and its readers sneered at, even by a critic of Frank Kermode's urbanity and sense of proportion: 'the copy in the local children's library seems to be taken out at least once a fortnight, from what strange motives of pubescent piety or hypocrisy I do not understand'. Ballantyne's three castaways, 'godly, regenerate, empire building boys who know by instinct how to turn paradise into a British protectorate', are altogether unlikely; they talk in semi-colons; Peterkin's jokes are not amusing; the difference is not just of 'different talents', he concludes; 'our minds have darker needs and obscurer comforts'.[13]

The popularity of *Coral Island* among the readers it was (and is) meant for is easy to see. Golding recalls how he formerly enjoyed it: 'remember how you *lived* in that island with Ralph and Jack and Peterkin'. The book is not meant to be grasped by its readers as a literary artefact; but to *be*, for them, an island, with pigs, sharks, underwater caverns, cannibals and pirates, completed by a satisfactory amount of slaughter and a happy ending. The same conventions which require that sharks be escaped from and cannibals vanquished provide Jack (who is meant to be eighteen) and Ralph (fifteen) with an idealised semi-adult self-reliance, although the thirteen-year-old Peterkin, closer to the reader's presumed age, is 'realistically' afraid of underwater swimming, and likes 'fun'; the same conventions arrange that tropical island discomforts can be forgotten about; 'this is not a stroll through a nineteenth-century English wood' say Kinkead-Weekes and Gregor of Golding's jungle (p. 23), but *Coral Island* does in a sense take place in the local woods, like the adventures in *Bevis*. Ballantyne's prose style strikes Golding critics as ponderous and his dialogue unnatural, compared to the brilliantly captured prep-school voices of *Lord of the Flies*. Ballantyne's writing was designed to be understood and inconspicuous as a style; it is a kind of *degré zéro de l'écriture*.[14] Golding's own praise of the book, 'how you *lived* on that island', is all that needs to be said of it. The critics are certainly right about how the *Coral Island* expectations, in the boys at the beginning and in the naval officer at the end, are a part of Golding's meaning in *Lord of the Flies*. But the fact that some critics have been led systematically to compare the sophisticated 1950s intellectual fable with the 1850s adventure story indicates an exaggerated anxiety about the credentials and validity of modern fiction.

One can see the point of Frank Kermode's suggestion about using the two books in a history of ideas: *Coral Island* could be of interest to an historian for the role it played in education in the later nineteenth century. Its breezy, unsuspecting, early-Victorian blend of optimism and enterprise, of Christianity and Free Trade was doubtless interpreted throughout the following century as a justification for an imperial jingoism in which Ballantyne himself, a free-trader, did not in fact indulge. But Golding writes in a tone of superiority to the mid-Victorian period which seems over-insistent: 'It is worth looking for a moment at the great original of boys on an island. This is *The Coral Island*, published a century ago, at the height of Victorian smugness, ignorance, and prosperity'.[15] In the same tone of superiority Oldsey and Weintraub think in terms of a century's decline into sober wisdom:

> While Ballantyne's characters, for instance, are stout English lads who overcome evil introduced into their worldly paradise by natives and pirates, Golding's characters find evil within themselves and almost go under, until finally extricated by a *deus ex machina*. The officer who is the long arm of that godly machine underscores the difference between Golding's novel and Ballantyne's when he says with Old Boy naïveté: 'Jolly good show. Like the Coral Island.' Ralph looks at the officer dumbly, uncomprehendingly and his look measures the distance between generations as well as the distance between the fictional visions of 1857 and 1954.[16]

This is a perfect example of modern critics summing the Victorians up. If it meant only the vision of Ballantyne's Ralph living on in the officer's mind, as opposed to that of Golding's Ralph, then the look might be said to measure their distance, though it is a reflection that arises in writing criticism rather than in reading the novel. But if we think of the fictional visions of 1857 and 1954 it is clearly misleading, although it is only an explicit assertion of what is implicit in many other critical accounts. *Coral Island*, conceived of as a Victorian 'experiment' which has been proved 'inane' by modern methods, is the focus of a number of current oversimplifications of what the Victorians were 'like' and of our own relative enlightenment and emancipation.

The year 1954 was a good one for novels: it produced *Lucky Jim*, *Under the Net*, *Lord of the Flies* and *Passage de Milan*. The year 1857 produced *Little Dorrit*, *Madame Bovary*, *Barchester Towers* and George Eliot's *Scenes of Clerical Life*, besides Mrs Gaskell's *Life of Charlotte Brontë* and Champfleury's *Le Réalisme*. Darwin's *Origin of Species* was ready for publication two years later. The decade ended with *Mill on the Floss* and *Great Expectations*. Almost any mid-nineteenth-century year will overwhelm one like this with its variety and energy of creative enterprise.

Almost all Golding critics effectively make the same oversimplification, so that Golding's reasonable observation that *Coral Island* coincided with and reflected a public mood of smugness in 1857 is developed into a contrast between 1857 and 1954 which attributes to a single adventure story the 'fictional vision' of the 1850s. Certainly *Coral Island* oversimplifies an ethos and an ideology which, in more complex form, were once widespread in the world. Individuals like Livingstone could, given the background of British economic and military power, though not always directly dependent on it, exercise a 'Coral Island mentality' with astonishing consequences, good and ill. At the same time, Darwin and Dickens would have been impossible without something of the exuberance and overconfidence which belonged both in *Coral Island* and in the infinitely more complex and self-critical civilisation behind it. The urge to 'place' the 1850s — as the decade of Jingoism — seems to be connected with the desire to justify a contemporary pessimism and knowingness, post-Christian, post-Freudian, perhaps 'post-cultural'. Martin Green's attack in 'Distaste for the Contemporary' should have been directed against a certain tone in the critical chorus around the novel rather than at *Lord of the Flies* itself.

There are two areas of human life in particular in which Golding's vision in the 1950s is supposed to be more mature than the vision of the 1850s: savagery and childishness. These related and basic forms of behaviour are, so it is claimed, better understood in 1954 than they were in the past. *Lord of the Flies* is certainly impressive in revealing connections between them. But Golding's originality is constantly misrepresented. That can be seen even in Martin Green's account which is unsympathetic: 'In other words, Golding is a belated recruit to the ranks of those writers who have rediscovered for this century man's essential savagery; who have triumphantly rejected science and hygiene, liberalism and progress . . .'[17] Eliot, Greene and Waugh are the others he cites as 'those writers'; they are all, like Golding, Christians. In fact the Christian basis of *Lord of the Flies*, stated in 'Fable' but clear enough in the novel, is not far from the Christian basis of *Coral Island*. Ballantyne's Ralph identifies himself with the dying pirate, Bill (in Chapter 27); he is a greater sinner than the pirates or the cannibals because he was brought up a Christian and they were not. Christianity offers them all the chance to be civilised; without it they are all savages in the eyes of God. This is one of the book's occasional solemn moments of course, but it shows the underlying belief: a fairly orthodox Christianity about which Ballantyne is franker than Golding, whose characters are all strangely a-religious, despite the fact that half of them come from a choir-school. But in 'Fable' Golding explains that 'the boys are suffering from the terrible disease of being human' and that by the end Ralph can see 'the fallen nature of man'. Ballantyne would not have disagreed with this, though he would have said that his own was not a serious devotional work, but written to amuse.

John S. Whitley's sixty-page essay on the novel in the responsible 'Studies in English Literature' series is an excellent introduction for students, but it too misrepresents the Victorian view of evil:

At times Ballantyne seems to teeter on the brink of a 'modern' subtlety. There are horrific descriptions of atrocities, and Ralph, upon witnessing a tribal war, remarks: 'I felt my heart grow sickened at the sight of this bloody battle, and would fain have turned away, but a species of fascination seemed to hold me down and glue my eyes upon the combatants.' Such a remark (and there are several) could be taken to suggest a tendency towards atavism lurking *within* the characters but, as in many minor Victorian novels, this remains an element which the writer has not recognised or cannot bring himself to countenance. [p. 16]

This is not far from being a modern smugness. Ballantyne as usual knows what his reader will recognise: 'it's horrible, but you can't help watching'. (The 'fain' is just story-book language of the sort Tom Sawyer enjoys.)

Elsewhere John S. Whitley refers to Peter Coveney's *The Image of Childhood* (first published as *Poor Monkey* in 1957). Coveney treats the theme of childhood in Victorian fiction and discovers a dialectical relationship between the opposed concepts of 'miserable sinner' and 'holy innocent'. Allowing that the insights of Dickens and George Eliot were exceptional, then, fairly close to the fictional vision of 1857, the following passage offers an example of how this worked in practice.

But perhaps Samuel was the general favourite; and dear little Soapy, as he was familiarly called, was as engaging a child as ever fond mother petted. He was soft and gentle in his manners and attractive in his speech: the tone of his voice was melody and every action was grace; unlike his brothers, he was courteous to all; he was affable to the lowly, and meek even to the very scullery maid. He was a boy of great promise, minding his books and delighting the hearts of his masters. His brothers, however, were not particularly fond of him; they would complain to their mother that Soapy's civility all meant something; they thought that his voice was too often listened to at Plumstead Episcopi, and evidently feared that, as he grew up, he would have more weight in the house than either of them; there was, therefore, a sort of agreement among them to put young Soapy down. This, however, was not so easy to be done; Samuel, though young, was sharp; he could not assume the stiff decorum of Charles James, nor could he fight like Henry; but he was a perfect master of his own weapons, and contrived, in the teeth of both of them, to hold the place which he had assumed. Henry declared that he was a false, cunning creature; and Charles James, though he always spoke of him as his dear brother Samuel, was not slow to say a word against him when opportunity offered. To speak the truth, Samuel was a cunning boy, and those even who loved him best could not but own that for one so young, he was too adroit in choosing his words, and too skilled in modulating his voice.

'To speak the truth, Samuel was a cunning boy' shows a refreshing freedom from cant about childhood on Trollope's part. This passage from Chapter 8 of *The Warden* (1855) is unusual, for Trollope rarely says much about children. David Skilton's *Anthony Trollope and his Contemporaries* (Longman, 1972) shows how his work was involved in delicate adjustments of mid-Victorian ideas: 'realism' and 'idealism'; 'moral proportion'; 'truth to nature'; 'false conventionality'; 'duty to elevate'. Certainly Trollope's readers would never have tolerated any elaborate investigation into schoolboy malice. But Henry's always speaking of his 'dear brother Samuel' catches both the atmosphere of Doctor Grantly's household and the stresses of teenage life. Trollope is quite clear-sighted about this trio of middle-class boys: the urge to dominate, lurking in the prosperous, snug coral island of Plumstead Episcopi and under the cheerful appearance of the Archdeacon's 'happy thriving family' (just what he should have) is unmistakable: a viciousness in human nature plainly recognised by Trollope and quite compatible with his 'idealised' presentation of the Grantlys. It seems improbable that any minor Victorian who had known school experiences like those of Trollope and Thackeray could be unaware of how an 'experiment in youthful isolation' would be likely to turn out. As for saying that the 'atavistic' impulse in Ballantyne's Ralph is 'as in many minor Victorian novels . . . an element which the writer either has not realised or cannot bring himself to countenance', Marryat's novels come to mind as a good example of a minor Victorian who also wrote adventure stories understanding the bloodthirsty inclinations of the young. We can see in this judgement of Whitley's an example, in a well-informed and sensitive critic, of a widespread modern myth about what the Victorians were like.

Certainly the interest in children which has followed the discoveries of Freud has led in twentieth-century novelists like L. P. Hartley to an observation of children's behaviour and a power to record their inner experience unprecedented in earlier fiction despite the insights that Victorian novelists could achieve. The real difference between Golding and Ballantyne is that Golding understands and fully accepts what V. S. Pritchett observes in the first volume of his autobiography, *A Cab at the Door* (1968):

Between the ages of ten and fourteen a boy reaches a first maturity and wholeness as a person; it is broken up by adolescence and not remade until many years later. That early period between ten and fourteen is the one in which one can learn anything. Even in the times when most children had no schooling at all, they could be experts in a trade: the children who went up chimneys, worked in cotton mills, pushed coster barrows may have been sick, exhausted and ill-fed, but they were at the height of their intelligence and powers.[18]

This was intuitively known by Dickens (and by the Elizabethan dramatists) but not fully appreciated by any nineteenth-century novelist. Ballantyne, of course, ignores it, and Trollope's miniature portraits in *The Warden* do not tell us the characters' ages, as if — between eight and eighteen — they scarcely mattered. Trollope is interested in the men the boys are growing into; like Ballantyne he sees them as partly formed adults. Golding is typical of modern novelists in seeing his child characters as belonging to their own order of being.

The wish to establish *Lord of the Flies* as a modern classic by contrasting it with alleged Victorian delusions has produced, in the pages of Golding's critics, strange occurrences of what the French call intertextuality. *Coral Island*'s actual relevance to *Lord of the Flies* can be quickly explained: there is the coincidence of names — Jack, Ralph and Piggy-Simon/Peterkin; also of certain activities like pig-hunting; there is the point that Ballantyne's characters fight against alien savages while Golding's become savages themselves; and there is the irony of the boys at the start and the officer at the end expecting things to be 'like *Coral Island*'. If this counterpointing is examined closely, its validity weakens. Ballantyne wrote a different sort of book; his Jack and Ralph are not children; his Ralph *does* realise that he is linked through his humanity with the pirates and cannibals. Yet although Golding's text mentions *Coral Island* only twice, many critics mention it on every other page. For Whitley and for Kinkead-Weekes and Gregor, *Coral Island* has to be kept in mind throughout one's reading of Golding. Kinkead-Weekes and Gregor comment on gaps in the narrative which the reader is supposed to fill in. The naval officer rescues Ralph from the stick sharpened at both ends which Jack has intended for his severed head; they insist that 'the murder of Ralph takes place in the imagination' (p. 62); the sharpened stick certainly remains horrifically in the reader's mind. Elsewhere Golding does evoke fear and disgust from what is left undescribed; this leaving of the worst scenes to the imagination is obviously a feature of the book. But, for these critics, 'gaps' of a different kind are meant to be filled by reference to *Coral Island*, and

Ballantyne's book threatens to turn into an obsession. After all, *Lord of the Flies* suggests a remarkable range and variety of analogues, apart from Ballantyne. It has been pointed out that the French translation never mentions *Coral Island*, substituting vaguely '*les robinsons*', and while it is true that Crusoe and the Swiss Robinsons are not proper substitutes for the other Jack and Ralph, a reader of Lola Tranec's version, *Sa Majesté-des-Mouches*, would lose little from these changes, and more probably from the absence of the cutting tone of Golding's boys:' "After all, we're not savages. We're English; and the English are best at everything."' ('"*Après tout, on n'est pas des sauvages. On est des Anglais, et les Anglais sont épatants en tout*"') (Chapter 2). Jack sounds more human in French. As for the minute details like Jack and Ralph talking over Simon's (or Peterkin's) head, which have been discovered hidden in the text, these are evidence of Golding's concern to make his book teachable. If they were more conspicuous we should wonder why the boys don't notice the accident of the *Coral Island* names turning up again, which would interfere with the mimetic integrity that Golding depends on. Annotators like recapturing the parallels and this helps to 'interweave' the two texts. It is hard to think of any equivalent to this intrusion between the lines of one novel of fragments from another so different in kind.

Lord of the Flies would be another suitable text to refute the distinction between the readable and the writerly since it is very accessible and endlessly 'open' to readings. The necessary background reading for an examinee is formidable, even according to the requirements of the strictest *Coral Island*ers. John Whitley sets the novel in its place in the cultural tradition: it is an island book (like *Robinson Crusoe*, *Swiss Family Robinson*, *L'Ile Mystérieuse*); a novel about children (he cites *Emile*, *Mill on the Floss*, *Alton Locke*, *Huckleberry Finn*, *What Maisie knew*, *The Catcher in the Rye*); and a novel about the problem of evil (*Pilgrim's Progress*, *Oliver Twist*, *The Turn of the Screw*, *The Red Badge of Courage*, *Heart of Darkness*). All these appear in Whitley's lively and thoughtful study: all or any of them could easily come to mind in reading. So could another work he refers to: *Freud's Three Essays on the Theory of Sexuality* (1905); and to cite that opens up a whole range of possibilities for interpretation in reading with reference to contemporary theories of human behaviour.

Golding said in 'Fable' that 'the boys were below the age of overt sex, for I did not want to complicate the issue with that relative triviality', which sounds very sane coming from a 1950s novelist but has not deterred critics from analysing the sexual connotations of the one passage where the author risks using them, the killing of the sow: 'Jack found the throat and the hot blood spouted over his hands. The sow collapsed under them and they were heavy and fulfilled upon her' (Chapter 8). Most writers on Golding at least refer to E. L. Epstein's discussion of this as an 'Oedipal wedding night'.[19]

Freudian analysis can be misapplied to any work, of course, but Golding's characters have such an allegorical look to them that it's tempting to try seeing Jack as the Id, Ralph as the Ego and Piggy as the Superego. There are many alternative approaches available: Virginia Tiger, in *William Golding: The Dark Fields of Discovery* (Calder and Bayars, 1974), sees the novel as preoccupied with a proverb — 'where there is no vision, the people perish'.[20] A. D. Fleck, in 'The Golding Bough: Aspects of Myth and Ritual in *Lord of the Flies*', applies Frazer, seeing Simon as a scapegoat and the pigs as reminders of the corn-spirit in European folk-lore.[21] The novel adapts itself easily to these different accounts; indeed it often yields new interest in response to the most far-fetched comparisons. Article titles are sometimes enough to suggest what can be attempted: 'Mute Choirboys and Angelic Pigs'.[22]

No doubt Golding wrote with Freud, Frazer, Darwin and the Bible at the back of his mind. His novel eludes any single account of it and attracts new readings in terms of theories developed since it was published. Marthe Robert's two archetypes, *l'enfant trouvé* and *bâtard*, in *Roman des origines* mentioned above in Chapter 7, might well be found in *Lord of the Flies*, and her discussions of '*l'identification classique du sauvage et de l'enfant*' (p. 152) or the idea of the island as a rebirth might be thought relevant. Recent books in other fields confirm the claims about how close Golding's novel is to contemporary thinking. Professor Norman F. Dixon's *On the Psychology of Military Incompetence* (Cape, 1976) offers an account of how armies attract and advance individuals psychologically prone to making disastrous decisions, and he lists the characteristics of an authoritarian but inept make-up in people like Himmler or Redvers Buller. Some of these — conventionalism, submission to authority — are fairly obvious, but the full list — superstition, fantasies about dangers that don't exist, inability to reconsider — accurately describes Golding's Jack, whose emergence as the Chief is the outcome of the personal shortcomings which make him so terrible when he is in command.[23] Professor Dixon's work was published twenty years later than Golding's novel but the fable could be readily explained in terms of the thesis. Robert Ardrey's *The Hunting Hypothesis* (Collins, 1976) is a less authoritative sort of work, popularising theories in anthropology about a prehistory in which man developed qualities — cooperativeness, sharing, self-sacrifice, courage, loyalty, responsibility — necessary to a hunting animal. Escaping from Jack's hunters, Golding's Ralph 'obeyed an instinct he did not know he possessed and swerved over the open space so that the spears went wide' (Chapter 11). A reader coming to *Lord of the Flies* after Ardrey's book might wonder if Golding wasn't showing the boys reverting to 'normal' behaviour.

Frank Kermode is right to say that this novel is attuned to contemporary consciousness. It makes clear once again that a creative writer can intuitively anticipate scientific theories of man. But the more attention is paid to this 'relevance' in *Lord of the Flies*, the more bizarre its alleged relationship to *Coral Island* comes to seem. It possesses an autonomy as a 'modern fable' which frees it from the story that originally provoked it in the author's mind. There is no good reason, with a novel so broadly in touch with modern views, to present it in relation to a Victorian tale which reveals its own cultural background only narrowly and obliquely. But there are reasons why we do so, which need to be recognised.

We have seen how novels dealing with present-day society are in various ways conceived in relation to society in Victorian fiction. With *Lord of the Flies*, a novel set outside the normal social world, we find a strong desire to explain it as the correct version of a misleading Victorian predecessor, even at the cost of reinforcing half-truths or mistakes about nineteenth-century culture. It seems to be impossible for us to interpret our own novels independently of 'the classics' of the last century and hard to be honest about these when ours are at stake. We are prevented from making a proper estimate of the novel today (hence the talk about its 'death') so long as we remain unwilling to look at Victorian civilisation without prejudice.

George Steiner begins *In Bluebeard's Castle* by saying that we are ruled by images and myths of the past. Yet his own summaries can reveal such myths: 'to most intelligent men and women of the nineteenth century, a prediction that torture and massacre were soon to be endemic again in "civilised" Europe would have seemed a nightmarish joke' (p. 43). This belief is widespread, as we have seen: V. S. Pritchett writes, 'in *Coral Island* we see the safe community'; Frank Kermode writes that '*The Coral Island* . . . belongs to the period preceding the breaking of the great wave of primitivism which has so altered the features of the modern mind'. Golding himself, in 'Fable', takes the same view: 'we are commonly dressed, and commonly behave as if we had no genitalia . . . it seems to me that in nineteenth-century and early twentieth-century society of the West, similar taboos grew up round the nature of man. He was supposed not to have in him the sad fact of his own cruelty and lust.'

Dickens knew how far his sexless characters were from the lives of men at the Garrick Club, just as he knew what street-urchins were really like. Trollope knew of the malpractice, laxity and immorality within even such a civilised community as that of Victorian clergymen, but he was surprised that Jane Austen's Emma could be shown to imagine a clergyman drunk (in Mr Elton, as his notes on the endpapers of his *Emma* record). It was because they lived so close to primitive, violent and sensual behaviour — accustomed to scenes in the streets, in clubs, in schools, in the army, in country villages, which would nauseate us — that Victorian writers and readers were determined to impose a humane and polite culture on the world they created in their novels. Revolution and terrorism were the background to their age and they tried to bring a stable order into being through their fiction, to forge a 'new man' as Alain Robbe-Grillet has lately recommended as a task for the novelist. *Coral Island* is a typical Victorian novel in presenting truth in the sense of *pravda* which (John Bayley points out to us) means what ought to be as well as what is. In this century we have derided Victorian 'smugness' and 'ignorance' and been unwilling to acknowledge how well the Victorians understood their own world and tried to civilise it. We assume that 1914 proved that they had failed: Golding's generation which grew up after the Great War felt a need to dissociate themselves from the 'Victorian'. Yet their own assumptions were the creations of the nineteenth century. The decency, order and responsibility which the boys take for granted in the early stages of *Lord of the Flies* are the achievement of Victorian civilisation. In our own precarious state of affairs the real value of Golding's book can be seen, not in the refuting of an imaginary false complacency a century ago, but in asserting that megalomaniacs and mobs must be resisted by the individual who has (like Ralph) 'some sense', even if without success. That was a basic belief of the Victorians, with whom Golding has more in common than he likes to admit.

10 Afterword

We have seen that relations between contemporary English novelists and their predecessors are more complex and creative (and better equipped for survival) than is recognised by the usual distinction between 'experiment' and 'tradition'. Hartley's *The Go-Between* is too subtle for Roland Barthes's crude contrast of 'the modern' and 'the classical'; and even among pragmatic English critics the case of Golding's *Lord of the Flies* reveals a misleading determination to present 'progress' in fiction in terms of an abrupt break with a Victorian past. Among the best of recent novelists, from Anthony Powell to John Fowles, a more interesting relationship with the past has developed which reflects the irregular and unsystematic conditions of change in English society.

The mingling of Victorian and contemporary ideas in *The French Lieutenant's Woman* has turned out to be typical of present-day writers' ability to develop the novel with a full sense of what has been done before. It seems to be typical of reading habits too: Philip Larkin's remarks about the novel, in an interview in the *Observer* on 16 December 1979, are significant coming from our leading poet, both in their confidence about fiction and in the choice of authors. Novels, he says, 'are so much more interesting than poems . . . a novel is so spreading'. Among novelists he reads he mentions Amis and Powell and also 'Dickens, Trollope — sometimes you go back to them for about three novels running'. In a similar way, we look back at Victorian works in sociology, in political and economic theory when considering new developments in the social sciences. We are far from having 'grown out of' the nineteenth century in the sense of jettisoning its cultural achievements; their relevance is too easily rediscovered. The achievement of Amis, Powell and their contemporaries is not in having preserved antiquated types of narrative, but in having responded to the full incongruity of a culture in which both Dickens and 'anti-novelists' are relevant to our experience of life.

However the terms 'tradition' and 'experiment' are used, there is clearly a wish among novelists to have both, and not only, of course, among those I have considered. Doris Lessing's *The Golden Notebook* (Michael Joseph, 1962) has been much discussed as an experimental novel breaking down barriers between fiction and other modes. In the Introduction to *Shikasta* (Jonathan Cape, 1979), she writes: 'I feel as if I have been set free both to be as experimental as I like, and as traditional.' The freedom in *Shikasta*, and in its sequel, *The Marriages Between Zones Three, Four and Five* (Jonathan Cape, 1980), has come from science fiction: these are the first volumes in a projected series dealing with the history of the Earth from the point of view of extraterrestrial intelligences who 'colonised' us long ago. William Golding's *Darkness Visible* (1979) also uses fantasy (with many echoes of Dickens) to disturb the reader's sense of the normal. Both books explicitly assert a 'traditional' opposition of good and evil forces, and both are keen to find new ground for the conflict. Science fiction is likely to remain a stimulating adjunct to the contemporary novel, and Doris Lessing's preface to *Shikasta* gives the best reason why: 'these dazzlers . . .' she says, 'have played the indispensable and (at least at the start) thankless role of the despised illegitimate son who can afford to tell the truths the respectable siblings either do not dare, or, more likely, do not notice because of their respectability' (p. x). This is a menippean quality of science fiction, providing, through fantasy, surprising and disturbing perspectives on ordinary experience. But the everyday is stranger than fantasy and in several other specialised forms of fiction the strong human interest we have seen in the mainstream novel is present, in reinvigorating menippean dealings with tradition, based on the healthiest kind of faith: in real life.

The historical novel is nowadays a robust minor genre. It was the most obvious significant failure of Victorian prose literature. When Trollope was waiting in a publisher's office, one day in 1857, he was given advice by a porter: 'I hope it's not historical, Mr Trollope. Whatever you do, don't be historical. Your historical novel is not worth a damn'.[1] They do very well, often as frankly light literature, nowadays. Tim Jeal, the author (between 1967 and 1974) of three ingenious, witty novels set in modern Britain,[2] has recently turned to 'historical epics'. *Until the Colours Fade* (Hamish Hamilton, 1976) is a vivid re-creation of life in exciting milieux in the mid-nineteenth century. There is clearly still a large readership for novels which make a traditional appeal out of adventure and romance. More open to new possibilities and more in touch with present-day life are stories like Matthew Vaughan's *Chalky* (Secker and Warburg, 1975) and Carolyn Slaughter's *The Story of the Weasel* (Hart-Davis, McGibbon, 1976), which investigate previously veiled areas of Victorian social and sexual life. There seems no end to our curiosity about what lies behind the reticence of the Victorian novels.

The reason why may perhaps be seen in George Macdonald Fraser's *Flashman* (Barrie and Jenkins, 1969) and its sequels which are among the liveliest of recent 'entertainments' set in the nineteenth century. Fraser is fully aware of the mythology of the period and he derives a well-thought-out comedy from the gap between our images of the Victorians and their images of themselves. *Tom Brown's Schooldays* (1857) created the ideology of the public-school man — muscular and Christian, based on Thomas Arnold — among the new middle-class clients of the public schools. Its drunken caddish bully (personifying an earlier, Regency, school type) becomes Fraser's Flashman, who cheats and swaggers his way through an army career to end up as a major-general and governor of Rugby School. Swinburne, who hated Hughes's novel, would have enjoyed Fraser's. Its popularity today is partly due to the skill of the story-telling and the sense of fun, and partly to the way it overthrows the older myth of Tom Brown, the plucky moralist. It substitutes our virtue of honesty — Flashman owns up to cowardice and lust, cruelty and greed — for all the virtues Tom represents to his society which we see as pervaded by falseness. The owning up is done in secret memoirs, found, Fraser tells us, in a packing-case. This device is what Barthes would call an *objet mythique*:[3] out of it come 'secret papers' which reinterpret the past and, like the memoirs of *My Secret Life*,[4] discredit past pretensions, as we clearly want to do.

Flashman both continues a Victorian tradition of adventure and romance and subjects it to satirical appraisal, exposing its conventions and telling the truth about heroes, and the British army — in this case in the First Afghan War. Within its own limited genre it reflects the relations we have seen between much more ambitious novels and their predecessors, a relationship obvious here because of the Victorian setting. Simon Raven's sequence, *Alms for Oblivion* (Blond and Briggs, 1964–76), ten novels set in the contemporary world, which are partly adventure stories, partly satires on upper-class and professional life done from a coolly classical moralist's pose, deal with the kind of circles which Thackeray lampooned in his satirical sketches and short novels up to *Vanity Fair*: the army, politics, journalism, club-life, financiers, academics, gamblers —

the borderland between high society and crime. Simon Raven gets closer to Juvenalian or menippean frankness in representing vice, of course, though he clings to the same ideal of the honourable officer as Thackeray does, and has similar sentimental foibles — about schooldays for example. But Raven is quite outside the Victorian Christianity which not only censored Thackeray but bemused him intellectually (as one sees in his own comments on the danger of despair arising from too caustic a view of social life). *Alms for Oblivion* shows the basic position of stoical scepticism which might have enabled Thackeray, in the fifteen years after *Vanity Fair*, to go on to fulfil his talent as a satirist.

The different conditions — apart from the question of talent — make it absurd to think of Simon Raven as 'a modern Thackeray'. Michael Frayn is fond of ridiculing such facile comparisons ('modern Gogol', 'the new Maupassant'), which persist as a symptom of our dependency on the nineteenth century. Margaret Drabble is frequently compared with George Eliot or Mrs Gaskell.[5] The way that her characters think of themselves in relation to Victorian fiction reminds us of how separate she is from the earlier writers with whom she is compared. C. P. Snow is no 'modern Trollope', and not merely because he lacks Trollope's understanding of women and Trollope's involvement with his characters' inner lives. To be a realist, after Joyce, is quite feasible, as Snow demonstrates in his effective study of power among dons, *The Masters* (Macmillan, 1951), but Lewis Eliot's manner of narrating is better suited to the somewhat archaic Cambridge community of this novel than to some of the others in the *Strangers and Brothers* sequence (Faber and Macmillan, 1940–70). Bergonzi contrasts Snow's unconscious 'rewriting of Trollope' (*The Situation of the Novel*, p. 33) with John Barth's wholly conscious use of earlier forms. 'Rewriting' seems unfair to both Snow and Trollope. But Snow is good at discovering where behaviour patterns known to Trollope survive in the contemporary world.

This habit of opposing the ultra-modern foreigner with the allegedly Victorian Englishman is one key to the failure of most criticism of the last thirty years to do justice to the achievements of English novelists. There are others. Some critics would say that the community of interest linking Trollope and Snow is limited to a bourgeois society not likely to survive, as was widely hoped, feared or taken for granted in the modernist 1920s and 1930s, but this has seemed less arguable with every decade since. F. R. Karl comments on Powell's ruling classes that they are not 'doomed' but changing, and working-class life, as pictured for example by David Storey, is also changing in relation to the novel. Lawrence and Hardy are suggested by his recent *Saville* (Jonathan Cape, 1976), but the changing society which produced this book can be seen in the closeness of its characters' dialogue to the narrative prose. Another failure to look clearly at the prospects of the novel has come from neglect of writers from Commonwealth countries and the best of them, V. S. Naipaul, much of whose early work was set in the West Indies, writes novels which might, like Storey's, be wrongly classed as 'conventional realism' except for the vital transforming influence of the cultural and linguistic background. But Naipaul relies on the central English tradition too. In *A Bend in the River* (Deutsch, 1979) a knowledge of Conrad's *Heart of Darkness* is expected for full appreciation of the originality of the picture of modern Africa. In Naipaul and in Africans like Chinua Achebe and James Ngugi, the community of novel readers is in the process of expanding. John Bayley has compared the situation in Africa with that of Russian novelists in the early nineteenth century: urgently wanting to catch up.[6] But it is possible for African writers to see contemporary and Victorian fiction in relation to each other and both in relation to older non-European types of narrative. The possibilities of intertextuality are expanding all the time.

'The higher a genre develops and the more complex it becomes,' says Bakhtin optimistically in *Dostoevsky's Poetics*, 'the better and more fully it remembers its past.'[7] This may not hold as a literary law, but his theory of menippean literature is a good corrective to the restricted outlooks which ignore popular forms and writing in 'backward' countries, and look on English fiction as a self-contained phenomenon bounded by Defoe and Virginia Woolf; to all accounts of the novel as an exhausted genre. The vitality of our best thrillers and romances is connected with that of the novel itself. Both are in touch with their past and this is an attraction for writers in English elsewhere in the world. The last thirty years have seen the novel alive and vigorous in England, and criticism, in an Age of Critics, unable to acknowledge the fact. Fortunately, the creative writers have not been put off.

Biographical Notes

Kingsley Amis was born in 1922 and educated at the City of London School and St John's College, Oxford. He served in the Royal Corps of Signals, 1942–5, and was a Lecturer in English at University College, Swansea from 1941 to 1961; then Fellow in English, Peterhouse College, Cambridge from 1961 to 1963. He has worked as a journalist, reviewer, editor and broadcaster.

John Fowles was born in 1926 and educated at Bedford School and New College, Oxford (where he read modern languages). He served in the Royal Marines, and taught for a while in Greece. He lives in Lyme Regis.

William Golding was born in 1911 and educated at Marlborough Grammar School and Brasenose College, Oxford. He served in the Royal Navy from 1940 to 1945, and taught at Bishop's Wordsworth's School, Salisbury, from 1945 to 1951. He has lectured and taught in America.

L. P. Hartley was born in 1895 and educated at Harrow and at Balliol College, Oxford. He served in the Norfolk Regiment in the First War and worked as a reviewer, on the *Spectator*, the *Observer* and other papers. He lived in Venice before 1939 and in England afterwards. He died in 1972.

Iris Murdoch was born in 1919 and educated at Badminton School, Bristol, and Somerville College, Oxford. She worked at the Treasury and for the United Nations, during the war, and taught philosophy as a Fellow of St Anne's College, Oxford, from 1948 to 1963. She was a Lecturer at the Royal College of Art from 1963 to 1967. Her most recent novel *The Sea, the Sea*, won the Booker Prize in 1978. She is married to John Bayley.

Anthony Powell was born in 1905 and educated at Eton and Balliol College. He served in the Welch Regiment from 1939 to 1941 and in the Army Intelligence Corps from 1941 to 1945. He worked at Duckworth (the publishers) from 1926 to 1935, and as a scriptwriter for Warner Brothers in 1936. He was Literary Editor of *Punch*, 1953–8, and reviewed for the *Daily Telegraph* and the *TLS*.

Angus Wilson was born in 1913 and educated at Westminster School and Merton College, Oxford. He worked at the Foreign Office from 1942 to 1946 and was Deputy Superintendent of the Reading Room of the British Museum from 1949 to 1955. In 1966 he became Professor of English Literature at the University of East Anglia. He has been a member of the Arts Council, Chairman of the National Book League and President of the Powys Society and of the Dickens Fellowship. Angus Wilson was knighted in 1980.

Notes and References

Bibliographical references are given here only for publications not detailed in the Select Bibliography.

CHAPTER I

1. See Chapter 7.
2. Juliet McMaster, *Trollope's Palliser Novels* (Macmillan, 1978); R. C. Terry, *Anthony Trollope: The Artist in Hiding* (Macmillan, 1977); Robert Tracy, *Trollope's Later Novels* (Berkeley: University of California Press, 1978).
3. *The Situation of the Novel* (2nd ed., 1979), p. 60. Page references are to this edition.
4. This introduction can be found in *The Novel Today* (ed. Bradbury).
5. 'Putting in the Person', *The Contemporary English Novel* (ed. Bradbury and Palmer), p.183.
6. 'François Mauriac', *Collected Essays* (Penguin, 1970), p. 91.
7. *The Novel Today* (ed. Bradbury).
8. *The Sovereignty of Good*, p. 76.
9. See *The Contemporary Writer*, ed. L. S. Dembo and C. Pondrom (Madison: University of Wisconsin Press, 1972).
10. In Chapter 5, 'Society and Authenticity', pp. 113–14.
11. In the Preface to *Mythologies*, for example.
12. *Roland Barthes: A Conservative Estimate*. See Chapter 7.
13. *The Situation of the Novel*, p. 65, from a BBC recording 1967: 'Novelists of the Sixties'.
14. *Problems of Dostoevsky's Poetics*, p. 93 (Chapter 4).
15. Ibid., p. 97.
16. *Anatomy of Criticism: Four Essays* (new ed., 1971), p. 309 (Princeton: Princeton University Press, 1957, 1971).
17. See *New Writings by Swinburne*, ed. Cecil Y. Lang (New York: Syracuse University Press, 1964).
18. See Chapter 1 of Bergonzi, *The Situation of the Novel*, for an account of this attitude.
19. *North British Review*, May 1951, p. 30. Quoted by Carl Dawson, *Victorian Noon: English Literature in 1850* (Baltimore and London: Johns Hopkins University Press, 1979), p. 153.

CHAPTER 2

1. In the 2nd ed., p. 32 (Chapter 1).
2. 'Notes on an Unfinished Novel', *The Novel Today* (ed. Bradbury), p. 136;

reprinted from *Afterwords*, ed. Thomas McCormack (New York: Harper and Row, 1969).
3. *The Other Victorians: A Study of Sexuality and Pornography in Mid-Nineteenth-Century England* (Weidenfeld and Nicolson, 1966).
4. *Fragments d'un discours amoureux* (Paris: Editions de Seuil, 'Tel Quel', 1977), p. 53, for example.
5. See 'Notes on an Unfinished Novel', op. cit., p. 136.
6. In 'Against Dryness'. See *The Novel Today* (ed. Bradbury), p. 27.
7. Ibid., p. 27.
8. Ibid., p. 31.

CHAPTER 3

1. *Spectator*, 11 June 1954.
2. *New Statesman*, 5 June 1954.
3. *The Fire and the Sun: Why Plato Banished the Artists*.
4. In Chapter 1.
5. Vol. XIII, pp. 265–73.
6. See Chapter 1 and n. 6.
7. See Chapter 2 and n. 6.
8. *Possibilities*, p. 246.
9. 'Writers and Their Work', *Iris Murdoch* (1976), pp. 29–30.
10. See *Possibilities*, p. 243, n. 1.
11. Chapter 37. The whole scene is reminiscent of late Victorian melodrama. Biranne pleads: 'So you haven't decided? Or do you want me on my knees? *Oro supplex et acclinis*. Yes, you do think you're God!' — 'Just a few questions, my dear Biranne.'
12. Following Samuel Beckett. See *The Novel Today* (ed. Bradbury), pp. 156–68.
13. *The Situation of the Novel*, p. 40. Yeats wrote in 'Lapis Lazuli' (*Last Poems*): 'They know that Hamlet and Lear are gay;/Gaiety transfiguring all that dread'.
14. Page 152 of Paladin ed., 1974. (First published 1970 by Chatto.)
15. *The Fire and the Sun*, p. 13.

CHAPTER 4

1. *The Novel Today* (ed. Bradbury), p. 154.
2. *The Contemporary English Novel* (ed. Bradbury and Palmer), p. 37.

CHAPTER 5

1. *Modern English Literature*, p. 154.
2. *The Novel Today* (ed. Bradbury), pp. 28–9.
3. *Repertoire* I, p. 193.
4. 'Dracula, Frankenstein, Sons and Co', *What Became of Jane Austen?*
5. *The Situation of the Novel*, p. 164.
6. *In Bluebeard's Castle* (1971). See Chapter 7.

CHAPTER 6

1. James Tucker, *The Novels of Anthony Powell*, pp. 1–5.
2. Arthur Mizener, *The Sense of Life in the Modern Novel*, Chapter 4; Frederick R. Karl, *A Reader's Guide to the Contemporary English Novel*, rev. ed. (1972).
3. *The Situation of the Novel*, pp. 118–19.
4. See Jonathan Culler, *Structuralist Poetics*, for an account of such views.
5. Op. cit., p. 89 ff. Arthur Mizener notes the 'anachronistic' nature of Powell's characters, especially Uncle Giles 'who has been an anachronism all his life' (p. 99).
6. *The Situation of the Novel*, p. 133.
7. 'The Uses of Polite Surprise: Anthony Powell', *Essays in Criticism*, April 1962.
8. See 'Aspects of the Novel, 1930–1960' in 'The Sphere History of Literature in the English Language', Vol. 7, *The Twentieth Century*, ed. Bernard Bergonzi.
9. In his 'Writers and Their Work' pamphlet (No. 221), *Anthony Powell*, p. 24.

CHAPTER 7

1. *Linguistics and the Novel*, pp. 124–5.
2. Bernard Bergonzi notes that James's precepts were under attack in the *T L S* in 1967; see *The Situation of the Novel*, pp. 70–1.
3. See his introduction to *The French New Novel*.
4. *Lire*, April 1979, p. 36
5. *Roland Barthes: A Conservative Estimate*, pp. 119–120. Professor Thody has also written 'Jeeves, Dostoyevsky and the Double Paradox', in the *University of Leeds Review*, October 1971.
6. *Lire*, op. cit.
7. *The Contemporary English Novel* (ed. Bradbury and Palmer), p. 111.
8. *The Situation of the Novel*, 2nd ed., Chapter 8.
9. *In Bluebeard's Castle*, p. 13.
10. Ibid., pp. 14–16.
11. '*Il est libre de n'être qu'une enfilade de phrases sans Histoire ni histoires, libre de ne dire que le vertige narcissique de sa propre écriture . . .*' *Roman des origines*, p. 363 (final section).

CHAPTER 8

1. *Repertoire*, I, p. 8.
2. 'Against Dryness', *The Novel Today* (ed. Bradbury), p. 28.
3. *Passim*; although Hartley is over-vague as part of a deliberate manner and this can cause him to be underestimated.
4. Like that of analysis in Robbe-Grillet; see *Pour un nouveau roman* (*Towards a New Novel*); as something more mystical in Butor.
5. 'Against Dryness', op. cit., p. 27.
6. *L'Ere du Soupçon* (Paris: Gallimard, 1964), p. 82.
7. *Modern English Literature*, p. 156.
8. Barthes's terms are '*lisible*' (readable) and '*scriptible*' (writerly); he complains of

'un conformisme de l'illisibilité' (*Lire*, April 1979, p. 36).

9. In a television interview, 1971.
10. *L. P. Hartley*, Chapter 5.
11. See W. C. Booth, *The Rhetoric of Fiction*, for an account of the techniques involved.
12. *In Bluebeard's Castle*, p. 15. See Chapter 7 above.

CHAPTER 9

1. 'The Novels of William Golding', *International Literary Annual*, III, 1961, p. 14.
2. *William Golding* (Edinburgh: Oliver and Boyd, 1969), p. 38.
3. See *College English*, XXVI, p. 481; and Oldsey and Weintraub, p. 36.
4. *Golding, Lord of the Flies*, ('Studies in English Literature'), p. 41.
5. *William Golding* ('Columbia Essays in Modern Writing'), p. 8.
6. *The Art of William Golding*, p. 37.
7. 'Distaste for the contemporary', *The Nation*, CXC, 21 May 1960.
8. 'The Coral Island Revisited', *College English*, January 1961, p. 241.
9. See William Nelson, *William Golding's 'Lord of the Flies'; A Source Book* (New York: Odyssey Press, 1963), p. 39 ff; *Spectator*, 22 August 1958; *New Statesman*, 2 August 1958.
10. See 'The Novels of William Golding', op. cit., p. 16.
11. *Daniel Martin*, p. 451.
12. Eric Quayle, *Ballantyne the Brave: A Victorian Writer and his Family* (Hart-Davis, 1967). Quayle points out that *Coral Island* derives from *The Island Home* by James Bowman (Edinburgh, 1852).
13. *Spectator*, op. cit.
14. The title of Barthes's first book, and his terms for the 'style-less' writing he claimed to admire.
15. *The Hot Gates*, p. 88.
16. Op. cit., p. 37.
17. 'Distaste for the Contemporary', op. cit.
18. Chapter 6, p. 102 (Chatto, 1968).
19. See, for example, Whitley, p. 47.
20. Proverbs 23, 18; Tiger, p. 15.
21. In *On the Novel, A Present for Walter Allen on his Sixtieth Birthday*, ed. B. S. Benedikz (Dent, 1971), p. 189 ff.
22. J. D. O'Hara, *Texas Studies in Literature*, Winter 1966, pp. 411–20.
23. Chapter 22, pp. 256–79.

CHAPTER 10

1. Michael Sadleir, *Trollope: A Commentary*, Oxford ed. (1961), p. 182.
2. *For Love or Money* (Macmillan, 1967); *Somewhere beyond Reproach* (Macmillan, 1968); *Cushing's Crusade* (Heinemann, 1974).
3. See *Mythologies* (passim).
4. See Marcus, *The Other Victorians* (n. 3 of Chapter 2, above).

5. In, for example, Lorna Sage, 'Female Fictions: The Women Novelists', *The Contemporary English Novel* (ed. Bradbury and Palmer), p. 27.
6. *Tolstoy and the Novel*, p. 27.
7. Op. cit., p. 99.

Select Bibliography

The place of publication, unless otherwise stated, is London.

I SEVEN NOVELISTS

1. Kingsley Amis

NOVELS
Lucky Jim (Gollancz, 1954); *That Uncertain Feeling* (Gollancz, 1955); *I Like It Here* (Gollancz, 1958); *Take a Girl Like You* (Gollancz, 1960); *One Fat Englishman* (Gollancz, 1963); *The Anti-Death League* (Gollancz, 1966); *I Want It Now* (Cape, 1968); *The Green Man* (Cape, 1969); *Girl, 20* (Cape, 1971); *The Riverside Villas Murder* (Cape, 1973); *Ending Up* (Cape, 1974); *The Alteration* (Cape, 1976); *Jake's Thing* (Hutchinson, 1978); *Russian Hide and, Seek* (Hutchinson, 1980)
With Robert Conquest: *The Egyptologists* (Cape, 1965)
As Robert Markham: *Colonel Sun: A James Bond Adventure* (Cape, 1968)
Kingsley Amis's novels are also available in Penguin and Panther paperbacks.

SHORT STORIES
My Enemy's Enemy (Gollancz, 1962); *Penguin Modern Stories, 11* (with others) (1975)

POETRY
A Case of Samples (Gollancz, 1957); *A Look Round the Estate* (Cape, 1967); *Collected Poems, 1944–1979* (Hutchinson, 1979)

GENERAL
New Maps of Hell: a survey of science fiction (Gollancz, 1960); *The James Bond Dossier* (Cape, 1965); *What Became of Jane Austen? and other questions* (Cape, 1970); *Rudyard Kipling and his World* (Thames

and Hudson, 1975); *The New Oxford Book of Light Verse* (ed.), (1978)

2. John Fowles

NOVELS
The Collector (1963); *The Magus* (1966, rev. 1977); *The French Lieutenant's Woman* (1969); *Daniel Martin* (1977)

NOVELLA
The Ebony Tower (1974)

GENERAL
The Aristos: A Self-portrait in Ideas (1965)
John Fowles is published by Jonathan Cape and in paperback by Panther.

3. William Golding

NOVELS
Lord of the Flies (1954); *The Inheritors* (1955); *Pincher Martin* (1956); *Free Fall* (1959); *The Spire* (1964); *The Pyramid* (1967); *The Scorpion God* (1973); *Darkness Visible* (1979)

DRAMA
The Brass Butterfly (1958)

GENERAL
The Hot Gates, and other Occasional Pieces (1965)
William Golding is published by Faber (in hardback and paperback).

4. L. P. Hartley

NOVELS
Simonetta Perkins (1925); *The Shrimp and the Anemone* (1944); *The Sixth Heaven* (1946); *Eustace and Hilda* (1947); *The Boat* (1949); *My Fellow Devils* (1951); *The Go-Between* (1953); *The Perfect Woman* (1955); *The Hireling* (1957); *Facial Justice* (1960); *The Brickfield* (1964); *The Betrayal* (1966); *Poor Clare* (1968); *The Love Adept* (1969); *My Sister's Keeper* (1970); *The Harness Room* (1971)

SHORT STORIES
The Complete Short Stories of L. P. Hartley (1973)

CRITICISM
The Novelist's Responsibility (1967)
L. P. Hartley is published by Hamish Hamilton and in paperback
by Penguin.

5. Iris Murdoch

NOVELS
Under the Net (1954); *The Flight from the Enchanter* (1956); *The
Sandcastle* (1957); *The Bell* (1958); *A Severed Head* (1961); *An Unofficial
Rose* (1962); *The Unicorn* (1963); *The Italian Girl* (1964); *The Red and
the Green* (1965); *The Time of the Angels* (1966); *The Nice and the Good*
(1968); *Bruno's Dream* (1969); *A Fairly Honourable Defeat* (1970); *An
Accidental Man* (1971); *The Black Prince* (1973); *The Sacred and Profane
Love Machine* (1974); *A Word Child* (1975); *Henry and Cato* (1976); *The
Sea, the Sea* (1978)
Iris Murdoch's novels are published by Chatto and Windus and in
paperback by Panther.

PHILOSOPHY
Sartre: Romantic Rationalist (Bowes, 1953); *The Sovereignty of Good*
(Routledge, 1971); *The Fire and the Sun; Why Plato Banished the Artists*
(Oxford University Press, 1977)

LITERARY THEORY
'Against Dryness', *Encounter*, January 1961; reprinted in *The Novel
Today*, ed. Malcolm Bradbury (Fontana, 1977)

6. Anthony Powell

NOVELS
Afternoon Men (Duckworth, 1931); *Venusberg* (Duckworth, 1932);
From a View to a Death (Duckworth, 1933); *Agents and Patients*
(Duckworth, 1936); *What's Become of Waring?* (Cassell, 1939)
A Dance to the Music of Time:
A Question of Upbringing (1951); *A Buyer's Market* (1952); *The
Acceptance World* (1955); *At Lady Molly's* (1957); *Casanova's Chinese
Restaurant* (1960); *The Kindly Ones* (1962); *The Valley of Bones* (1964);

The Soldier's Art (1966); *The Military Philosophers* (1968); *Books Do Furnish a Room* (1971); *Temporary Kings* (1973); *Hearing Secret Harmonies* (1975)
All the volumes of *Music of Time* are published by Heinemann and in paperback by Fontana.

PLAYS
The Garden God and *The Rest I'll Whistle* (Heinemann, 1971)

GENERAL
John Aubrey and his Friends (Heinemann, 1948); *Novels of High Society from the Victorian Age* (ed.) (Pilot Press, 1947); *Brief Lives and other Selected Writings* (ed.) (Crescent Press, 1949)

MEMOIRS
To Keep the Ball Rolling:
1. *Infants of the Spring* (Heinemann, 1976)
2. *Messengers of Day* (Heinemann, 1978)

7. Angus Wilson

NOVELS
Hemlock and After (1952); *Anglo-Saxon Attitudes* (1956); *The Middle Age of Mrs Eliot* (1958); *The Old Men at the Zoo* (1961); *Late Call* (1964); *No Laughing Matter* (1967); *As If By Magic* (1973); *Setting the World on Fire* (1980)

SHORT STORIES
The Wrong Set (1949); *Such Darling Dodos* (1950); *A Bit Off the Map* (1957)

PLAY
The Mulberry Bush (1956)

GENERAL
Emile Zola: An Introductory Study of his Novels (1952, rev. ed. 1965); *The Wild Garden: or, Speaking of Writing* (1963); *The World of Charles Dickens* (1970).
Angus Wilson is published by Secker and Warburg (the novels and short stories in paperback by Panther).

II CRITICAL STUDIES

Allen, Walter. *Tradition and Dream* (Phoenix House, 1964)

Auerbach, Erich. *Mimesis*; trans. W. Trask (Princeton: Princeton University Press, 1953)

Bakhtin, Mikhail, *Problems of Dostoevsky's Poetics* (1929, 1963); trans. R. W. Rotsel (Ann Arbor: Ardis, 1973)

Barthes, Roland. *Mythologies* (Paris: Editions du Seuil, 1957). Twenty-eight *mythologies* and the essay 'Myth Today' trans. Annette Lavers (Cape, 1972; Paladin, 1973)

Barthes, Roland. *S/Z* (Paris: Editions du Seuil, 1970); trans. Richard Miller (Cape, 1975)

Barthes, Roland, *Le Plaisir du Texte* (Paris: Editions du Seuil, 1973); trans. Richard Miller (Cape, 1976)

Bayley, John. *Tolstoy and the Novel* (Chatto and Windus, 1966)

Bergonzi, Bernard. 'Sphere History of Literature in the English Language' (ed.), Vol. 7, *The Twentieth Century* (Barrie and Jenkins and Sphere Books, 1969). See especially the chapter 'Aspects of the Novel, 1930–1960' by Stephen Wall.

Bergonzi, Bernard. *The Situation of the Novel* (Macmillan, 1970, 1979)

Bien, Peter. *L. P. Hartley* (Chatto and Windus, 1963)

Booth, W. C. *The Rhetoric of Fiction* (Chicago: Chicago University Press, 1961)

Bradbury, Malcolm. *Possibilities; Essays on the State of the Novel* (Oxford University Press, 1973)

Bradbury, Malcolm. *The Novel Today: Contemporary Writers on Modern Fiction* (ed.) (Fontana, 1977)

Bradbury, Malcolm and Palmer, David. Stratford-upon-Avon Studies No. 18, *The Contemporary English Novel* (eds.) (Edward Arnold, 1979)

Burgess, Anthony. *The Novel Now* (New York: Norton, 1967)

Butor, Michel. *Repertoire* (Paris: Editions de Minuit, 1960)

Byatt, A. S. *Degrees of Freedom: The Novels of Iris Murdoch* (Chatto and Windus, 1965)

Byatt, A. S. *Iris Murdoch*, 'Writers and Their Work' (Longman, for the British Council, 1976)

Cox, C. B. *The Free Spirit* (Oxford University Press, 1963)

Culler, Jonathan. *Structuralist Poetics* (Routledge and Kegan Paul, 1975)

Fowler, Roger. *Style and Structure in Literature* (ed.) (Oxford: Basil Blackwell, 1975)

Fowler, Roger. *Linguistics and the Novel*, 'New Accents' (Methuen, 1977)

Fraser, G. S. *The Modern Writer and His World*, rev. ed. (Penguin Books, 1964)

Gindin, James. *Postwar British Fiction: New Accents and Attitudes* (Cambridge University Press, 1962)

Gindin, James. *Harvest of a Quiet Eye: the Novel of Compassion* (Bloomington: Indiana University Press, 1971)

Gransden, K. W. *Angus Wilson* (Longman, 1969)

Halio, Jay. *Angus Wilson* (Edinburgh: Oliver and Boyd, 1964)

Harvey, W. J. *Character and the Novel* (Chatto and Windus, 1965)

Hayman, Ronald. *The Novel Today: 1967–1975* (Longman, for the British Council, 1976)

Heath, Stephen. *The Nouveau Roman* (Elek, 1972)

Hynes, Samuel. *William Golding* (New York: Columbia University Press, 1964)

Iser, W. *The Implied Reader* (Baltimore: Johns Hopkins University Press, 1974)

Josipovici, Gabriel. *The World and the Book: A Study of Modern Fiction*(Macmillan, 1971)

Josipovici, Gabriel. *The Modern English Novel: the Reader, the Writer and the Work* (ed.) (Open Books, 1976)

Karl, Frederick R. *A Reader's Guide to the Contemporary English Novel*, rev. ed. (Thames and Hudson, 1972)

Kinkead-Weekes, Mark and Gregor, Ian. *William Golding: A Critical Study* (Faber, 1967)

Leavis, F. R. *The Great Tradition* (Chatto and Windus, 1948)

Leavis, F. R. and Q. D. *Dickens the Novelist* (Chatto and Windus 1970)

Lodge, David. *Language of Fiction* (Routledge and Kegan Paul, 1966)

Lodge, David. *The Novelist at the Crossroads* (Routledge, 1971)

Lodge, David. *The Modes of Modern Writing* (Edward Arnold, 1977)

Mercier, Vivian. *A Reader's Guide to the New Novel from Queneau to Pinget* (New York: Farrar, Straus and Giroux, 1971)

Mizener, Arthur. *The Sense of Life in the Modern Novel* (Heinemann, 1965)

Mulkeen, Anne. *Wild Thyme, Winter Lightning: the Symbolic Novels of L. P. Hartley* (Hamish Hamilton, 1974)

Oldsey, Bernard and Weintraub, Stanley. *The Art of William Golding* (Bloomington: Indiana University Press, 1968)

Preston, John. *The Created Self: The Reader's Role in Eighteenth-Century Fiction* (Heinemann, 1970)

Rabinovitz, Rubin. *The Reaction against Experiment in the English Novel, 1950–1960* (New York: Columbia University Press, 1967)

Robbe-Grillet, Alain. *Pour un nouveau roman* (Paris: Editions de Minuit, 1966)

Robert, Marthe. *Roman des origines et origines du roman* (Paris: Gallimard, 1972)

Robson, W. W. *Modern English Literature* (Oxford University Press, 1970)

Russell, John. *Anthony Powell: A Quintet, Sextet and War* (Bloomington: Indiana University Press, 1970)

Scholes, Robert. *The Fabulators* (New York: Oxford University Press, 1967)

Scholes, Robert and Kellogg, Robert. *The Nature of Narrative* (Oxford University Press, 1966)

Steiner, George. *In Bluebeard's Castle: or, Some Notes towards a Redefinition of Culture* (Faber, 1971)

Sturrock, John. *The French New Novel* (Oxford University Press, 1969)

Tanner, Tony. *City of Words: American Fiction, 1950-1970* (Cape, 1971)

Thody, Philip. *Roland Barthes: A Conservative Estimate* (Macmillan, 1977)

Trilling, Lionel. *Sincerity and Authenticity* (Oxford University Press, 1972)

Tucker, James. *The Novels of Anthony Powell* (Macmillan, 1976)

Whitley, John S. *William Golding*, 'Studies in English Literature', 42 (Edward Arnold, 1970)

III FURTHER READING

The best-known French new novelist, in the anglophone world, is Alain Robbe-Grillet, whose novels are *Les Gommes* (1953); *Le Voyeur* (1955); *La Jalousie* (1957); *Dans le labyrinthe* (1959); *La Maison de rendez-vous* (1965). *Les Gommes* is available as *The Erasers*, trans. R. Howard (Calder, 1966); *Dans le labyrinthe* as *In the Labyrinth*, trans. Christine Brooke-Rose (Calder, 1968). Michel Butor's novels are *Passage de Milan* (1954); *L'Emploi du temps* (1957); *La Modification* (1957); *Degrés* (1960). *L'Emploi du temps* is available as *Passing Time*, trans. J. Stewart (Calder, 1965). Butor's *Degrés* is published in Paris by Gallimard. All the other novels of Butor and Robbe-Grillet, like almost all works of the *nouveau roman*, are published in Paris by Les Editions de Minuit.

John Barth is published in England by Secker and Warburg. *Giles Goat Boy; or, the Revised New Syllabus* (1967) is his best-known book, but seems to be found less enjoyable, in England, than the more recent *Lost in the Funhouse* (1968) and *Chimera* (1974, Quartet paperback, 1977). The following novels by John Hawkes are published in London by Chatto: *The Beetle Leg* (1967; US, 1951); *Second Skin* (1966); *The Blood Oranges* (1971); *Death, Sleep and the Traveller* (1974); *Travesty* (1976). The most brilliant of 'emphatically fictive' novels claimed by American literature are by the late Anglo-Russian, Vladimir Nabokov: *Pale Fire* (1962) and *Ada, or Ardor: A Family Chronicle* (1969), published by Weidenfeld and Nicolson, and in paperback by Penguin. The most popular new American novels are Thomas Pynchon's: *V* (1963), *The Crying of Lot 49* (1967) and *Gravity's Rainbow* (1973), published by Cape, and in paperback by Picador. William Burroughs's work is reminiscent of Jean Genet in content — violent, anarchic, homosexual — and connects the breaking down of conventional narrative order with the breakdown of consciousness under the influence of drugs. *The Naked Lunch* (Paris: Olympia Press, 1959), *The Soft Machine* (Olympia, 1961) and *The Wild Boys* (New York: Grove Press, 1971) are available in Corgi paperbacks.

Christine Brooke-Rose, Robbe-Grillet's translator, is an English 'new novelist': *The Sycamore Tree* (Secker and Warburg, 1958); *Such* (Michael Joseph, 1966) and *Thru* (Hamish Hamilton, 1975). The Irish postmodernist writer Flann O'Brien is rightly becoming better known in England: *At Swim-Two-Birds* (MacGibbon and Kee, 1960; new ed., Hart-Davis, 1976) is by far his best; next best is *The Third Policeman*, new ed. (Hart-Davis, 1975); published in paperback by Picador. B. S. Johnson's *Travelling People* (Constable, 1963) and *Albert Angelo* (Constable, 1964) illustrate Johnson's anti-novelistic ideas but do so entertainingly; he died in 1973. The more austere interpreters of postmodernism might object to Flann O'Brien because he is so entertaining and the same objection could be made to many technically original English novels: Brigid Brophy, *In*

Transit (Macdonald, 1969); Anthony Burgess, *Tremor of Intent* (Heinemann, 1966), *Inside Mr Enderby* (Heinemann, 1963) and *Enderby Outside* (Heinemann, 1968; Penguin have paperbacked some of his novels); Michael Frayn, *The Tin Men* (Collins, 1965) and *Sweet Dreams* (Collins, 1973; both Fontana paperbacks); Muriel Spark, *The Abbess of Crewe* (Macmillan, 1974) and *The Takeover* (Macmillan, 1976; both Penguin paperbacks).

All these writers are still in mid-career. So is Margaret Drabble: *The Needle's Eye* (Weidenfeld and Nicolson, 1972) and *The Ice Age* (Weidenfeld, 1977; both Penguin paperbacks). Malcolm Bradbury and David Lodge move with the times, though they publish fiction too infrequently. Bradbury's *The History Man* (Secker and Warburg, 1975; Arrow paperback) and Lodge's *Changing Places* (Secker and Warburg, 1975; Penguin paperback) are good evidence for the survival of the novel. The best evidence of all, perhaps, is the work of a writer who uses overseas settings in most of his books and whom I have, therefore, reluctantly left out: V. S. Naipaul's *A House for Mr Biswas* (Deutsch, 1961; Penguin paperback) transcends the differences of 'period' and his recent, disturbing *In a Free State* (Deutsch, 1977; Penguin paperback) looks at Britain as part of a larger world. *A Bend in the River* (Deutsch, 1979) was perhaps the best novel of the year.

Index